ALSO BY **Roger Crowley**

1453: THE HOLY WAR FOR CONSTANTINOPLE AND
THE CLASH OF ISLAM AND THE WEST

EMPIRES *of the* SEA

RANDOM HOUSE | NEW YORK

# EMPIRES *of the* SEA

THE SIEGE OF MALTA,

THE BATTLE OF LEPANTO,

AND THE CONTEST FOR

THE CENTER OF THE WORLD

*Roger Crowley*

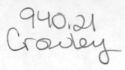

940.21
Crowley

Published in the United States by Random House,
an imprint of The Random House Publishing Group,
a division of Random House, Inc., New York.

RANDOM HOUSE and colophon are registered
trademarks of Random House, Inc.

Originally published in the United Kingdom by
Faber and Faber Ltd., London.

LIBRARY OF CONGRESS CATALOGING-IN-PUBLICATION DATA

Crowley, Roger.
Empires of the sea: the siege of Malta, the battle of Lepanto,
and the contest for the center of the world / Roger Crowley.
p.    cm.
Includes bibliographical references and index.
ISBN 978-1-4000-6624-7
1. Naval battles—History—16th century.    2. Naval history, Modern.
3. Europe—History, Naval.    4. Islam—Relations—Christianity.
5. Christianity and other religions—Islam.    I. Title.
D215.C76 2008        940.2'1—dc22        2007033794

Printed in the United States of America on acid-free paper

www.atrandom.com

9 8 7 6 5 4

*Book design by Barbara M. Bachman*

To George,

*who also fought in this sea, and who took us there*

The inhabitants of the Maghreb have it on the authority of
the book of predictions that the Muslims will make a successful
attack against the Christians and conquer the lands of the European
christians beyond the sea. This, it is said, will take place by sea.

~IBN KHALDUN, FOURTEENTH-CENTURY ARAB HISTORIAN

# Contents

# Ptolemy's Map

Long before the office blocks across the Golden Horn, before even the mosques, there was the church. The dome of Saint Sophia stood alone against the skyline for a thousand years. If you had made your way up onto its roof anytime in the Middle Ages, you would have been afforded an unimpeded view of "the city garlanded by water." From here it is quite clear why Constantinople once ruled the world.

On the afternoon of May 29, 1453, Mehmet II, sultan of the Ottoman Empire, made this ascent. It was the end of a momentous day. His army had just taken the city by storm in fulfillment of Islamic prophecy and destroyed the last vestiges of the Christian empire of Byzantium. Mehmet climbed, in the words of the Ottoman chronicler, "as the spirit of God ascending to the fourth sphere of heaven."

The sultan gazed upon a scene of melancholy devastation. Constantinople had been wrecked and thoroughly looted, "despoiled and blackened as if by fire." The city's army had been routed, the churches ransacked; its last emperor had perished in the massacre. Long lines of men, women, and children were being roped together and herded off. Flags fluttered from empty buildings, a sign to looters that the spoils had already gone. Above the pitiful wailing of the captives, the call to prayer rose in the spring air. It signaled the emphatic end of one imperial dynasty, the legitimization of another by right of conquest. The Ottoman Turks, a nomadic, tribal people from the heart of Asia, had now consolidated the presence of Islam on the European shore in the city they called Istanbul. Its capture confirmed Mehmet both as heir to Byzantium and as the undisputed leader of holy war.

From his vantage point the sultan could contemplate the past and future of the Turkish people. To the south, beyond the Bosphorus straits, lay Anatolia, Asia Minor, the road up which the Turks had made their long migration; to the north, Europe, the object of their territorial ambitions. But it was the prospect to the west that was to prove most challenging to the Ottomans. In the afternoon sun, the Sea of Marmara glittered like beaten brass; beyond lay the wide expanse of the Mediterranean, the place the Turks called the White Sea. With the conquest of Byzantium, Mehmet was not just inheriting a landmass; he was also heir to a maritime empire.

THE EVENTS OF 1453 were part of a larger ebb and flow in the struggle between Islam and Christianity. Between the eleventh and the fifteenth centuries, Christendom, on the impetus of the Crusades, had dominated the Mediterranean. It had created a patchwork of small states on the shores of Greece and the islands of the Aegean, which linked the enterprise of crusading to the Latin West. The direction of conquest had begun to reverse when the Crusaders lost their last major foothold on the shores of Palestine in 1291 at the fall of Acre. Now Islam was poised to strike back.

No one since the Romans had possessed sufficient resources to organize this sea, but Mehmet conceived himself as the inheritor of the Roman emperors. His ambitions were limitless. He was determined to create "one empire, one faith and one sovereignty in the world," and he styled himself the "sovereign of two seas"—the White and the Black. This was alien territory for the Ottomans. The sea is not solid ground. There are no natural frontiers, nowhere for nomads to pitch camp. It is uninhabitable. It remembers nothing: Islam had established footholds in the Mediterranean before and then lost them. But Mehmet had already set down a clear declaration of intent: he brought a large, if inexperienced, fleet to the siege of Constantinople, and the Ottomans were quick learners.

In the years after the conquest, Mehmet commissioned a copy of a map of Europe by the ancient geographer Ptolemy, translated for him into Arabic by Greeks. Here he studied the configuration of the sea in predatory detail. He ran his finger over Venice, Rome, Naples, Sicily, Marseilles, and Barcelona; he traced the Gates of Gibraltar; even faraway Britain fell under his gaze. The translators had prudently ensured that nowhere was marked as prominently as Istanbul, and Mehmet was as yet unaware that the Catholic kings in Spain were in the process of constructing a matching set of imperial ambitions at the map's western edge. Madrid and Istanbul, like giant mirrors reflecting the same sun, were initially too far apart to be mutually visible. Soon hostility would focus the light. Even Ptolemy's map, with its unfamiliar misshapen peninsulas and distorted islands, could not conceal an essential fact about the Mediterranean: it is really two seas, pinched at the middle by the narrow straits between Tunis and Sicily, with Malta sitting midstream, an awkward dot. The Ottomans would quickly dominate the eastern seas, the Hapsburgs of Spain the western. In time both would converge on the dot.

NOWADAYS YOU CAN FLY the length of the Mediterranean, from southern Spain to the shores of Lebanon, in three hours. From the air it is a peaceful prospect; the orderly procession of ships moves tamely over the glittering surface. The thousands of miles of crenellated coast on the northern shore reveal holiday villages, yacht harbors, and smart resorts, as well as the great ports and industrial complexes that provide the economic muscle of Southern Europe. Every vessel in this calm lagoon can be tracked from space. Ships travel at will, immune to the storms that wrecked Odysseus and Saint Paul. To our ever-shrinking world the place the Romans called the center of the world seems tiny.

Five hundred years ago people experienced the sea quite differently. Its shores were coasts of hunger, stripped early of trees, then soil, by men and goats. By the fourteenth century, Crete was able to furnish Dante with an image of ecological ruin. "In mid-sea sits a waste land," he wrote, "which once was happy with water and leaves. Now it is a desert." The sea is also barren. The Mediterranean has been formed by dramatic geological collapse, so that the entrancing transparent waters at its edge plunge away sharply into deep submarine gulfs. There are no continental platforms to rival the rich fishing grounds of Newfoundland or the North Sea. To those living on the shore, the million square miles of water, broken up into a dozen separate zones, each with its own particular winds and coastal irregularities and scattered islands, were intractable, vast, and dangerous—so big that the two halves of the Mediterranean were different worlds. A sailing ship might take two months to make the voyage from Marseilles to Crete in good weather, in bad six. Boats were surprisingly unseaworthy, storms sudden, pirates numerous, so that sailors generally preferred to creep around the sea's coastal margins rather than cross open water. Peril attended the voyage: no sane person would step up the gangplank without committing his soul to God. The Mediterranean was a sea of troubles. And after 1453 it became the epicenter of a world war.

On this terrain was played out one of the fiercest and most chaotic contests in European history: the struggle between Islam and Christianity for the center of the world. It was a drawn-out affair. Battle rolled blindly across the water for well over a century; the opening skirmishes alone, in which the Ottomans eclipsed Venice, lasted fifty years. The struggle assumed many forms: little wars of economic attrition, pirate raids in the name of faith, attacks on coastal forts and harbors, sieges of the great island bastions, and, rarest of all, a handful of epic sea battles. The struggle sucked in all the nations and special-interest groups that bordered Mediterranean waters: Turks, Greeks, North Africans, Spaniards, Italians, and Frenchmen; the peoples of the Adriatic Sea and the Dalmatian coast; merchants, imperialists, pirates, and holy warriors. All fought in shifting alliances to protect religion, trade, or empire. None could fly a neutral flag for long, though the Venetians tried hard.

The landlocked arena provided limitless possibilities for confrontation. North to south it is surprisingly narrow; in many places only a small strip of water separates alien peoples. Raiders could appear over the horizon at a moment's notice, and vanish again at will. Not since the lightning strikes of the Mongols had Europe experienced so abruptly the sudden terror of enemies. The Mediterranean became a biosphere of chaotic violence where Islam and Christianity clashed with unmatched ferocity. The battlegrounds were water, islands, and shores, where events were conditioned by wind and weather, the key weapon the oared galley.

FOR CHRISTENDOM, THE OTTOMANS, whose empire was multi-ethnic, were always simply the Turks, "cruellest enemy of Christ's name." Western Europe saw the contest as the source of ultimate war, and experienced it as trauma, a psychic struggle against the powers of darkness. Within the Vatican, they knew about Ptolemy's map. They imagined it as the template for Ottoman conquest and pictured the scene in the Topkapi Palace, high above the Bosphorus, in excruciating detail. The generic figure of the sultan, the Grand Turk, turbaned and caftanned, hook-nosed and genetically cruel, sits within the barbaric splendor of his tiled pavilion, studying the sea-lanes to the west. He thinks of nothing but the destruction of Christendom. To Pope Leo X in 1517, the menace of the Turk was as close as breathing. "He has daily in his hand a description and a painted map of the shores of Italy," he wrote with a shudder. "He pays attention to nothing but collecting artillery, building ships, and surveying all these seas and the islands of Europe." For the Ottomans and their North African allies it was pay-back time for the Crusades, the opportunity to reverse the flow of world conquest and control of trade.

This contest would be fought over a huge front, often far beyond the sea. Europe battled their enemy in the Balkans, on the plains of Hungary, in the Red Sea, at the gates of Vienna, but eventually, in the sixteenth century, the concentrated resources of the protagonists would converge on the center of the map. It would be a sixty-year struggle, directed by Mehmet's great-grandson Suleiman. War broke out in earnest in 1521 and reached its climax between 1565 and 1571, six years of unparalleled bloodshed that saw the two heavyweights of the age—the Ottoman Turks and the Hapsburgs of Spain—hold up the battle standards of their faiths and fight to the death. The outcome would shape the boundaries of the Muslim and Christian worlds and condition the future direction of empires.

It began, if anywhere, with a letter.

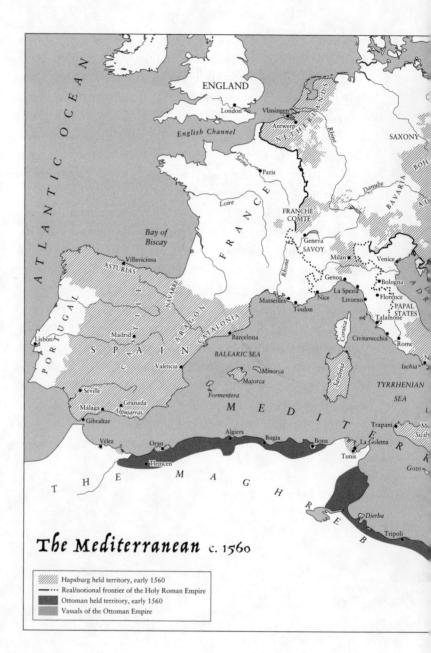

## The Mediterranean c. 1560

Hapsburg held territory, early 1560
- - - - Real/notional frontier of the Holy Roman Empire
Ottoman held territory, early 1560
Vassals of the Ottoman Empire

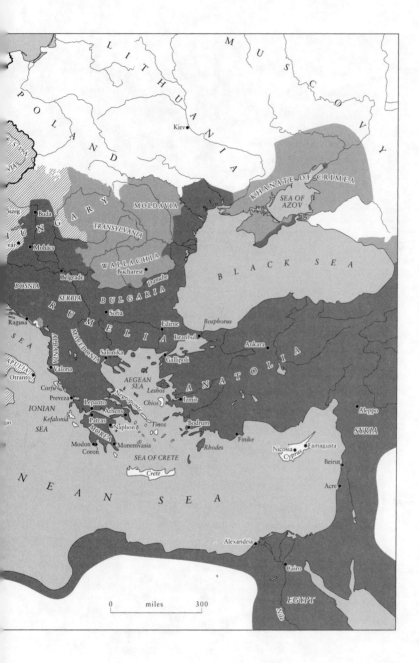

POLAND

LITHUANIA

MUSCOVY

Kiev

KHANATE OF CRIMEA

SEA OF AZOV

HUNGARY

MOLDAVIA

TRANSYLVANIA

Buda

Mohács

WALLACHIA

Bucharest

Danube

BLACK SEA

BOSNIA

Belgrade

SERBIA

BULGARIA

Sofia

RUMELIA

Ragusa

MACEDONIA

ALBANIA

Edirne

Bosphorus

Istanbul

Ankara

ANATOLIA

Salonika

Gallipoli

Valona

Otranto

APULIA

AEGEAN SEA

Lesbos

Corfu

Negroponte

Chios

Izmir

Preveza

Lepanto

IONIAN

Athens

Kefalonia

SEA

Patras

Naplion

Tinos

Bodrum

MOREA

Modon

Monemvasia

Finike

Rhodes

Coron

SEA OF CRETE

Nicosia

Famagusta

Cyprus

Aleppo

SYRIA

Beirut

Crete

Acre

MEDITERRANEAN SEA

Alexandria

Cairo

EGYPT

Nile

0        miles        300

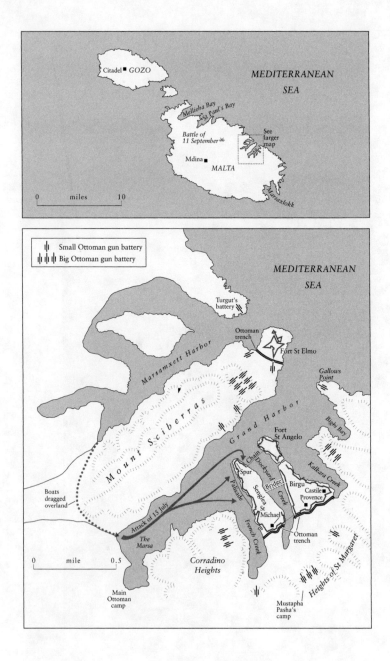

## The Siege of Malta:

MAY TO SEPTEMBER 1565

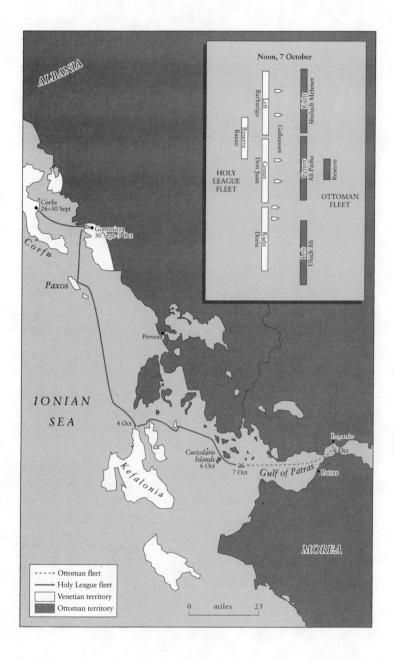

The Battle of Lepanto:

OCTOBER 7, 1571

## Part One

## CAESARS: THE CONTEST FOR THE SEA

SÓLIMANVS · IMPERATOR
· TVRCHARVM ·

1521–1560

# CHAPTER 1

# The Sultan Pays a Visit

1521–1523

FIRST THE DRUMROLL of imperial titles. Then the threat:

> Suleiman the sultan, by the grace of God, king of kings, sovereign of sovereigns, most high emperor of Byzantium and Trebizond, very powerful king of Persia, of Arabia, of Syria, and of Egypt, supreme lord of Europe, and of Asia, prince of Mecca and Aleppo, lord of Jerusalem, and ruler of the universal sea, to Philip de L'Isle Adam, Grand Master of the island of Rhodes, greetings.
>
> I congratulate you upon your new dignity, and upon your arrival within your territories. I trust that you will rule there prosperously, and with even more glory than your predecessors. I also mean to cultivate your favour. Rejoice then with me, as a very dear friend, that following in the footsteps of my father, who conquered Persia, Jerusalem, Arabia and Egypt, I have captured that most powerful of fortresses, Belgrade, during the late Autumn. After which, having offered battle to the Infidel, which they had not the courage to accept, I took many other beautiful and well-fortified cities, and destroyed most of their inhabitants either by sword or fire, the remainder being reduced to slavery. Now after sending my numerous and victorious army into their winter quarters, I shall myself return in triumph to my court at Constantinople.

To those who could read between the lines this was not an expression of friendship. It was a declaration of war. Suleiman, great-grandson of Mehmet the Conqueror, had just inherited the Ottoman throne. According to custom and tradition, he was obliged to mark his accession with victories; each new sultan had to legitimize his position as "Conqueror of the Lands of the Orient and the Occident" by adding fresh territories to the world empire. He could then distribute booty, secure the loyalty of the army, and indulge in the ritual forms of propaganda. Victory letters—assertions of imperial power—were sent out to impress the Muslim world and intimidate the Christian one, and the new sultan could then start building his mosque.

An accession also had to be accompanied by death. The sultan was required by law to kill all his brothers "in the interest of the world order," to scotch the possibility of civil war. A mournful line of children's coffins would be carried out of the palace harem to the muted sobbing of women, while stranglers with bowstrings were dispatched to distant provinces to hunt down older siblings.

In Suleiman's case there were no such deaths. He was the sole male heir. It is likely that his father, Selim, had executed all his other sons six years earlier to snuff out preemptive coups. The twenty-six-year-old was uniquely blessed in his inheritance. He acquired a powerful, unified empire possessed of unrivaled resources. To pious Muslims, Suleiman was the harbinger of good fortune. His name—Solomon—chosen by opening the Koran at random, presaged a ruler dedicated to wisdom and justice. In an age of portents, all the circumstances of Suleiman's accession were significant. He was the tenth sultan, born in the tenth year of the tenth century of the Muslim era. Ten was the cipher of perfection: the number of the parts of the Koran, the number of disciples of the Prophet, the commandments in the Pentateuch, and the astrological heavens of Islam. And Suleiman stepped onto the world stage at a moment of imperial destiny.

His reign would overlap and compete with the claims of a jostling crowd of rival monarchs: the Hapsburgs, Charles V and Philip II of Spain; the French Valois kings, Francis I and his son Henry II; in England the Tudors, Henry VIII and Elizabeth I; in Muscovy, Ivan the Terrible; in Iran, Shah Ismail; in India, the Mogul emperor Akbar. None would have a keener sense of imperial mission or make for themselves more lofty claims.

From the start Suleiman made a powerful and calculated impression on the foreign ambassadors admitted to his court. "The sultan is tall and slender but tough, with a thin and wiry face," wrote the Venetian Bartolomeo Contarini. "Rumour has it that Suleiman is aptly named . . . is knowledgeable and shows good judgement." His countenance was sober, his gaze steady, his caftans simple but magnificent. His height and physical presence were enhanced by the size of the enormous spherical turban pulled low over his forehead, and by his pale face. He meant to impress with the splendor of his person and his court. Soon he would lay claim to the title of Caesar and envisage control of the Mediterranean.

He had two immediate victories in mind. Keenly aware of the achievements of his forebears, Suleiman had dreamed, since boyhood, of completing the twin conquests that had eluded his great-grandfather Mehmet. The first was the storming of the fortress of Belgrade, the gateway to Hungary. Within ten months of his accession, the sultan was encamped before the city walls; by August 1521 he was saying prayers in its Christian cathedral. The second conquest was intended to advance his claim to be "Padishah of the White Sea." It was to be the capture of Rhodes.

THE ISLAND TO WHICH Suleiman now turned his attention was a strange anachronism—a freak Christian survivor from the medieval Crusades located within touching distance of the Islamic world. Rhodes is the most substantial and fertile of a belt of limestone islands—the Dodecanese, the twelve islands—that stretches for a hundred miles along the coast of Asia Minor. Rhodes lies at the southwest end of the group; the northern marker is the whitewashed monastery island of Patmos, one of Orthodox Christianity's holy sites, where Saint

*The young Suleiman*

John the Divine received the revelations of the New Testament. These islands are so closely intertwined with the bays and headlands of the Asian shore that the mainland is always a presence on the horizon. From Rhodes the crossing is a bare eleven miles, just a couple of hours' sailing time with a smart wind, so near that on clear winter days the snowy Asian mountains, refracted through the thin air, seem almost within touching distance.

When Mehmet took Constantinople in 1453, Christian powers still held the whole of the Aegean Sea in a defensive ring, like an arch whose strength depended on the interdependence of each stone. By 1521, the entire structure had collapsed; yet against gravity, Rhodes, the keystone, survived as an isolated Christian bastion that menaced the Ottomans' sea-lanes and cramped their maritime ambitions.

Rhodes and its accompanying islands were held in the name of the pope by the last remnant of the great military orders of the Crusades, the Knights of Saint John—the Hospitallers—whose fortunes closely mirrored the whole crusading enterprise. Originally founded to provide care for sick pilgrims in Jerusalem, they had also become, like the Templars and the Teutonic Knights, a military fighting order. Its members took lifelong vows of poverty, chastity, and obedience to the pope; their cardinal purpose was to wage unceasing war on the infidel. The Order of Saint John had fought in every significant action in the long wars of the Holy Land until they were cut down, almost to a man, with their backs to the sea at Acre in May 1291. In exile they searched for a means to continue this struggle, and their eyes alighted on the Greek Christian island of Rhodes. In 1307 they attacked and captured it. Rhodes became Western Christendom's deep position against the Islamic world, a launchpad from which a new counteroffensive for Palestine could be prepared at some point in the unspecified future.

In the town of Rhodes the knights created a small feudal bastion, a last outpost of the Latin Crusades, subject only to the pope, paid for from the rents on the Order's huge land holdings in Europe, and dedicated to holy war. The Holy Religion, as the knights called themselves, understood fortified places; they had generations of experience of frontier defense in Palestine. They had constructed Crac des Chevaliers, the greatest of the Crusader castles, and they now fortified the town with bravado and reinvented themselves as sea raiders, building and equipping a small squadron of heavily armed galleys, with which they plundered the Ottoman coasts and sea-lanes, taking slaves and booty.

For two hundred years, the Hospitallers maintained an uncompromising piratical presence on the edge of the Muslim world, holding the Dodecanese as a chain of fortified islands to pen in the Turks. The knights even managed to keep a toehold on the mainland itself, at the fortress the Turks called Bodrum—the castle of Saint Peter the Liberator. The fortress served both as an escape route for Christian slaves and as a propaganda tool for raising funds for the Order's mission throughout Europe. The knights, well aware of the fate that had befallen the Templars, managed their image carefully as the Shield of Christendom.

European opinion of the knights was mixed. For the Papacy, Rhodes carried a huge symbolic weight as the outer line of defense against the infidel, manning a maritime frontier in continual contraction as the Byzantine inheritance crumbled before the Islamic advance and one by one the bright ring of islands fell to the Ottomans. Pope Pius II lamented that "if all the other Christian princes . . . had shown themselves as tireless in their hostility to the Turks as the single island of Rhodes had done, that impious people would not have grown so strong." Even after the fall of Constantinople, Rhodes continued to nourish the Holy See's most cherished project—the possibility of an eventual return to the Holy Land. Others were less charitable: to Christian maritime traders, the Hospitallers were a dangerous anachronism. The Order's acts of piracy and blockades of Western trade with Muslims threatened to destabilize the delicate peace on which commerce depended. The Venetians thought the knights indistinguishable from corsairs and regarded them as a menace second only to Ottoman imperial ambitions.

The knights' impact certainly outstripped their resources. There were never more than five hundred on Rhodes, drawn from the aristocracy of Europe, supported more or less willingly by the local Greek population and mercenaries. They comprised a small well-organized military elite with a powerful sense of mission whose nuisance value was out of proportion to their number. Their galleys lurked in the aquamarine lagoons and rocky inlets of the Asian shore, quick to snatch passing traffic—boatloads of pilgrims from Istanbul bound for

Mecca; timber for Egypt from the Black Sea; cargoes of spices from Arabia; honey, dried fish, wine, and silk. Their reputation was fearsome among friend and foe alike. To tackle a Hospitaller galley was to take on a scorpion. "These corsairs are noted for their energy and daring," wrote the Ottoman chroniclers. "They disrupt life, causing all sorts of losses to merchants, and capturing travelers." To Muslims, they were, and always had been, the archenemy, the "evil sect of Franks, the worst sons of Error, the most corrupted of the Devil's spawn"; the Muslim general Saladin had slaughtered his Hospitaller captives without compunction during the Crusades. Their allegiance to the pope made them doubly loathsome in Ottoman eyes. Worse still, they ran a market on the island for the sale of Muslim slaves. "How many sons of the Prophet are captured by these children of lies?" mourned the Muslim chroniclers. "How many thousand of the faithful are forced to turn infidel? How many wives and children? Their wickedness knows no end."

Successive sultans perceived Rhodes as a menace, an affront to sovereignty—and unfinished business. Mehmet had sent a large invasion force to take it and been humiliated. When Selim, Suleiman's father, captured Egypt in 1517, the position of Rhodes astride the sea route to Istanbul increased the island's strategic threat. The early decades of the sixteenth century were a time of hunger in the Eastern Mediterranean, and food supplies for the capital were critical. "The said Rhodians are inflicting great losses on the sultan's subjects," noted the Venetian diarist Sanudo in 1512, the year the knights captured eighteen grain transports bound for Istanbul and forced up the prices there by 50 percent. Complaints to the sultan grew audible: "They don't let the ships of merchants or pilgrims bound for Egypt pass without sinking them with their cannon and capturing the Muslims." To Suleiman this was not just a strategic threat; his position as "head of Muhammad's community" was at stake. The taking of Muslim slaves on the very doorstep of his realm was intolerable. He now decided to crush "the vipers' nest of Franks."

NINE DAYS AFTER SULEIMAN had written his victory letter in Belgrade, the man to whom it was addressed set foot in Rhodes. His name was Philippe Villiers de L'Isle Adam, a French aristocrat who had just been elected grand master of the Order of Saint John. He was fifty-seven years old, the descendant of a family with a long history of dying

for the Crusades. His ancestor had conducted the order's last-ditch defense at Acre in 1291. L'Isle Adam must have been under few illusions
about the task ahead. The voyage from Marseilles to take up his post
had been ominous with portents. Off Nice, one of his vessels caught
fire; in the Malta Channel, the Order's great flagship, the *Saint Mary*,
was blasted by a lightning bolt. Nine men fell dead; a crackle of elec-
tricity flashed down the grand master's sword, reducing it to twisted
scrap, but he stepped away from the scorched deck unharmed. When
the ships put in at Syracuse to repair the storm damage, they found
themselves shadowed by the Turkish corsair Kurtoglu, cruising offshore with a powerful squadron of galleys stripped for war. Under
cover of darkness, the knights quietly slipped from the harbor and out-
ran their pursuers on a westerly wind.

When he read Suleiman's letter, L'Isle Adam framed a terse response, distinctly short of pleasantries and any recognition of the sultan's grander titles. "Brother Philippe Villiers de L'Isle Adam, Grand
Master of Rhodes, to Suleiman, sultan of the Turks," it began. "I have
right well comprehended the meaning of your letter, which has been
presented to me by your ambassador." The grand master went on to
recount the attempt by Kurtoglu to capture the ship on which he was
traveling, before concluding with an abrupt "Farewell." At the same
time, he dispatched a parallel letter to the king of France: "Sire, since
he became Grand Turk, this is the first letter that he has sent to
Rhodes, and we do not accept it as a token of friendship, but rather as a
veiled threat."

L'Isle Adam was well aware what was likely to unfold—the knights'
intelligence was excellent and they had been bracing themselves
against attack for forty years. The early years of the sixteenth century
ring with their appeals to the pope and the courts of Europe for men
and money. After the Ottoman capture of Egypt in 1517, the menace of
the Turk loomed larger than ever. The Christian sea began to tremble
in dreadful anticipation. Pope Leo was almost paralyzed by fear: "Now
that the Terrible Turk has Egypt and Alexandria and the whole of the
Roman eastern empire in his power and has equipped a massive fleet in
the Dardanelles, he will swallow not just Sicily and Italy but the whole
world." It was obvious that Rhodes was the front line in a gathering
storm. The grand master renewed his appeals for help.

The unified response of Christendom was exactly zero. Italy, as

Suleiman well knew, was a battleground between the Hapsburg kings of Spain and the Valois of France; Venice, bloodied in her earlier struggle with the Turk, had opted for treaties of friendship; while Martin Luther's reformation was beginning to split the Christian world into fractious shards. Successive popes unceasingly jabbed the conscience of the secular potentates of Europe to no avail, and dreamed up fantasy schemes for crusades. In more lucid moments the popes bewailed the disarray of Christendom. Only the knights themselves rallied from their command posts across Europe, but their numbers were pitifully small.

Undeterred, L'Isle Adam began preparing for siege. He dispatched ships to Italy, Greece, and Crete to buy wheat and wine. He oversaw the clearing out of ditches and the repairing of bastions and the operation of gunpowder mills—and tried to stifle the hemorrhaging of information across the narrow straits to the sultan's lands. In April 1522, the unripe wheat was harvested and the ground outside the town stripped of cover and scorched. A pair of massive iron chains was hauled across the harbor mouth.

Four hundred fifty miles away in Istanbul, Suleiman was gathering a huge army and fitting out his fleet. The hallmark of any Ottoman campaign was the ability to mobilize men and resources on a scale that paralyzed their enemy's powers of calculation. Chroniclers tended to double or triple the reasonable estimate of a force that could be assembled and supplied for war—or simply gave up; "numerous as the stars" was a common epithet of appalled defenders crouching behind their battlements at the sight of the vast host of men and animals and tents camped outside. In this spirit, the expedition to Rhodes was put at an inflated two hundred thousand men and a mighty armada of ships, "galleasses, galleys, pallandaries, fustes and brigantines to the number of 300 sails and more." L'Isle Adam decided against counting his men too carefully. There were so few of them, it would be bad for morale, "and he feared that the Great Turk might have knowledge by goers and comers into Rhodes." In all likelihood there were five hundred knights and fifteen hundred mercenaries and local Greeks to defend the town. The grand master decided on a series of morale-raising parades, whereby the various companies "decked their men with colours and devices" and mustered "with the great noise of trumpets and drums." The knights in their red surcoats bearing white crosses made a cheerful array.

When Mehmet had besieged Rhodes in 1480, he had not attended in person. He stayed in Istanbul and sent his commander. Suleiman resolved to make a personal call on "the damnable workers of wickedness." Any sultan's presence upped the stakes in a military campaign enormously. Defeat was inadmissible; failure by any corps commander meant dismissal—or death. Suleiman was coming only to win.

ON JUNE 10 THE KNIGHTS received a second letter, this time stripped of diplomatic niceties:

> The Sultan Suleiman to Villiers de L'Isle Adam, Grand
> Master of Rhodes, to his Knights, and to the people at large.
> Your monstrous injuries against my most afflicted people have
> aroused my pity and indignation. I command you, therefore,
> instantly to surrender the island and fortress of Rhodes, and
> I give you my gracious permission to depart in safety with the
> most precious of your effects; or if you desire to remain under
> my government, I shall not require of you any tribute, or do
> anything in diminution of your liberties, or against your reli-
> gion. If you are wise, you will prefer friendship and peace to
> cruel war. Since, if you are conquered, you will have to undergo
> all the miseries as are usually inflicted by those that are victori-
> ous, from which you will be protected neither by your own
> forces, nor by external aid, nor by the strength of your fortifica-
> tions which I will overthrow to their foundations. . . . I swear
> this by the God of heaven, the Creator of the earth, by the four
> Evangelists, by the four thousand prophets, who have descended
> from heaven, chief amongst whom stands Muhammad, most
> worthy to be worshipped; by the shades of my grandfather and
> father, and by my own sacred, august and imperial head.

The grand master did not deign a reply. He concentrated his efforts on the manufacture of gunpowder.

On June 16 Suleiman crossed the Bosphorus with his army and proceeded to make his way down the Asian coast to the crossing place to

Rhodes. Two days later the fleet set sail from its base at Gallipoli, carrying heavy guns, supplies, and more troops.

DESPITE THE HUGE DISCREPANCY in numbers, the contest was less one-sided than it appeared. When Ottoman armies had surrounded the town of Rhodes in 1480, they looked up at a typical fortress of the medieval world. The thin, high walls, designed to resist scaling by ladders and siege engines, were horribly vulnerable to sustained gunfire. By 1522, the defenses had been largely remodeled. The knights may have been backward-looking in their ethos and sense of mission, but when it came to military engineering, they were early adopters. In the forty years of peace, they had spent their spare cash commissioning the best Italian engineers to strengthen their redoubts.

This work was undertaken on the cusp of a revolution in military architecture. The gunpowder age and the development of accurate bronze cannon that fired penetrative iron balls were revolutionizing fortress design. Italian military engineers developed their discipline as a science. They mapped geometric angles of fire with compasses and used knowledge of ballistics to design radical solutions. At Rhodes, the engineers constructed prototypes of this new military engineering: massive walls, angled bastions of immense thickness that commanded wide fields of fire, slanted parapets to deflect shot, mountings for long-range guns, splayed gun ports, inner defensive layers with concealed batteries, double ditches excavated to the depth of canyons, counterscarps that exposed an advancing enemy to a torrent of fire. The new principles were depth defense and cross fire; no enemy could advance without being hit from multiple vantage points, nor could he be sure what traps lay within. Rhodes in 1522 was not just the best-defended city on earth, it was also a laboratory of siege warfare. The labor for this enterprise was largely supplied by enslaved Muslims, one of whom was a young seaman called Oruch, destined neither to forget nor forgive the experience.

In layout, the town was as round as an apple with a bite taken out of one arc, where the protected harbor was let into the town. The knights fought in national groups so that the defense of the circle was divided into eight sectors, each with its tower, managed by a particular country. England held one sector, Italy another; Auvergne commanded the most redoubtable bastion of all; then Germany, Castile, France, Provence, and Aragon.

Despite failing to draw substantial Western aid, L'Isle Adam had a small stroke of luck. From Crete he managed to recruit the services of one of the great military engineers of the day, Gabrielle Tadini, "a most brilliant engineer and in the business of war a supreme expert in mathematical science." Tadini was nominally in the pay of the Venetians, who were utterly opposed to his participation, which would be seen as a breach of their neutrality. The knights smuggled him off the island at night from a deserted cove. It was a cheering coup. Tadini, craggy, spirited, innovative, and brave, was worth a thousand men. He set to work adjusting the defenses, measuring distances and fields of fire, fine-tuning the killing zones.

It was on the feast day of Saint John, June 24—the most holy day in the knights' year—that the Ottoman fleet made a first tentative landing on the island. Two days later the fleet came to anchor six miles south of the town and started the lengthy process of unloading equipment and ferrying men and materials across from the mainland. In a solemn ceremony, the grand master laid the keys to the city on the altar of the saint's church, "beseeching St John to take keeping and protection thereof and of all The Religion ... and by his holy grace to defend them from the great power of enemies that had besieged them."

It took two weeks for the Ottomans to bring everything across. Onto the shore they unloaded a comprehensive lexicon of artillery pieces: bombards and basilisks, serpentines, double guns, and pot guns. These fired an exotic range of projectiles intended to fulfill specific purposes in the pattern of attack: giant stones nine feet in circumference, and penetrative iron balls propelled at explosive velocity, for battering and puncturing walls; brass firebombs that fragmented and spread flaming naphtha "to make murder of the people'; high-trajectory mortar bullets. Even biological weapons: some cannon were expressly designed to hurl rotting corpses over the walls.

No army in the world could match the Ottomans in the art of siege warfare; through espionage they came to Rhodes quite well informed about the defenses, and had made a realistic assessment of the task. The Turks accordingly placed their ultimate confidence less in their siege guns than in subterranean devices: the use of explosive mines. To this end, a substantial portion of the men unloading onto the bright beaches were armed only with picks and shovels. Suleiman had scoured his Balkan territories for skilled miners, mainly Christians, to tunnel under the walls. Inflated figures suggested sixty thousand—a third of the total army. They would dig their way under the cunningly designed Italian bastions yard by painstaking yard.

On July 28 the defenders could see the Ottoman ships draping celebratory banners from their tops: Suleiman had crossed the straits in his galley. Once the sultan had established his camp and ceremonial tent beyond the reach of gunshot and overseen the arrangements, the siege could formally begin.

INITIALLY IT WAS a contest for the ground beyond the walls; later for the walls themselves. The miners were put to work constructing trenches parallel to the town's defenses and erecting wooden palisades in front of them; a second phase involved the digging of saps—deep narrow trenches—spidering forward to the walls themselves. From the start it was a brutal affair. The wretched miners, digging in the open, were massacred by Tadini's pinpoint gunfire; unexpected sorties killed more. It was of little import to the Ottoman commanders—men were plentiful and expendable. Trenches were established, guns dragged into position behind the protective screens, and the firing began. Heavy cannon pummeled the walls night and day for a month; mortars bombed the town with flaming missiles and "falling to the ground they broke and the fires came out of them and did some harm"; sharpshooters with arquebuses—matchlock muskets—attempted to sweep the battlements clean of defenders. One eyewitness noted that "the handgun shot was innumerable and incredible." The immense supply of human labor enabled prodigious feats of excavation. The miners brought "a mountain of earth" from half a mile away to construct two huge ramps that overtopped the walls, on which they mounted five cannon to fire into the town.

So large was the army that it encircled the landward perimeter in a Turkish crescent that stretched from shore to shore, a distance of one and a half miles. An extensive network of trenches started to inch forward day by day, their open tops covered with screens of wood and skin, while the miners worked below.

Tadini mounted energetic countermeasures. As the tunnels advanced, he constructed ingenious listening devices: skin membranes were stretched tight across frames to which bells were attached. These were so sensitive that even the minutest vibrations from beneath the ground set the alarm tinkling. He dug countermines to intercept the tunnels and killed the intruders in the dark, blasted the miners out of their covered saps with gunpowder, and set up elaborate traps to catch the advancing enemy in a murderous cross fire. In case a tunnel should be missed, he bored spiral vents in the walls' foundations to disperse the force of explosive charges.

The newly constructed Italian bastions resisted the pummeling of the guns well, but some of the older sections, particularly the English zone, were more vulnerable. And the miners were indefatigable. By early September, Tadini had neutralized some fifty tunnels, but on September 4 the whole town was rocked by an explosion under the English bastion. An undetected tunnel had allowed the Turks to detonate mines and blast a thirty-foot hole. Infantry poured forward; for a while Suleiman's men established a bridgehead and planted banners on the walls, before being beaten back with great loss of life. Successive days saw the bloodshed escalate. Mines exploded—mainly with little damage, because of Tadini's system of vents—direct attacks were mounted and repulsed, unknown thousands of Ottoman troops perished. Suleiman's master gunner had his legs blown off by a cannonball—a loss said to have been more grievous to the sultan than that of any general. The men became reluctant to attack; on September 9 they had to be driven to the walls "with great strokes of the sword." Casualties within the city were far fewer but much more serious—each man killed was an irreplaceable loss. On September 4 alone, the knights lost three leading commanders: the captain of the galleys, the standard-bearer Henry Mansell, and the grand commander Gabriel de Pommerols, who "fell from the walls as he went to see his trenches . . . and hurt his breast."

Suleiman watched from a safe distance beyond the reach of gunshot and recorded the unfolding battle in a series of laconic entries in his campaign journal. For the end of August he simply noted: "26 and 27, combat. 28, order given to fill in the ditch with branches and rocks. 29, the batteries of Piri Pasha, which the infidel had knocked out, start firing again. 30, the ditch is filled in. 31, bitter combat." A sense of Olympian detachment pervades these pages; the sultan speaks of himself only in the third person, as if the man who was the Shadow of God on Earth were too elevated to admit to human emotions, but in the journal it is possible lightly to trace a trajectory of expectation. His general, Mustapha Pasha, had told the sultan that the siege would take a month. As the town was shaken by a succession of explosive mines during September and breaches widened, it seemed likely that a final assault was not far off. On September 19, Suleiman recorded that some troops managed to get inside a sector of the walls. "On this occasion, certain knowledge was acquired that inside there was neither a second ditch nor a second wall." On September 23, Mustapha Pasha decided the moment had come. Heralds went among the army to announce an imminent all-out attack; Suleiman addressed the men, stirring them to deeds of valor. He had a viewing platform erected from which to follow the final push.

In the predawn of September 24, "even before the hour of morning prayer," a massive bombardment opened up. In the concealing smoke, the janissaries, Suleiman's crack troops, began their advance. The defense was taken by surprise. The janissaries established themselves on the walls and planted banners. A furious battle ensued. The ground was contested for six hours, but the grand master managed to rally the defenders, and a hail of cross fire hit the intruders from the bastions and concealed positions within the outer wall. Eventually the Ottomans wavered and fell back. No threats could return them to the breach. They fled the field, leaving the rubble smoking and bloody. Suleiman wrote just one sentence in his journal: "The attack is repulsed." Next day he declared his intention to have Mustapha Pasha paraded in front of the whole army and shot full of arrows. The following day Suleiman reversed the decision.

MUFFLED NEWS OF THE SIEGE was relayed across the Mediterranean world. Though they did nothing, the potentates of Europe understood how much Rhodes mattered. It was the dam holding back the Ottoman maritime advance. The Holy Roman Emperor Charles V foresaw that the island's loss would open up the central seas; the Ottomans would proceed to a seaborne assault on Italy, "and finally to ruin and destroy all Christendom." Unfortunately for Rhodes, this brilliant strategic insight had no material consequences. During October just a couple of small ships broke the blockade, bringing a few knights. In Italy the Order had raised the cash for two thousand mercenaries, who made it to Messina on Sicily but no farther; without armed escorts they dared not sail. In faraway Britain, some English knights prepared an expedition. It departed too late in the season and foundered with the loss of all hands in the Bay of Biscay.

The attacks went on. The walls were repeatedly undermined and assaulted; five attempts on the English sector were beaten back in ten days; by early October most of the English knights were either wounded or dead. On October 10, events took a more serious turn. The Spanish wall was breached and the intruders could not be dislodged; they were contained by a hastily constructed inner wall, but the Ottomans were there to stay. "It was an ill-starred day for us," wrote one of the knights, "the beginning of our ruin." Further bad news next day: a marksman spotted Tadini studying the defenses through an embrasure and shot him in the face. The ball smashed his eye socket and exited out of the side of his skull. The doughty engineer, though grievously wounded, proved too tough to die. He was out of action for six weeks. In the meantime the number of serviceable cannon was dwindling by the day, and powder supplies were running so low that the grand master ordered no gun to be fired without permission.

The town succumbed to a witch hunt for spies. In a mixed population of Latins, Greeks, and Jews, supported by a sullen gang of enslaved Muslims, everyone could imagine a fifth column of enemy sympathizers. Early in the siege, a plot by the Turkish women slaves to set fire to the houses had been foiled and the ringleaders put to death. Despite being closely guarded, the male slaves continually escaped; they dropped over the wall at night or slipped into the sea and swam out of the harbor. Suleiman learned from a deserter that the attack of September 24 had cost the lives of three hundred men and the significant loss of key commanders. The same month a Jewish doctor, a deep mole planted in the town by Suleiman's father years earlier, was caught firing a crossbow bolt over the wall with a message attached to it. The jittery population started to imagine spies everywhere; rumors of treachery and prophecies of doom spread like wildfire. In late October a second Jew was caught preparing a crossbow message; he was the servant of the chancellor of the Order, Andrea D'Amaral, a surly, unpopular figure who had been passed over for the office of grand master. The knights were now prepared to believe anything. D'Amaral was arrested and tortured. He refused to confess to aiding the enemy but was found guilty and hanged, drawn, and quartered. The head and dismembered body parts were spitted on pikes on the walls. Fear stalked the camp.

AS THE LIKELIHOOD of relief slipped away, the knights had one last hope: the weather. Campaigning throughout the Mediterranean basin was a seasonal affair. By late autumn, once the rains start, soldiers dream of a return to their barracks, conscripted men of their villages and farms. The seas become too rough for the low-slung war galleys—disaster awaits the fleet that outstays its welcome. No one observed this calendar as prudently as the Ottomans; the traditional campaigning season began each year on the Persian New Year's Day—March 21—and was over by the end of October. On Rhodes it began to rain on October 25. The trenches filled with water, churning the ground to mud. The battlefield resembled the Somme. The wind swung east, whipping the cold straight off the Anatolian steppes. The miners found it difficult to grip their shovels with frozen fingers. Men began to die of disease. It became harder to urge them on. The attackers were losing heart.

Any Ottoman commander left to his own devices would now cut his losses. With the fear of having his fleet smashed on the rocks and his army murmuring and weakened by disease, he would turn for home and risk the sultan's wrath. With Suleiman in attendance, this was not an option: the sultan had come to win. A failure so early in his reign would severely dent his authority. At a council on October 31, the fleet was dispatched to a secure anchorage on the Anatolian shore; Suleiman commanded a stone "pleasure-house" to be constructed to provide his winter quarters; the siege would continue.

It straggled on through the whole of November. The knights were now too few to guard every sector of the wall, nor did they any longer possess sufficient slave labor to repair defenses or move guns. "We had no powder," wrote the English knight Sir Nicholas Roberts, "nor [any] manner of munitions, nor vittles, but ... bread and water. We were as men desperate." No substantial help arrived by sea, and the Ottomans were securely lodged in the Spanish breach. By now the gap was wide enough for forty horsemen to enter side by side. Further attacks were made, but the bitter weather and slashing rain dampened morale: "insistent and interminable downpours; the raindrops froze; large quantities of hail fell." On November 30, the Ottomans made their last major assault. It failed, but they could not be pushed back. The contest had reached an impasse. Realists within the town "could not think the city any longer tenable, the enemy being lodged forty yards one way and thirty yards another way within the city, so that it was impossible for them to retire any further, nor for the enemy to be beaten out." Suleiman, on the other hand, was watching his army being decimated by the day. Modern fortress design had been remarkably effective in evening up the contest. He knew his soldiers' endurance was finite. He had to find a solution.

On December 1 a Genoese renegade appeared unexpectedly at the gates, offering to act as an intermediary. He was chased away but returned two days later. It was the start of a cagey attempt to broker negotiated surrender, in which the sultan could not be seen to be involved. It was beneath the dignity of the most powerful ruler on earth to seek peace. Mysterious letters repeating the terms were delivered to the grand master, which Suleiman denied sending, but gradually a pattern of diplomacy emerged. The knights debated the issue at length in closed council. L'Isle Adam would have preferred to go down fighting; so distressed was he at the prospect of surrendering the island that he collapsed in a faint. But Tadini knew that militarily their case was hopeless, and the citizens of the town, remembering the fate of the civilian population at Belgrade, made tearful supplications. The defenders were surprised and initially suspicious of the terms: the knights could depart with honor, taking with them their possessions and arms, with the exception of artillery. The freedom and religion of the remaining townspeople would be respected; there would be no forced conversion to Islam, nor would the churches be turned into mosques. No tribute would be required for five years. In return the knights were required to surrender all their islands and fortresses, including the fort of Saint Peter the Liberator on the mainland. The generosity of the terms suggested that Suleiman also needed an end to winter warfare: he had been fought to a standstill. He even offered to provide the ships for the knights' departure.

Stop-start talks dragged on for a fortnight. L'Isle Adam tried to play for time and had to be brought back to negotiation by another attack. In the end he accepted the inevitable. Suleiman was firm: he would have the fortress, even if "all Turkey should die," but he convinced the Christians of his good faith. To create a climate of trust,

*The aging L'Isle Adam*

Suleiman withdrew the army a mile back from the city, and hostages were exchanged. Among these was Sir Nicholas Roberts, the first Englishman to record a meeting with a sultan. The experience left a deep impression: "The Great Turk is very wise, discreet ... both in his words and deeds," he wrote. "We were brought first to make our reverence unto him, we found ... a red pavilion ... marvellous rich and sumptuous." Here he made obeisance to Suleiman, who was "sitting in a chair, and no [other] creature sat in the pavilion, which chair was of fine gold." Even in makeshift camp, Suleiman overawed.

The treaty was finally signed on December 20. Four days later L'Isle Adam went to make his submission to Suleiman in a plain black habit, the garb of mourning. The meeting was almost gentlemanly. Suleiman was apparently moved by the bearded melancholy figure who stooped to kiss his hand, and by the knights' gallant defense. Through an interpreter, he consoled the visibly ageing L'Isle Adam with sympathetic words on the vagaries of life—that "it was a common thing to lose cities and kingdoms through the instability of human fortune." Turning to his vizier, he murmured, "It saddens me to be compelled to cast this brave old man out of his home." Two days later, in a further remarkable gesture, he made a visit to view the city he had captured, almost without guards and trusting to the knights' honor. As he left, he raised his turban in salute to his adversary.

Not everything went so smoothly. On Christmas Day, a detachment of janissaries entered the city, ostensibly to guard it, and indulged in some looting and desecration of the churches. Far away in Rome, the imminent loss of the Christian bastion was marked by an ominous coincidence. During the Christmas Day service in Saint Peter's, a stone detached itself from the cornice high up in the arch and crashed at the feet of the pope. The faithful saw in this a clear sign: the cornerstone of Christian defense had collapsed; the infidel's way into the Mediterranean lay open. And for the Muslims, there was the triumphant entry into the city to cries of "Allah!" The janissaries' standard—one of the victorious flags of Islam—was raised, and the imperial drums and music sounded. "In this way, the city that had been subjected to error was incorporated into the lands of Islam."

AS AFTERNOON FADED into winter dusk on New Year's Day 1523, the knights still left alive—those able to walk and those who had to be carried, one hundred eighty in all—boarded their great carrack, the *Saint Mary*, and their galleys, the *Saint James*, the *Saint Catherine*, and the *Saint Bonaventura*. With them they took the records of their Order and their most holy relics: the right arm of John the Baptist in its jeweled casket, and a venerable icon of the Virgin. Tadini, whom Suleiman had been eager to retain for his army, had already been spirited away.

As the ships put off from the embracing harbor, the knights could look back at the snowy mountains of Asia Minor and four hundred years of Crusader history, emphatically ended now with the fall of Rhodes and the surrender of Bodrum. Rhodes would remain for the knights a kind of paradise in the following decades; nostalgic dreams of regaining it died hard. Ahead lay an uncertain future and night running toward them over the Sea of Crete. Among those watching from the rail was a young French aristocrat, Jean Parisot de La Valette. He was twenty-six years old—the same age as the sultan. Among those on the shore was a young Turkish soldier called Mustapha who had distinguished himself in the campaign.

SULEIMAN RETURNED TO Istanbul in triumph. In just eighteen months, the taciturn young ruler had laid down an emphatic statement of imperial intent. Belgrade opened up Hungary and central Europe; Rhodes stripped the Eastern Mediterranean of its last militant Christian stronghold. Ottoman ships, "agile as serpents," were poised to sweep the central seas. These were the opening shots in a huge contest that would stretch from the gates of Vienna to the Gates of Gibraltar.

The reign that sprang from these conquests was destined to be the longest and most glorious in Ottoman history. The man the Turks called the Lawgiver and Christians the Magnificent would wage war on an epic scale and lift his empire to the summit of power. None would equal the tenth sultan for majesty, justice, and ambition. Yet Suleiman's golden age would be tarnished by the troublesome Knights of Saint John: forty years later, they would return to haunt him, in the person of La Valette. The sultan's youthful act of generosity at Rhodes was to prove a costly mistake. And if after 1522 Suleiman claimed to be advancing under the legitimate banners of heaven, he was not alone. At the far western edge of Ptolemy's map, there was a Christian counterweight.

# CHAPTER 2

# A Supplication

1517–1530

*Five years earlier. Fifteen hundred miles west. Another sea.*

IN NOVEMBER 1517, a fleet of forty sailing vessels was dipping and plunging across the Bay of Biscay in dirty weather. They were Flemish ships from Vlissingen in the Netherlands bound for the north coast of Spain. These stout carracks were built to withstand the long Atlantic rollers. Each one carried yards of canvas; their mainsails swelled in the fierce winter blow. Fists of squally rain whipped across the gray water, blotting out the vessels, then revealing them again in the dull light. A coastline slowly formed through the mizzle.

Even from a distance, one ship stood out from the rest. The *Real* was carrying the young Charles, duke of Burgundy, to claim his crown as king of Spain, and its sails were elaborately decorated with symbols of religious and imperial power.

On its mainsail was painted a picture of the crucifixion, between the figures of the Virgin Mary and St John the Evangelist, the whole enframed between two pillars of Hercules which appear on the royal arms, together with the king's motto "Further," written on a scroll twined around the said pillars. On the topsail was painted a representation of the Holy Trinity, and at the mizzen that of St Nicholas. On the foresail was a picture of the Virgin with her Child, treading on the moon, and surrounded by the rays of the sun, with a crown with seven stars above her head; and over it all there was painted the figure of St James, the lord and patron of Castile, slaying the infidels in battle.

CHARLES WAS SEVENTEEN YEARS OLD. Through the complexities of dynastic succession, he was the inheritor of the largest domain in Europe since the time of Charlemagne. His realms were the mirror image of the Ottoman Empire, and he claimed a litany of titles to equal

Suleiman's. It took scribes two long-winded pages to record them: king of Aragon, Castile, and Navarre, Naples and Sicily; ruler of the Burgundian territories; duke of Milan; head of the house of Hapsburg, of Franche-Compte, Luxemburg, and Charolais; and so on. His territories, dotted across Europe like the black squares on a chessboard, stretched from Hungary in the east to the Atlantic in the west, from Amsterdam to the shores of North Africa, and beyond—to the newfound Americas.

The imagery on the sails had been carefully chosen by the young king's Flemish advisers both to appeal to his new Spanish subjects and to declare their king's claim to empire and leadership of holy war. In the Spanish age of discovery, Charles's domains would extend far beyond the Gates of Gibraltar—they would encompass the earth. With the crown, he inherited the honorific title of the Catholic King and the commitment to crush the moon of Islam and trample its soldiers underfoot in the name of Saint James.

From the start his advisers promoted the idea that their sovereign had been chosen by God to be emperor of the world. He inherited from the Austrian Hapsburgs the motto "It is for Austria to rule the entire earth." Two years later, in 1519, he would be elected, not without heavy bribes, to the office of Holy Roman Emperor. It was a purely honorific title, to which neither lands nor revenue attached, but in an age of imperial epithets, it conferred enormous prestige. It designated Charles as the secular champion of Catholic Europe against Muslims and heretics. And Charles would soon be described as the ruler of the empire on which the sun never sets. In the year of his election Magellan departed on the voyage that would throw a Spanish girdle around the earth.

UNFORTUNATELY, NONE OF THIS imperial splendor was apparent in Charles's farcical landfall in November 1517. As the ships drew near the Spanish coast, the Flemish navigators were mortified to discover that they were a hundred miles west of their true objective. They made an unannounced arrival at the small port of Villaviciosa, where the local inhabitants failed to read the majestic symbols on Charles's sails and mistook them for pirates. The townspeople panicked and fled into the hills with their belongings and prepared for battle. Shouts of "Spain, it's the king" failed to clarify the situation—it was well known that pirates would descend to any ruse to lull the unwary—and it was a good while before the banners of Castile were recognized by someone braver than the rest, "approaching covertly through the bushes and hedgerows." Charles's thunderstruck subjects finally pulled themselves together and laid on an impromptu bullfight.

It was not a glorious start. Nor did the seventeen-year-old groggily setting foot on Spanish soil cut any kind of figure. Where the young Suleiman's calculated imperial demeanor struck all who saw him, Charles just looked an imbecile. Generations of inbreeding within the Hapsburg dynasty had bequeathed an unkind legacy. His eyes bulged; he was alarmingly pale. Any redeeming physical features that he did possess—a well-formed body, a broad forehead—were immediately off-set by the long protruding lower jaw that frequently left his mouth hanging open, which to those impolite enough or royal enough to re-mark on it, lent the young man an aspect of vacant idiocy. His grandfa-ther Maximilian bluntly called him a heathen idol. Facial deformity made it impossible for Charles to chew food properly, so that he was troubled all his life by digestive problems, and the deformity left him with a stammer. The king spoke no Spanish. He seemed grave, tongue-tied, stupid—hardly the prospective emperor of the terrestrial globe. The Venetians considered him the pawn of his advisers. But appear-ances would prove deceptive. The unprepossessing exterior hid an in-

*The young Charles*

dependence of mind, the taciturn silence an unblinking commitment to imperial duty and the protection of Christendom. "There is more at the back of his head," a papal legate judiciously observed, "than appears in his face."

Charles's landfall was symbolic of all the difficulties that instantly confronted him. It was said that only those regions that had not set eyes on their French- and Flemish-speaking king refrained from revolt at the start of his reign. And in addition to the internal problems of the Iberian Peninsula, Charles was almost immediately plunged into the whole entangled history of Christian Spain's relations with Islam. The Gates of Gibraltar that featured so prominently on Charles's sails were not only the portal to the Americas and the Indies; they were also the frontier with an increasingly hostile Muslim world, just eight miles across the straits. Soon after Charles's arrival, the situation was laid out in detail by the marquis of Comares, the military governor of Oran on the North African shore. He came in the company of a man in Arab dress to pay homage and present a petition that promptly tested the king's ambitions.

THE ROOTS OF COMARES'S suit lay centuries deep, in the Arab occu-pation of southern Spain and the long Christian counter-crusade, the *reconquista*, but it also involved the Knights of Saint John. The water-shed year was well within living memory—1492, the year of Colum-bus—when Isabella and Ferdinand, monarchs of Aragon and Castile, had dislodged the last Moorish kingdom in Granada. The Muslims who had lived peacefully on the Iberian Peninsula for eight hundred years were at once out of place. Many crossed the straits to North Africa. The tens of thousands who remained were subject to increasing restrictions in an atmosphere of growing Christian intolerance. By 1502 the Muslims of Castile were given a stark choice: convert or leave Spain. Many embittered subjects again departed; those who stayed— the so-called Moriscos or New Christians, often converted only in name—remained suspect to their increasingly twitchy masters.

These events had a galvanizing effect across the water in the land the Europeans called the Barbary Coast and the Arabs the Maghreb (the West)—that strip of North Africa occupying the footprint of mod-ern Morocco, Algeria, and Tunisia. Sea robbery had always been en-demic on both sides of this maritime frontier. Now the expulsion of a vengeful Muslim population injected a new bitterness. Piracy was no longer an act of random plunder; it was holy war. From secure havens of the Barbary shore, raids were becoming intense and grievous. Christian Spain began to reap the whirlwind of its internal crusade. The new breed of Islamic corsairs knew the coasts of Spain ominously well; they spoke the language and could pass themselves off as Spanish; worse still, they had the active cooperation of disaffected Moriscos on the northern shore. Christian Spain started to feel itself under siege. In response, the Christians seized the pirate strongholds on the Barbary coast and constructed a chain of forts as a defensive Maginot Line against Islam.

The policy proved to be half-baked and badly executed. The Spanish forts, clinging tenuously to an alien shore, were poorly resourced and hemmed in by a resentful, unassimilated population. Spain had more pressing interests in Italy and the New World. North Africa possessed no ready wealth to reinforce the zeal of Spain's crusading bishops; it remained a largely forgotten frontier. And now Spain was paying the price in the shape of a band of Turkish adventurers who were threatening to turn the whole of the Western Mediterranean into a major war zone. It was about the Barbarossas that Comares had come to petition.

The two brothers Oruch and Hizir, whom the Christians called the Barbarossas—the Redbeards—were adventurers from the Eastern Mediterranean. They had been born on the island of Lesbos on the fragmenting maritime frontier between Islam and Christendom before the siege of Rhodes, and they spanned both worlds. Their father was an Ottoman cavalryman, their mother a Greek Christian. Their commitment to piracy in the name of Islam had been shaped by the Knights of Saint John. Oruch was captured by the knights in an encounter that left another brother dead. He toiled for two years as a shackled slave on the new fortifications at Rhodes and as an oarsman in their galleys, until he filed off his chains and swam away. It was a formative experience that would shape his self-projection as an Islamic warrior.

The brothers appeared abruptly on the shores of the Maghreb sometime around 1512. They were adventurers with nothing to lose, caught on the wrong side of an Ottoman civil war and forced to flee the Aegean. They came with nothing but their skill as sailors: their ability to navigate by the stars, to read the sea and take risks. They were the

Ottoman equivalent of the Spaniard Cortez, about to conquer Mexico in the name of a parallel faith, and like Cortez, they would fall on their western frontier with the force of destiny. "It was the start of all the evils that our Spain received at the hands of the corsairs," the chronicler López de Gómara wrote later, "the moment that Oruch Barbarossa began to sail our seas, robbing and pillaging our land."

Oruch and his band established themselves on the island of Djerba, hard against the shore of modern Tunisia—a sandy, palm-fringed haven with a secure deepwater lagoon on its landward side, ideal for piracy. From here the enterprising corsairs were well placed to plunder traffic passing between North Africa and the Italian coast. The annual pattern quickly became familiar. When the spring sailing season began, they would strike out in a handful of ships—usually one large galley rowed by Christian slaves and several small galliots to do the fighting—and raid the shipping lanes between Spain and Italy. Their initial targets were lone merchantmen carrying bulk goods—cloth, arms, wheat, and iron—ambushed in the lee of islands with bloodcurdling shouts of "Allah!" Everything they seized was used to advance their position in the Maghreb. The ships would be sailed back to Djerba, broken up, and the timbers used to build more raiding vessels on the treeless shore. The Barbarossas cut a commercial deal with the sultan of Tunis to operate from the city's port, La Goletta, and wooed both sultan and populace with slaves and gifts, the religious leaders with their appeal to holy war. They prowled the coasts of Spain, evacuating Spanish Muslims across the straits and using their knowledge to raid Christian villages. The coastline of southern Italy and the great islands—Majorca, Minorca, Sardinia, and Sicily—also started to live in waking fear of these corsairs. Their sweeps were sudden, unpredictable, and terrifying, the damage immense. In one month Hizir claimed to have taken twenty-one merchant ships and thirty-eight hundred men, women, and children.

As the fame and notoriety of the Barbarossas' exploits spread, so did the legends. Oruch, short, stocky, powerful, given to explosions of rage, with a gold ring in his right ear and with his red beard and hair was a figure of inspiration and dread. In the oral history and poetry of the Maghreb and among the oppressed Muslims of Spain, he was an Islamic Robin Hood with the talismanic powers of a sorcerer. It was whispered that his resources were limitless, that God had rendered him

*Oruch*

invulnerable to sword thrusts, that he had signed a pact with the devil to make his ships invisible. These were matched by fantastic accounts of cruelty. Oruch was said to have ripped out the throat of a Christian with his teeth and eaten the tongue, killed fifty men with his scimitar, tied the head of a Hospitaller knight to a rope and twirled it like a globe until the eyeballs popped. In Spain and Southern Italy people crossed themselves at his name. The new printing presses of Southern Europe hurried out lurid pamphlets detailing his atrocities. Immense sums were offered to privateers for his capture, dead or alive.

The brothers consciously promoted these myths. They sought legitimacy on the North African coast as warriors in a holy war under the protection of God. Hizir claimed that "God had made him to frighten Christians so that they dared not sail" and that he was directed by prophetic dreams. Terror and cruelty were weapons of war. When Hizir raided Minorca in 1514, he left a horse on the shore with a message pinned to its tail: "I am the thunderbolt of heaven. My vengeance will not be assuaged until I have killed the last one of you and enslaved your women, your daughters, and your children." Such presence had the power to terrify the Christian sea.

———

ORUCH, THE OLDER OF the two, had ambitions beyond mere piracy. He had arrived in the Maghreb when the traditional kingdoms in North Africa were starting to fragment. The tensions between a group of rival city-states—Tunis, Tripoli, and Algiers—and the surrounding tribal groupings of Arabs and mountain Berbers caused continuous and chaotic conflict. It was the power vacuum in the Islamic heartlands that the brothers were poised to exploit with the ruthlessness of conquistadors, bent on carving out kingdoms for themselves in this new world. In 1515, Oruch established a link with the imperial center in Istanbul. He dispatched the navigator and cartographer Piri Reis back to the city with the present of a captured French ship to beg for the protection of Sultan Selim, Suleiman's father. The sultan reciprocated by bestowing his favor on the enterprising corsairs. He sent honorific gifts—titles, caftans, and jeweled swords—and, more usefully, he dispatched two heavy war galleys with a full complement of troops, gunpowder, and cannon. It was a significant moment: this first contact with the imperial center was the start of a process that would soon draw the Maghreb into the Ottoman Empire.

The following year Oruch seized control of Algiers in a stunning inter-Islamic coup. He strangled the city's sultan in his bathhouse with his own hands and flooded the streets with his newly acquired Ottoman troops, heavily armed with muskets. It was the kind of colonial land grab that Spanish privateers were themselves conducting in the New World with a similar use of gunpowder.

The Spanish were now thoroughly alarmed by this triangulation of power between the Ottoman corsairs, the Moriscos, and the sultan in Istanbul. Spanish forts on the North African shore were under continuous pressure. Oruch made two failed attempts on their outpost at Bougie; a Spanish counteroffensive to dislodge the Barbarossas from Algiers ended in hideous failure and the loss of most of the ships and men. Oruch and his Ottoman usurpers, now firmly entrenched, continued their territorial expansion inland. They captured Tlemcen, the old capital city of the central Maghreb, murdered seventy members of the ruling Arab dynasty, and further isolated the forts at the Peñón of Algiers and neighboring Oran. Oruch was quickly master of nearly all the land that constitutes modern Algeria. And the debilitating raids on shipping and coastlines went on; Muslim corsairs took to dumping mutilated captives on the Christian shore with the mocking instruction "Go and tell your Christian kings: 'This is the crusade you have proclaimed.'" The Spanish felt severely threatened. After several years of warfare, their only triumph had been to smash Oruch's arm with an arquebus ball at Bougie. Henceforth he gained another nickname: Severed Arm—or in yet another version that reflected the nightmarish image projected into the minds of Christians: Silver Arm. He was said to have had a forearm and hand of pure silver made to replace the amputated limb.

IT WAS AT THIS MOMENT that the young Charles V received the petition from the marquis of Comares and his Arab ally, the deposed king of Tlemcen. The marquis explained the deteriorating situation in North Africa, the present and future danger to Spain. He now begged the young king to seize a rare moment of opportunity. Comares realized that Oruch had for once overreached himself in Tlemcen. The city lay two hundred miles inland from the corsair's base at Algiers; his band of Turkish adventurers was small and they had inflamed Arab sentiment against them to the point of revolt. It was an ideal moment to strike back and rid the western seas of the pirates for good. It was a challenge that the young king, pledged to crush the infidel underfoot, could not refuse. He authorized his first Mediterranean venture.

Charles granted Comares ten thousand men and the money to inspire a full-blown Arab revolt. For once the Spanish acted decisively. Moving fast, they cut the supply route to Algiers, blockaded Tlemcen, and subjected it to a long siege. As the defenses crumbled, Oruch played out his last act. With Arabic voices shouting "Kill him!" the corsair king slipped the city with a small band of followers and galloped away. They were spotted and pursued by Spanish troops. Oruch scattered the treasure of Tlemcen behind him in the dust. Many of the rank and file stopped to gather the trail of gems and coins, but a determined group pressed on and finally cornered Oruch in an arid stretch of upland country. Calling on Saint James for aid, they closed in for the kill. The Turks fought to the last man, Oruch wielding an axe with his one good arm until he was run through with a pike. He managed to inflict a last savage bite on the man who dispatched him; Don Garcia Fernandez de la Plazza carried the legendary wound for the rest of his days. The Spaniards hacked off the metal arm as a trophy and mounted the head on a lance. The body they nailed to the walls of Tlemcen by torchlight. It was an act of superstitious dread, like impaling a vampire. The grotesque red-bearded head, its eyeballs still glaring defiance, was processed throughout the Maghreb as proof of death, before being sent, now putrescent, to Spain. People stared at it, crossed themselves, and recoiled.

IT WAS A SIGNAL TRIUMPH for Charles at the opening of his reign, but the advantage was almost immediately lost. Spain never had a coherent policy for solving the North African problem; instead of marching on Algiers and eliminating the corsair threat, the army retired to Spain. The ghost of Oruch, nailed to the walls, rose almost immediately from the dead in the person of his younger, and more astute, brother. Hizir, who never forgot or forgave an injury or insult, carried forward the commitment to holy war in the western seas. His first act was literally to take on the mantle and myth of his older brother: the dark-haired Hizir hennaed his beard. His second was even more astute.

Hizir realized that his position in the Maghreb was parlous. He needed not only men and equipment but religious and political authority if he were to survive as a foreign intruder on the Arab shore. He decided to abandon his brother's dream of an independent state. He sent a ship back to Istanbul with new gifts and a formal submission to the sultan. He requested that Algiers should be included within the territories of the Ottoman Empire. Sultan Selim made a gracious response: he formally appointed Hizir governor-general of "Algeria of the Arabs" and sent him the customary badges of office—a horse, a scimitar, and the ceremonial horsetail banner. When Selim died shortly afterward, it was Suleiman's name that was honored in Friday prayers in the mosques of Algiers and minted on the city's coins. At a stroke Algeria became a province of the Ottoman Empire, won by enterprising seamen from the Eastern Mediterranean at almost no cost to the imperial treasury. With this act, Hizir acquired both political legitimacy and new resources: gunpowder, cannon, two thousand janissaries. Four thousand volunteers also joined the cause, eager for the spoils of war under this talismanic commander. And it was Suleiman who conferred a new honorific on the young corsair: Hayrettin—"Goodness of the

Faith"—so that he would become known in time as Hayrettin Barbarossa.

These were to prove decisive acts. From the moment that Hayrettin made formal obeisance to Suleiman, "kissing the imperial decree and placing it respectfully on his head with due reverence," the whole nature of the struggle changed. Henceforth, North Africa was no longer a local difficulty between Spain and a band of troublesome pirates; it became the front line in a contest between Suleiman and Charles that would lead inexorably to full-scale sea war.

# The King of Evil

Tнᴇ ɪᴅᴇᴀ ᴏꜰ ᴘᴛᴏʟᴇᴍʏ'ꜱ ᴍᴀᴘ frightened the potentates of Europe, but shortly after the fall of Rhodes, one of the sea captains at the siege presented Suleiman with a remarkable volume that would have doubled Christians' apprehension, had they known of its existence. Its author was a geographically curious Turkish navigator called Piri Reis—Piri the Captain. He had already produced for the sultans a world map of astonishing accuracy, which included copies of the Columbus maps. *The Book of Navigation* did something more immediately useful. Alongside accounts of the discoveries of Columbus and Vasco da Gama, it contained a practical guide to sailing the Mediterranean, drawn from Piri Reis's voyages. Two hundred ten portolan charts—diagrammatic maps with sailing instructions—expounded the coastal seas. The book explained how to navigate all the coastal waters of the infidel to the straits of Gibraltar. Crucially for oared galleys, which could travel for only a few days without taking on water, it located the position of springs on coasts and islands. Piri showed where a galley might water within a hundred miles of Venice, and right around the coasts of Italy and Spain. His book was a blueprint for fighting naval wars.

In the years ahead, the *The Book of Navigation* would be widely carried by Suleiman's fleets, yet at the time the sultan seems to have regarded it, and its author, with a disdain indicative of his attitude toward the sea. In the 1520s Suleiman was largely indifferent to the Mediterranean, beyond claiming it for his own. His ambitions were firmly territorial. The sea was alien and barren—better left to the corsairs. Only the conquest of territory could bring glory, new titles, and the land and booty to appease his army. Rhodes was to prove Suleiman's only personal Mediterranean venture; it was against Hungary and Charles's Austrian dominions that he swung into the saddle in 1526. Initially the Mediterranean war would be fought by frontiersmen such as Hayrettin.

DESPITE THE INFUSION of military aid, the corsair's immediate position remained precarious, but Charles was in no position to profit. He

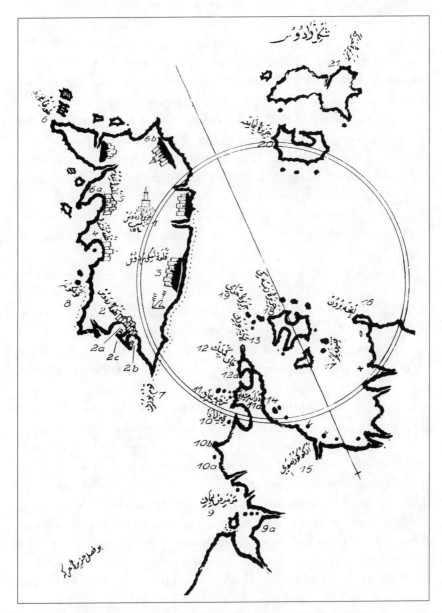

*Rhodes and the coast of Asia Minor in* The Book of Navigation

was beset by other difficulties. Anticipating the Ottoman onslaught along the Danube, he passed control of his Austrian domains to his brother Ferdinand, and turned his attention to yet another war—with his Christian neighbor, Francis I of France, piqued by failure to win the post of Holy Roman Emperor. It was a hampering contest that would continue on and off for the rest of both their lives. With this distraction, the years after Oruch's death marked an unhalted decline for Spanish fortunes in the Maghreb. A succession of badly coordinated expeditions came to spectacular grief. An attempt on Algiers in 1519 ended in shipwreck and massacre. Its leader, Hugo de Moncada, escaped ingloriously by hiding among the butchered corpses on the shore. Barbarossa was fueled by anger at his brother's death and in no mood to ransom prisoners. When Charles offered a large sum for the captured officers, Barbarossa had them killed. Offered another sum for the return of the bodies, he threw them into the sea, so that "if the parents of any of the dead ever came to Algiers, they would not know the burial place of their father or brother, nor be able to see the ashes, but only the waves." With the Spanish fleet decimated, he could now raid Charles's coasts at will.

Hayrettin's position continued to wane and wax—he was briefly ousted from Algiers by a coalition of Arabs and Berbers in 1520—but the Spanish failed to prosper. They never mastered the complex winds of the Barbary Coast and invariably sailed too late in the year. A second Moncada expedition in 1523 led to a more spectacular shipwreck, "which destroyed twenty-six great ships and many small ones." Algiers was doomed to be a place of collective grief for Christian crusaders. The Spanish managed to retain some kind of hold over the city through their looming fort on the Peñón, but morale throughout the chain of fortresses on the Barbary Coast was dangerously low. North Africa was the forgotten frontier; there were other priorities and prizes that demanded more urgent attention. It was a war no one wanted to fight. The soldiers were badly paid, if they were paid at all. Supplies for the forts were so irregular that it was not unknown for men to die of hunger. Soldiers looked enviously over their shoulders at reports from the New World. "It's not Peru, where you can go out and collect precious stones," muttered one military commander. "It's Africa and all we have here are Turks and Moors." Soldiers would defect and renounce their faith, enlist for service in the Americas, or pay people-smugglers to ferry them back to Spain. Only the political instability of the Maghreb permitted the Spanish to cling on.

In the Eastern Mediterranean, the Maghreb *was* the New World. As Hayrettin's reputation continued to grow, a stream of corsairs sailed west in his wake. The motivation was not lost on the Spanish themselves. "Because of the story of the great riches ... gained on the Barbary Coast, men hurried there with the same fervor that compelled the Spanish to the mines of the Indies," wrote the chronicler Diego de Haëdo. By the late 1520s there were at least forty corsair captains on the Barbary Coast, deployed by Hayrettin to harry the Christian sea. Hayrettin himself assumed an awesome presence: invincible, frightening, brilliant. He projected himself as the manifestation of the will of God and the imperial authority of Suleiman, as one whose prescient dreams allowed him to escape ambushes, dodge storms, and capture cities. He came, in his own words, among the Christian fleets, "like the sun among the stars, at whose appearance, their light vanished." His flagship, the *Algerian*, rowed by 108 men, carried at its masthead a red banner studded with three silver moons and at its stern two interlaced inscriptions in Arabic. One said: "I will conquer"; the other, "God's protection is better than the strongest armor and the tallest tower." At its approach, Christian ships surrendered without a struggle, or their crews hurled themselves overboard, preferring a quick death to the protracted torture of the galleys. His stratagems were said to be legion, his cruelties refined, his anger volcanic. Hayrettin's knowledge of the sea, drawn from thousands of voyages, was unmatched, and his intelligence on enemy intentions, gathered from the interrogation of captured crews and from the freely given advice of Spanish Muslims, allowed him to strike unpredictably and at will. He made one or two sweeps a year with a flotilla of eighteen vessels, snatching merchant ships, burning coastal villages, and abducting populations. Over a ten-year period, he took ten thousand people from the coastline between Barcelona and Valencia alone—a stretch of just two hundred miles.

Hayrettin's skill and propaganda burned a deep hole in the popular imagination of Christian Europe. With the reputation of Oruch fading, he became known simply as Barbarossa, the lurid subject of countless stories and songs. The printing presses fed this avid horror with a stream of news sheets and woodcut likenesses. The French writer Rabelais sent one to a friend from Rome in 1530, "drawn," he assured its

*Contemporary print of Hayrettin*

recipient, "from life." Prints show an imposing turbaned figure, clad in an opulent caftan, whose massive hands grasp a scroll and hawk-headed scimitar. The eyes are deep set and glaring, with the frizzled beard of an ogre and an expression of vulpine rapacity. New technology let Europe gaze on the mythic pirate and find there its template for cruelty. "Barbarossa, Barbarossa, you are the king of evil," they sang up and down the Spanish coast.

THE CORSAIRS WHO accompanied him and answered to his iron will—and gave him 12 percent of their takings—trailed their own smaller appalling legends across the sea. They came from all points of the compass. Many were renegade Christians for whom there was no way back, exiled from their native lands through crime or capture by corsairs, and converted, at least nominally, to Islam. They lived and died by the sea and gave their ships beautiful names—the *Pearl*, the *Door of Neptune*, the *Sun*, the *Golden Lemon Tree*, the *Rose of Algiers*— that belied their purpose. The corsairs' short, vivid careers summarized the poverty, violence, and dislocation of the Mediterranean world. Salah Reis, who tied his captives over the mouth of a cannon and blasted them to pieces, died of plague. Ali the Karaman, "Scarface," lacked two fingers and was so hated along the coasts of Italy that the Genoese had sworn to display him in an iron cage. Al Morez, "the Cretan," beat his oarsmen with a severed arm. "More cruel than Al Morez?" Tunisian peasants would ask when trying to determine the exact measure of a man's brutality. Elie the Corsican, a master of marine ambushes, was crucified on his own mast; Aydin the Ligurian, "the Devil Hunter," drowned in an Algerian river. These men were the squadron commanders in Hayrettin's holy war, who gathered sacks of noses and hands as prizes and fought without rules.

During the 1520s the level of their maritime plunder grew steadily, but Charles only worsened his own plight. In the age of inquisition, the remnant Muslim population of Spain remained an unfinished project. The Moorish inhabitants of Valencia were conspicuously loyal to the emperor during an uprising in the early 1520s. They were cruelly rewarded. Charles was not fanatical by nature, but he was conscious of his responsibility before Christendom as Holy Roman Emperor. In 1525 he authorized the proclamation known as the Purification of Aragon—an edict that required the conversion or exile of all the Muslims in that part of Spain. Baldly put, the terms were: convert or die. Barbarossa promptly answered the plight of the Valencian Moors. Large numbers were ferried across to the Maghreb to swell the pirate wars and suggest suitable targets for revenge attacks. There was no bay, no coastal village, no island unvisited. The complaints of Spanish subjects to their king became ever louder.

In May 1529, all these forces came to a head when Spain's neglect of its African outposts brought a defining catastrophe. The Peñón of Algiers, the small fort that throttled the city and its port, ran short of gunpowder. Spies reported the situation to Hayrettin, who immediately stormed it. The commander, Martin de Vargas, was offered the choice of conversion to Islam or execution. He chose to die. He was beaten to death in front of the janissaries—a slow and painful end. Shortly afterward, a relief fleet of nine Spanish ships arrived at the Peñón, unaware of the catastrophe, and were all captured.

It was a loss that would have long-lasting consequences for the Western Mediterranean. Hayrettin demolished the castle, connected its island to the mainland by a causeway, and secured a safe harbor of immense strategic value. This victory strengthened the corsairs' hand enormously. Algiers the White, glittering above the blue sea, became the sea robber's kingdom and souk, the Baghdad or Damascus of the Maghreb, where ships could be safely harbored, booty collected, and human beings bought and sold. It was now a permanent problem for Charles. Algiers was the western marker of a war that stretched all the way to the Danube. Ten days before the Peñón fell, Suleiman departed from Istanbul with seventy-five thousand men to march on Vienna.

It was Charles's brother Ferdinand who braced himself for this onslaught. For once Charles was more pleasantly occupied. After an eight-year struggle with France, he was in the act of signing what he hoped would be a lasting peace. Temporarily free from the burden of war, he set off for the greatest triumph of his life: his coronation in Italy as Holy Roman Emperor, the champion of the Christian world. He departed from Barcelona with the imperial galleys under their general in chief, Rodrigo de Portuondo, to a volley of ceremonial cannon shot.

It was to prove a moment of hubris. Charles might aspire to be the ruler of the world, whose kingdom stretched from Peru to the Rhine, but on the coast of Spain he was horribly vulnerable. In the summer of 1529 there was suddenly no protecting fleet, and Hayrettin quickly knew it. Immediately he dispatched Aydin the Devil Hunter, his most experienced corsair, with fifteen galliots to ransack the Balearic Islands and the Spanish coast. Revenge centered on Valencia. After snaffling a succession of passing merchant ships, Aydin's pirates descended abruptly on a religious festival and seized a sizeable band of pilgrims, then rescued two hundred Muslims from the same coast, and made off.

Portuondo had delivered the emperor to Genoa and was on his way home when news of this raid reached him. Spurred on by a reward of ten thousand escudos for the return of the Muslim vassals, he turned to head off Aydin. He caught the corsair's ships, totally unprepared, beached on the shore of the deserted island of Formentera, southwest of Majorca. Portuondo's nine heavily armed war galleys had the lighter galliots totally at their mercy; he could and should have blasted them out of the water. But Portuondo had left half his complement of soldiers in Genoa to escort the emperor, and his ten thousand escudos depended on returning the Muslims alive. He decided not to use his guns, then dithered and missed his chance. Aydin's galliots were able to push off from the shore, catch the galleys sideways, and counterattack. The Spaniards were taken by surprise. Portuondo was killed by an arquebus shot; his flagship surrendered. Panic spread to the rest of the fleet. Seven galleys were taken in all; the eighth rowed away to tell the tale. Aydin's fleet, now doubled in size, returned to Algiers with guns firing and flags flying. The ships had so many Christian slaves on deck, including Portuondo's son, "that they could not move."

It was the first significant open sea engagement against Barbarossa's corsair fleet and it ended in humiliation. "It was the greatest loss that had ever happened to the Spanish galley fleet," wrote López de Gómara dramatically. The Spanish chronicler, not known for his objectivity, gave a ghastly account of the crew's fate. The son of Portuondo "Barbarossa impaled with many other Spaniards ... and they say that he subjected some of the captives to a form of torment and death that was as cruel as it was new. On a flat part of the countryside he had holes dug that were waist-deep and had the Spanish put in them; he buried them alive, leaving the arms and heads exposed, and he had many horsemen trample them." Barbarossa's own chronicle puts it differently: "Hayrettin spread his name and reputation through all regions and countries of both the Christians and Moors, and sent the sultan two galleys, one of these with Portuondo and all the other leading Christians." In the deeds of the great corsair, the boundaries of truth remain hard to establish.

THE SOLDIERS who might have made the difference to Portuondo's fate were at that moment preparing for Charles's festivities at Bologna. On November 5, 1529, Charles entered the city in preparation for his coronation two months later. It was a carefully staged set piece of imperial theatre, modeled on the triumphs of Roman emperors—an extraordinary declaration of the emperor's claim to the terrestrial globe. Charles rode through triumphal arches, accompanied by the pope and all the notables of his domains. Musicians played, drummers beat battering tattoos, and the populace, exuberant at the prospect of feasting, shouted "Caesar, Charles, Emperor!" Charles rode in stately procession under a brocaded canopy carried by four plumed knights. His own elaborate helmet was surmounted by a golden eagle, and he carried the imperial scepter in his right hand. Among the sea of banners embroidered with the emblems of emperor and pope was a Crusader's flag decorated with the crucified Christ. During the months of celebration that followed, the artist Parmigiano started work on an immense allegorical portrait of the emperor. It showed the infant Hercules offering Charles the globe, turned not to the Indies or his possessions in Europe but to the Mediterranean, the center of the world, and ordained to be ruled by Caesar.

IN TRUTH, THE HUMILIATION of the imperial galleys ten days earlier had revealed the hollowness of this pantomime. After twelve years of warfare with the Barbarossas, Charles's only tangible trophies were Oruch's skull and his crimson cloak, now displayed in Córdoba cathedral as an object of venerable dread. The Spanish position in the Maghreb was precarious; the seas had never been less safe. The Western Mediterranean was in danger of being overrun by these outriders of the Ottoman Empire. On November 15, Charles received a letter in Bologna from the archbishop of Toledo, outlining the situation in stark terms. Immediate action was now critical. "Unless this disaster is reversed," he wrote, "we will lose the commerce of the Mediterranean from Gibraltar to the east." Now only decisive action would suffice. He urged the emperor to construct a new fleet of twenty ships and "sailing with a great armada to hunt out Barbarossa in his own house [Algiers], for money spent solely for defence will otherwise be wasted." The Empress Isabella wrote in the same vein. Algiers was the key to Christian peace, but Barbarossa was the key to Algiers.

THERE WERE TWO balancing consolations for Charles as he contemplated these letters. The first was not inconsiderable. In the autumn rain, Suleiman's great siege of Vienna had ground to a halt. By early October it was getting cold; his supply lines were overextended and the season late. On the fourteenth of the month, Suleiman made a short entry in his campaign journal in customary telegraphic style, as if it were a detail of no import: "Explosion of mines and new breaches in the walls. Council. Fruitless attack. The orders are given to return to Constantinople." The briefest of notes sketch a bitter retreat: "17. The army arrives at Bruck. Snow. 18. We cross three bridges near Altenburg. A considerable quantity of baggage and part of the artillery are lost in the marshes. 19. Great difficulty in crossing the Danube. The snow continues to fall." It was the first Ottoman setback in two hundred years. Suleiman was compelled to organize his own face-saving victory celebrations for the people of Istanbul.

The second consolation for Charles was more immediate. In anticipation of Toledo's advice, the emperor had just provided himself with the means to strike back. In 1528 he managed to steal the services of Andrea Doria, the great Genoese admiral of the age, from Charles's rival the king of France. Doria was a member of the old nobility of the city and a condottiere, a soldier of fortune. Disillusioned with Francis I, Doria switched sides for a handsome fee, but he represented good value and would prove durably loyal. The admiral brought with him his own galley fleet, use of Genoa's strategic port, and immense experience of sea warfare and anti-corsair activity. Doria had his drawbacks. Because the galleys were his private property, he was excessively cautious in their use, but he was by far the most astute Christian naval commander in the emperor's domains. At a stroke the sea-lanes between Spain and its Italian possessions became safer—Genoa gave Charles strategic control of his coasts and a substantial fleet with which to defend them. It was through Doria that he intended to halt the Hapsburg decline in the Mediterranean and wage aggressive war.

Charles also buttressed the defenses on Italy's southern flank. Since the fall of Rhodes, the Knights of Saint John had been homeless wanderers in the Mediterranean. L'Isle Adam had petitioned the potentates of Europe, one by one, for a new base from which to carry on the Order's mission of holy war. In London, Henry VIII had received the old man graciously and given him guns, but only Charles provided the possibility of a permanent home. He offered the barren and impoverished island of Malta, south of Sicily, in the path of every corsair raid on the Italian coast. The present came with strings attached—Charles did not give something for nothing; the knights also had to defend the emperor's fort at Tripoli on the Barbary shore. It was an unattractive prospect but L'Isle Adam had no alternatives; without a base for piracy, the Order would certainly collapse. In 1530 Charles dispatched the fateful document to L'Isle Adam, "bestowing on the Knights in order that they may perform in peace the duties of their Religion for the benefit of the Christian community and employ their forces and arms against the perfidious enemies of Holy Faith—the islands of Malta, Gozo and Comino in return for the yearly presentation, on All Saint's Day, of a falcon to Charles, Viceroy of Sicily." This bargain placed the knights at the very center of the sea, in the eye of a rising storm.

# CHAPTER 4

# The Voyage to Tunis

1530–1535

CHARLES'S NEED TO STRIKE COUNTERBLOWS was not con-
fined to the shores of Spain and Italy. By 1530 warfare between sultan
and emperor stretched diagonally across the whole of Europe, and
Christendom perceived itself everywhere on the back foot. The central
metaphor of Martin Luther's famous protestant hymn, "A Mighty
Fortress Is Our God," was not randomly chosen: Suleiman was besieging Vienna at the time. Where the Ottomans thought of advance and
encirclement, the Christian mind-set was obsessively defensive. Exor-
bitantly expensive fortress chains dotted the Hungarian plains; the
Italians were busy constructing watchtowers along their vulnerable
shores; the Spanish forts clung precariously to the shipwrecking coasts
of the Maghreb. Everywhere the threat of Islam seemed to press.

THE SCALE OF THE CONFLICT dwarfed all preconceptions. The
early sixteenth century witnessed a new concentration of imperial
power: the Austrian Hapsburgs and the Ottoman Turks were able to
aggregate men and resources on an unprecedented scale—and to find
the means to pay for them. The engines of warfare were the centralized
bureaucracies in Madrid and Istanbul, which could raise taxes, levy
men, dispatch ships, organize supplies, manufacture cannon, and mill
gunpowder with a comparative efficiency unimaginable in the hand-
made wars of the Middle Ages. Armies became bigger, cannon more
powerful, logistics and resource allocation—within the limitations imposed by traveling times and communications—more sophisticated. It
was a struggle between empires with global reach; the 1530s would see
the Spanish conquistador Francisco Pizarro conquer Peru, the Ottomans attack India. A grid of interconnections between distant places
drew the world together. The Austrians sought treaties with the Persians, the Ottomans with the French; the cause of German Lutherans

was furthered by decisions taken in Istanbul; New World bullion paid for wars in Africa. If the commitment to holy war was the lever to empire, there were other forces at work. In Europe, the decline of Latin, new notions of national identity, and protestant revolt were shaking old certainties. The whole basin was prey to mysterious forces. Populations and cities grew rapidly, cash replaced barter, inflation effortlessly leaped the frontiers of faith.

In the 1530s, this sense of global disturbance was widely felt across the Mediterranean. Millennial expectations gripped the popular imagination. Within Islam it was thought that the tenth century of the Muslim era would usher in the end of history; in Christendom, 1533 was taken to be the fifteen hundredth anniversary of the crucifixion. Prophecies abounded on both sides of the religious divide. It was widely believed that Suleiman and Charles were embarked on a contest for the world. In 1531, the Dutch humanist Erasmus wrote to a friend, "the rumour here—indeed not a rumour, but public knowledge—is that the Turk will invade Germany with all his forces, to do battle for the great prize, whether Charles or the Turk be monarch of the entire globe, for the world cannot any longer bear to have two suns in the sky." The notion of a world ruler was much discussed by Charles's advisers, though the emperor himself, more prudent about how such claims might be received in France or Protestant Germany, was less explicit. He was the defender of the faith against the infidel, both Islamic and Protestant. Suleiman, in a more unified Islamic world, could be forthright. "Just as there is only one God in heaven, there can be only one empire on earth," his chief vizier, Ibrahim Pasha, roundly declared to visiting ambassadors. "Spain is like a lizard, pecking here and there at a bit of weed in the dust, while our sultan is like a dragon which gulps down the world when it opens its mouth."

BENEATH THE BRAGGING, there was popular fear in Istanbul of Charles's aggressive intentions. Anxiety and pessimism, amplified by the failures in Hungary, dogged the city; omens were widely cited to suggest that the wheel of fortune would reverse again and restore Christian Constantinople. Like plague and a shortage of bread, these were symptoms of troubled times, but they reflected matching fears. If Charles's dream was the restitution of Constantinople, Suleiman's was the capture of Rome. Both men were committed to leading their armies in person, though careful to choose their terrain. By 1530 this contest had become increasingly personal. It centered on their rival claims to the crucial title, Caesar, and ownership of the center of the world. Nothing enraged Suleiman as much as the accounts of Charles's coronation in 1530. "He detests the emperor and his title of Caesar, he, the Turk, causing himself to be called Caesar," declared Francis I of France. The sultan was set on a face-to-face trial of strength with the man he only ever called "the king of Spain." In the spring of 1532, Suleiman prepared to march his army up the Danube again and delivered a thunderous challenge: "The king of Spain has for a long time declared his wish to go against the Turks; but I by the grace of God am proceeding with my army against him. If he is great of heart, let him await me in the field, and then, whatever God wills, shall be. If, however, he does not wish to wait for me, let him send tribute." Charles's response appeared unequivocal. He wrote to his wife, "In the light of duty I have to defend the faith and the Christian religion in person."

Competition focused on the emblems of power. The details of Charles's entry into Bologna had been minutely reported to the sultan. On his march north, Suleiman staged his own rival triumphs, contriving a matching iconography. From the Venetians he had commissioned a set of ceremonial objects worthy of a Roman emperor: a scepter, a throne, and an extraordinary jeweled helmet-crown, which the Italians claimed had been a trophy of Alexander the Great. He entered Belgrade in a cavalcade of opulent pageantry, "with great ceremony and pomp and with pipes and the sound of different instruments, that it was an extraordinary thing to marvel at and he went through triumphal arches along the streets of his progress, according to the ancient customs of the Romans." It was propaganda war on a grand scale. Charles, detained by tetchy negotiations with the German Protestants, raised a substantial army and prepared to float it down the Danube. The stage seemed set for a final confrontation.

Yet the definitive battle never happened. Suleiman was held up for weeks by the heroic defense of the small fortress of Köszeg in central Hungary; Charles was probably too prudent to risk open-field warfare anyway. Bogged down in the rain, Suleiman was again forced to retreat. It was an exhausting slog home across mountain passes and swollen rivers: "continuous rain . . . difficult river crossing . . . the fog so thick it's impossible to tell one person from another"; the campaign diary has a familiar ring to it. There were the habitual celebrations in Istanbul on Suleiman's return—triumphant processions and nighttime illuminations to celebrate the happy conclusion to the war against the king of Spain. It was given out that "the miserable fugitive had fled to save his life and abandoned his unbelieving subjects." The Hapsburgs concocted their own fictional triumph: artists set to work on engravings that showed Charles liberating Vienna from the Turks. The gap between imperial rhetoric and reality was equally wide on both sides. The truth

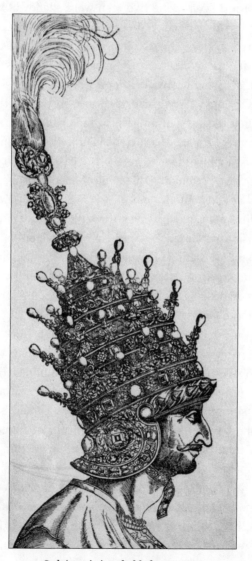

*Suleiman's jeweled helmet-crown*

was, the Ottomans were operating at the limits of their range within the span of a campaigning season, and Charles's globe was always turned toward the Mediterranean. He never personally chose the Danube basin as a theatre of operations. While Suleiman was at Köszeg, Charles was two hundred miles away. It was the closest the two men ever got.

SIMULTANEOUSLY CHARLES CHOSE this moment to shift the whole focus of the contest. While the two men were shadowboxing along the Danube, Charles authorized a diversionary attack. In the spring of 1532, he ordered Andrea Doria to ransack the coast of Greece. Forty-four galleys sailed east from Sicily. Doria was brutally effective. On September 12, as Suleiman was tramping home again, Doria stormed the strategic Ottoman stronghold of Coron in the southern Peloponnese and ravaged the surrounding coastline. A garrison secured Coron for the emperor. Suleiman was furious. The following spring, when he sent a hastily assembled fleet to retake the castle, Doria redoubled the humiliation. Sixty Ottoman galleys blockaded Coron; Doria simply broke the cordon and routed them.

These actions sent shock waves through the eastern Aegean. The Ottomans considered Greece to be their home waters but had been incapable of defending them. If Doria could take Coron, what was to prevent him from striking Istanbul? The shortcomings of the official Ottoman navy had been badly exposed; it represented a horrible vulnerability. For the sake of his security, as well as his honor, Suleiman grasped that the Mediterranean was no longer a sideshow—it was a principal theatre of war, and it must now be fought for.

The sultan's response was prompt. He summoned Hayrettin from Algiers as the only man with the experience to mount an adequate riposte. In the summer of 1533, the legendary corsair sailed fourteen galleys into the Golden Horn, "amid the firing of numerous salutes," and presented himself to the sultan, "taking with him eighteen captains, his companions, and rich presents, where he had the honour of kissing the royal hand, and had innumerable favours conferred upon him." With the backing of the chief vizier, Ibrahim Pasha, he was appointed the sultan's admiral and tasked with the construction of a new fleet, the reversal of Coron, and striking back at the impudent king of Spain. Hayrettin was not only given the official title of *kapudan-i-derya*, grand admiral of the Mediterranean fleet, Suleiman also created a new governorship for him—the Province of the Archipelago—formed from the coasts of the Ottoman Mediterranean. It was a measure of how seriously he now regarded the struggle for the sea.

HAYRETTIN WAS SIXTY-SEVEN or sixty-eight years old and at the height of good fortune, his energy apparently undiminished by age. In the winter of 1533–34 he set about reconstructing the Ottoman navy in the arsenal on the Golden Horn. He was able to harness all the natural advantages of the empire. Shipbuilding is a hungry consumer of raw materials; vast quantities of timber, pitch, tallow, iron, and sailcloth are required. All these things could be supplied from within the empire's own resources, and the manpower to build, sail, and row the vessels—a perennial problem for Christian fleets—could be efficiently levied by a centralized administration, unmatched in its reach and efficiency. With these resources, Hayrettin worked unceasingly to construct an imperial fleet worthy of the ruler of the White Sea. European spies and diplomats closely monitored his progress—no hard thing, as the arsenal was not surrounded by any enclosing wall. "Barbarossa was continually in the arsenal," it was reported back to the west, "where he did both eat and drink to lose no time."

On May 23, 1534, as Suleiman swung himself into the saddle for yet another campaign—against the shah of Persia—Barbarossa's new fleet nosed its way out of the Golden Horn, to the triumphal firing of cannon. The Flemish diplomat Cornelius de Schepper saw it go and wrote Doria an ominous report. Altogether there were seventy serviceable galleys, including three commander's ships with stern lanterns. Hayrettin's ornate flagship was rowed by one hundred sixty Christian slaves. "In all he had 1,233 Christian slaves . . . the rest of the oarsmen were Serbians and Bulgarians, all of whom were chained because they were Christians." Each galley had bronze cannon firing stone shot, and between one hundred and one hundred twenty fighting men, "many of whom were in his expedition without pay, because of his fame and the expectation of plunder." The fleet carried a substantial treasury to pay the salaried men: fifty thousand gold ducats, forty thousand ducats' worth of precious stones, three hundred bolts of gold cloth. Suleiman had been able to aggregate huge resources.

With hindsight, the French ambassador in the city was fully able to

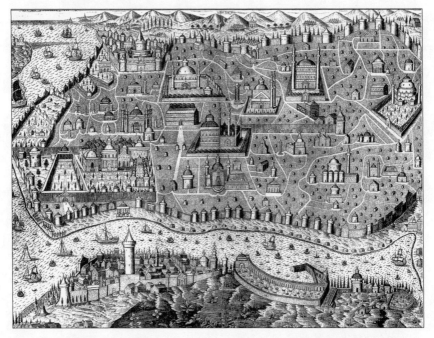

*Ottoman Istanbul, the Golden Horn, and the arsenal (foreground, center)*

grasp the significance of this moment. "The supremacy of Turkey dates from Hayrettin's first winter in the dockyards of the city," he wrote ten years later. The fleet rowing smartly down to Gallipoli represented a major escalation of naval power. It was the start of an era of full-blown sea warfare. Almost every spring for the next forty years European spies would send back ominous rumors of huge fleets preparing to devastate the vulnerable shores of Christendom.

Hayrettin's new fleet set a course for revenge. In the summer it struck the coast of Charles's domains in Southern Italy like a tidal wave. The sultan's new admiral was evidently well informed. Aware that the Adriatic shore had been fortified with watchtowers, he swung around the heel of Italy and ravaged the western coastline toward Naples, burning villages, destroying ships, enslaving whole settlements. The suddenness and terror of his mass landings, the impact of the churning galley squadrons closing on the unprotected shore, had the heart-stopping terror of Ottoman frontier raids. Detachments of Doria's fleet at Messina could only hug the harbor and watch the Ottoman fleet sweep by. Reggio, hard opposite Sicily, was abandoned on Barbarossa's approach. He took six transport ships and burned the town; he left the castle of San Lucido in flames and captured eight hundred people. At Citrero he burned eighteen galleys. Slipping past Naples, he sacked the fishing village of Sperlunga, then landed and struck twelve miles inland in an attempt to seize the beautiful countess of Fondi, Julia Gonzaga, as a present for the sultan's harem. When the prize eluded him, the corsairs left Fondi ablaze, "massacring many men and seizing all the women and children." Sixty miles away people began to flee Rome. Turning about, Barbarossa burned six imperial galleys under construction at Naples. And then before anyone could catch their breath, the fleet was gone, slipping off south into the blue, edging past smoldering Stromboli for Tunis. He took with him hundreds, perhaps thousands, of captives, a portion of whom he dispatched back to Suleiman in Istanbul.

It had been a commanding exercise in terror and revenge, but it was only the start. Hayrettin had his own personal objective on the shores of the Maghreb. On August 16 his flotilla dropped anchor at Tunis and landed his janissaries. The unpopular Arab ruler Muley Hasan abandoned the city without a shot fired. The capture of Tunis doubled Charles's agitation at a stroke. Situated on the collar of the Maghreb, the city commands the axis of the whole Mediterranean— the narrow straits, a hundred miles wide, that separate North Africa from Sicily, with Malta sitting midstream. It was just twenty hours' sailing time to the emperor's lands. Tunis provided a launchpad for massive raiding, or even the invasion of Southern Italy—the natural stepping-stone would be to seize Malta from the Knights of Saint John. It was the traditional route into Southern Europe; the Arabs had passed this way into Sicily in the ninth century. Hayrettin's "inner voice" had already predicted this move. During his raid on Italy he had been promised the island in a dream.

By the end of 1534 the whole of the Western Mediterranean was stark with terror at the exponential threat posed by Barbarossa's new fleet. Deepening unease gripped the littoral of Spain and Italy. Shipping insurance rates rocketed; coastal towns were refortified and villages abandoned, new chains of watchtowers constructed. Doria and the Spanish admiral Álvaro de Bazán tracked every scrap of rumor about Barbarossa's movements and readied their own galley fleets to scramble at a moment's notice. "From the Strait of Messina to that of Gibraltar no one in any part of Europe could eat in peace or go to sleep with any feeling of security," wrote the Spaniard Sandoval. Even the neutral Venetians in their secure lagoon felt uneasy and started to build new ships. This was no longer a case of daring pirate raids—it was the incursion of imperial warfare into the heart of the sea.

IF CHARLES HAD BEEN WOUNDED by the attack on Southern Italy, he was thoroughly alarmed by the new threat from Tunis. He was clear that it was Suleiman's riposte for the humiliation in Hungary and for Doria in Greece. And this, in its turn, could not go unanswered. Each action required a larger counterreaction. He was determined "to attack the enemy and chase him from the seas of Christendom." He resolved to organize a crusade against Barbarossa and lead it in person, even at the risk of his life.

Over the winter of 1534–1535 Charles threw himself personally into planning an expensive maritime expedition to Tunis. He requisitioned men and ships from across his empire. Transports sailed from Antwerp with chained Protestants to row the galleys. Troops marched from Germany, Spain, and Italy to the collection points at the coast. Doria assembled his galley fleet at Barcelona; Bazán sailed from Malaga. The Knights of Saint John came from Malta in their great carrack, the *Saint Anne,* the largest ship in the world; the Portuguese sent twenty-three caravels and another carrack; a detachment was funded by the pope. Genoa and Barcelona were a hubbub of men and ships, busy with the loading of barrels of biscuits, water, and gunpowder, horses, cannon, and arquebuses. Charles proved himself an accomplished military planner. The expedition was conceived on a huge scale and was unusually well coordinated by Hapsburg standards; for once it did not sail too late in the year. In early June 1535, the armada assembled off the coast of Sicily: seventy-four galleys, three hundred sailing ships, thirty thousand men. The fleet review was a calculated showpiece of religious iconography and imperial splendor. Charles had commissioned a ship worthy of his position as the defender of Christendom—a quadrireme, an immense galley rowed by four men to a bench, with a castellated and gilded poop and a canopy of red and gold velvet, flying heraldic flags from its masts. One depicted the crucified Christ with Charles's personal motto, "Further," another a radiant star surrounded by arrows and the legend "Show me your ways, O God." On June 14, this expedition departed from Sardinia with great show. The oarsmen propelled the splendid craft along a water lane through the anchored fleet, to the braying of trumpets and the thunderous cheering of the men. Charles took with him his own official war artist, Jan Vermeyen, to record the impending victory. The emperor was intent on controlling his own image.

The fleet took less than a day to reach the North African shore. By the morning of June 15, it had anchored off the site of ancient Carthage and was preparing to besiege La Goletta, "the throat," the fortress that controlled the channel into the inner lake on whose banks sat Tunis "the Green." Charles took a month to reduce this obstacle, harassed continuously by Hayrettin's sorties from the city. On July 14, after a furious bombardment from the great carrack and the galleys advancing in successive waves to pummel the defenses with their bow guns, the walls were breached and the fortress stormed with great loss of life. Among the ruins, the Spanish were surprised to find cannonballs stamped with the fleur-de-lis of France.

Hayrettin watched in consternation as the army advanced on Tunis. His position was becoming precarious; he was particularly concerned at the possibility of revolt by the thousands of chained Christian slaves. He proposed to kill them all, but this was strongly resisted by those around him. It was not squeamishness that prevented a massacre; slave owners were simply unwilling to destroy their own wealth. In the event, Barbarossa was justified. After fierce fighting, he withdrew his army to the walls of Tunis. Within the city, a group of renegades, sensing the drift of events, switched sides and started to slip the prisoners' shackles. The Christians seized the arsenal, armed themselves, and burst out into the streets. With no secure base behind him, Barbarossa had no option but to flee. He slipped away toward Algiers with several thousand Turks. On the morning of July 21, Charles entered Tunis in unopposed triumph, his horse high-stepping over the corpses of slaughtered Muslims.

The aftermath was bloody. Charles had promised his men the customary right to pillage, due in cases where a city had not surrendered; they accordingly subjected Tunis to a fearful massacre. The mosques were plundered and stripped; thousands of surrendering Tunisians, no more enthusiastic about Hayrettin than they had been about Muley Hasan, were cut down in the street; ten thousand more were sold into slavery. The savagery was fueled by personal and national vengeance for the raids on Italy, the taking of slaves, the twenty years of misery inflicted by the Barbarossas on the Christian shore. It was hate at a visceral level.

Charles emerged from the bloodbath with his reputation enormously enhanced in Catholic Europe. He had personally risked his life in the assault of Tunis and proved his courage, resolution, and military judgment. According to contemporary Spanish accounts, he had fought in the front line, advancing "with lance in hand, putting himself in the same danger as a poor common soldier," and had felt the bullets whistle past his head. His horse was shot from under him, while his page was killed by his side. The Spanish chroniclers ensured that his deeds were widely reported. Charles felt justified in calling himself the emperor of war.

The practical gains were considerable: the puppet ruler Muley Hasan was restored to the throne of Tunis, and La Goletta garrisoned with Spanish troops. Most significant of all, Charles had burned almost the complete fleet that had sailed so proudly out of Istanbul the previous spring. Eighty-two ships were destroyed in the lake at Tunis. Charles had wanted to follow Barbarossa and take Algiers, but the army had been struck down by dysentery. On August 17 he sailed back to Naples in pomp, confident that his adversary had been negated.

Charles was never a man to be constrained by cost in his pursuit of war, but the expenditure on Tunis had been immense. When planning the campaign, he had faced huge financial difficulties. Galley fleets were ruinously expensive and the emperor had just laid out nine hundred thousand ducats on the Danube campaign against Suleiman. In prospect, the armada to Tunis would cost another million, a sum of money Charles did not have. The expedition against Barbarossa took place only because of events on the other side of the world. On August 29, 1533, Francisco Pizarro had strangled Atahualpa, the last king of the Incas, at Cajamarca in the Andes, having extracted an immense quantity of gold for his ransom. Spanish galleons supplied Charles with a windfall 1,200,000 ducats of South American gold for "the holy enterprise of war against the Turk, Luther and other enemies of the faith." The treasure house of Atahualpa paid for Charles's crusade. It was the first time that the New World had altered the course of events in the Old.

To Charles, it was God who provided this means for his signal victory; and it was as God's champion that he sailed home again. "Your glorious and incomparable victory at Tunis seems to me, by my faith as a Christian, of a dignity which far surpasses all others of ever-lasting memory," wrote the toadying chronicler Paolo Govio. Charles's artist, Jan Vermeyen, designed a set of twelve tapestries commemorating scenes from the campaign that would travel with Charles wherever he went, to bear witness to this triumph. It was the high point of the emperor's military career.

THE DESTRUCTION of Barbarossa's power base and the cutting of the link between the Maghreb and Istanbul was a momentous event throughout the Western Mediterranean. Charles reached Naples amidst an explosion of popular rejoicing. There were widespread rumors that Barbarossa himself was dead; the coasts were in festive mood; the news was celebrated with church services, gunfire, pageants, and festivals. In Toledo and Granada processions of the faithful sang hymns and prostrated themselves at the feet of the Virgin. The Knights of Saint John held services of thanksgiving and ignited fireworks in the night sky over Malta, while for the Venetians, further removed from the consequences and generally of a more frivolous frame of mind, it provided the excuse for carnivals and masked balls. Nowhere was the joy more rapturous than on the Balearic Islands. Majorca and Minorca had suffered cruelly at the hands of the corsairs. At Palma, on Majorca, they staged a cheerful reenactment of their tormentor's downfall. A convicted criminal, with his beard hennaed and his tongue cut out, was dressed in Turkish costume and hustled into the main square. The startled man was burned alive to the screams of the crowd. Joy, cruelty, revenge, religious deliverance, exaltation, mystical fervor—powerful emotions swept across the sea.

It was in this carnival atmosphere that a flotilla of galleys flying Spanish flags rowed into the port of Mahon on the island of Minorca one day in October. Those watching from the shore shouted out cheerful greetings, thinking it was Doria back from a sweep of the North African coast. They could distinguish the Christians on board by their clothes and rang the church bells in welcome as the ships pulled steadily nearer. A Portuguese caravel lying at anchor in the harbor fired off a friendly salute. It was met by a furious burst of cannon fire. Astonished beyond surprise, the Portuguese ran to arm themselves but

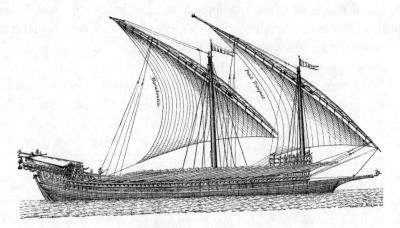

*Galley going with the wind*

it was already too late to register the galleys of Barbarossa bearing down on them. The old corsair was far from dead. He had slipped free from Tunis and regrouped; he had held fifteen galleys back at Bona, farther west. Here he had evaded Doria, sailed off to Algiers, and added more ships to his fleet. Now he was back to inflict terror on the Christian sea. The disguised galleys fell on Mahon like the vengeance of God. Barbarossa took the caravel, comprehensively sacked the town, and carried off eighteen hundred people. There was a glut of goods in the slave market of Algiers.

It was a sickening lurch back into nightmare for the Christian sea. An involuntary shudder ran along the coasts, passing from ship to ship, through the ports of Spain and Italy, the undefended islands and coastal towns. Charles's huge expenditure of effort and money had almost been negated. He had only scotched Barbarossa. By the end of the year the sultan's admiral was back in Istanbul. The usually intolerant Suleiman forgave him for the loss of his ships and ordered the construction of a new fleet.

# CHAPTER 5

# Doria and Barbarossa

1536–1541

CHARLES AND DORIA, SULEIMAN AND BARBAROSSA. After Tunis it was clear that the two potentates who would contest the Mediterranean had chosen their champions and were gathering their forces. If Barbarossa was the sultan's grand admiral, Doria was Charles's captain-general of the sea. Both seamen were the executors of their master's wars. The sea was no longer an outer frontier to be contested by pirates; it had become a major theatre of imperial conflict to rival the plains of Hungary. Year on year the violence grew. When Barbarossa struck Italy again in 1536, Doria responded by capturing Ottoman galleys off the coast of Greece the following year. And the fleets got bigger: in 1534, Barbarossa had built ninety galleys; in 1535, one hundred twenty. The two commanders had repeatedly sailed past each other, tracked each other's squadrons around the capes and bays of Italy, but they had never fought. The sea war was a series of uncoordinated punches, like a contest between amnesiac boxers. Many factors conspired to hinder coherent battle: the conditions imposed by the sea, the limits of the campaigning season, the logistical time lapses in preparing campaigns, the blind trawling for opponents before the age of radar, and not least the natural caution of experienced sailors. Both men understood the risks of naval warfare. Fractional disadvantages could aggregate great consequences that could hinge on a slight shift in the wind. A safe raid was always better than a chancy battle. Yet by the mid-1530s, the insistent pressure of imperial ambitions and the race for bigger fleets were shrinking the sea.

The French cannonballs at La Goletta were a disturbing portent for Charles of events about to unfold. In 1536 he embarked on another exhaustive two-year war with Francis, the Valois king of France. It was one of the bitter truths of a fragmented Europe that the Catholic King would spend more time, money, and energy fighting the French and the Protestants than he ever devoted to war with Suleiman. The perceived power of the Hapsburgs frightened rather than united Christendom, and in this climate Suleiman was able skillfully to affect the balance of power in the Mediterranean Sea.

The French had been flirting with an Ottoman alliance for years, either directly through furtive embassies or by means of the Barbarossas. As early as 1520, they sent an ambassador to Tunis to persuade the corsairs "to multiply the difficulties of the Emperor in his kingdom of Naples." They supplied Hayrettin with military technology—guns, powder, and cannonballs—and intelligence about the emperor. "I cannot deny," Francis admitted to the Venetian ambassador, "that I wish to see the Turk all-powerful and ready for war, not for himself—for he is an infidel and we are all Christians—but to weaken the power of the emperor, to compel him to make major expenses and to reassure all the other [Christian] governments who are opposed to [Charles]." In early 1536, Francis and Suleiman signed an agreement that granted mutual trading rights; behind it lay an understanding that they would fall on Italy in a pincer movement and destroy Charles. The Mediterranean moved center stage in the sultan's imperial war. Francis was evidently well informed on his ultimate objective. "The Turk will make some naval expedition," he told the Venetians, "going perhaps as far as Rome, for Sultan Suleiman always says 'to Rome! To Rome!' " The sultan ordered Barbarossa, now back in Istanbul, "to build two hundred vessels for an expedition against Apulia, to the completion of which he accordingly applied himself." It was a further escalation of sea power.

At the top of the Adriatic, the Venetians watched these developments with grave disquiet. An expedition aimed at Rome almost certainly involved encroaching on her home waters in the Adriatic. Venice maintained a queasy balancing act, trying to maintain her independence between two menacing superpowers. Charles had swallowed up all of Italy around her; Suleiman's navy threatened her maritime possessions. The republic's sole ambition was to trade profitably on a calm sea. Unable to compete militarily, she had built her security on adroit political maneuvering. No one courted the Grand Turk so assiduously, bribed his ministers so handsomely, spied on him so obsessively. The Venetians sent their top diplomats to Istanbul, where they kept a trained corps of Turkish speakers and cryptographers, who dispatched endless coded reports. It was a policy that had bought them thirty years' peace. The cornerstone was the special relationship with Ibrahim Pasha, the powerful chief vizier, born a Venetian subject on the shores of the Adriatic. He occupied a uniquely trusted position in the sultan's favor, but as Suleiman turned his intense gaze on the sea, all this started to unravel.

On the evening of March 5, 1536, Ibrahim came to the royal palace as usual to dine with Suleiman. As he was leaving, he was surprised to meet Ali the executioner and a posse of palace slaves: the ambitious vizier had overreached himself, almost assuming that the authority of the sultan was his own, and winning the particular disfavor of Suleiman's wife, Hurrem. When the hacked body was discovered the following morning, it was apparent from the bloody walls that Ibrahim had gone down fighting. The spattered room was left untouched for many years as a warning to ambitious viziers that it takes but a single Turkish consonant to fall from *makbul* (the favored) to *maktul* (the executed).

THE EXECUTION MARKED a pivotal moment in Suleiman's reign. Henceforth his style would become more austere; an Islamic piety would replace the previous brilliant ceremonial display of the man who would be Caesar. At a stroke, Ibrahim's death deprived Venice of an influential champion at court. It was clear that Suleiman was growing intolerant of the "Venetian infidels ... a people famous for their great wealth, their extensive commerce, and their deceit and perfidy in all their transactions." Edgy clashes in the Adriatic between Venetian galleys and Turkish corsairs provided a pretext for Ottoman aggression. At the start of 1537, Suleiman prepared a two-pronged assault on Italy, with the support of the French, and eyed the Venetian base at Corfu as a stepping-stone for invasion. The Venetian senate was sent a pointed request to join the alliance. The republic found itself between a rock and a hard place; the unspoken threat was the inevitable choice between Charles and Suleiman. The Venetians squirmed, declared their neutrality, politely declined the sultan's request, then armed a hundred galleys "as we observe that all the other princes in the world are doing." They waited to see what would happen next.

The French king's predictions proved entirely accurate. In May 1537, Suleiman set out with a sizeable army for Valona on the Albanian coast of the Adriatic; at the same time, Barbarossa was dispatched by sea. One hundred seventy galleys pulled out of Istanbul and beat down

*Pirates chasing a Christian ship*

on the Adriatic coast of Italy; for a month Barbarossa "laid waste the coasts of Apulia like a pestilence," burning castles, seizing slaves, spreading panic all the way back to Rome. Doria's fleet was too small to confront this shock force; he withdrew to Sicily and watched. In late August the sultan announced a change of tactic and ordered Barbarossa to take Corfu; twenty-five thousand men landed on the island and besieged the citadel, but to the Venetians' own surprise the defenses held. The much-anticipated linkup with the French failed to materialize, the siege guns got bogged down in the autumn rain, and the Venetians had prudently strengthened their bastions. After three weeks Suleiman called it off, but Venice was now irrevocably committed to warfare, and the emperor's cause. Over the winter of 1537, Pope Paul III brokered the terms of a Holy League against "the common enemy, the Tyrant of the Turks." It was to take the form of a maritime crusade, whose ultimate objective was the capture of Istanbul and the establishment of Charles as emperor of Constantinople. The Venetians, being pragmatists, tacitly preferred the notion of a quick defeat of Barbarossa and a return to peaceful trading with the Islamic world.

It was a crucial moment; Southern Europe felt itself hanging in the balance. A decisive Christian defeat now would lay the whole sea open to the merciless raids of the Ottoman fleet. In the spring of 1538, while the allies were maneuvering and organizing, Barbarossa was already at sea, giving the Venetians a taste of what failure would mean. As well as Cyprus and Crete, Venice held a string of small ports and islands across the Aegean—Naplion and Monemvasia in the Peloponnese, Skiathos, Skopelos, Skyros, Santorini, and a scattering more, each with its neat harbor, Catholic church, and dour bastion, with the lion of Saint Mark carved above the gateway. Hayrettin sacked them one by one, massacring their garrisons and carrying off other able-bodied men for galley service, before sailing on, leaving each one smoking and desolate beneath the hot sky. The Ottoman chroniclers tersely enumerated the extent of the republic's loss: "This year the Venetians possessed twenty-five islands, each having one, two or three castles; all of which were taken; twelve of the islands being laid under tribute, and the remaining thirteen plundered." Hayrettin was ravaging the south coast of Crete when a galliot brought news that the Christians were gathering a sizeable fleet in the Adriatic. He turned north to confront it.

IT HAD TAKEN AN AGE for the Holy League to assemble at Corfu. The Venetians and the pope's galleys were there by June, eager to fight. They then waited nearly three months for Doria, the overall commander, to drag himself tardily around from Genoa. He did not arrive until early September, by which time the weather was on the turn. There was instant bickering among the Italian and Spanish contingents. The Venetians were impatient and fretful at the long delay. The cost of the galleys was hurting the republic badly; they were anxious for a decisive strike before Barbarossa could inflict more damage on their islands. The politics of Christian Europe played heavily in the atmosphere; the parties had quite distinct strategic goals that even the optimistic pope, Paul III, had been unable to paper over. Venice was waging war to protect its possessions in the Eastern Mediterranean. For Charles the maritime frontier stopped at Sicily and he had little concern with Venetian interests farther east. Doria's tardiness was most likely at the emperor's behest. As for Doria, there was scarcely veiled distrust, bearing out the ancient grudge match between Genoa and Venice. None of this boded well.

It was early September before the assembled fleet moved out to seek a decisive encounter with Barbarossa. They had the weight of numbers on their side—139 heavy galleys and 70 sailing ships, to the enemy's 90 galleys and 50 light galliots—but the Ottomans had tucked themselves into an inlet on the west coast of Greece, the gulf of Preveza, and were well protected by shore-based guns. For nearly three weeks the Holy League blockaded Preveza, but it proved impossible to tempt Barbarossa out, and the season was getting late; the possibility of a gale wrecking his fleet concentrated Doria's mind. On the evening of September 27, he decided to weigh anchor and slip away. At this moment, Barbarossa, watching closely, saw his opportunity. Doria and Barbarossa had been playing cat and mouse in the Mediterranean for years; now the moment had come to try conclusions for control of the sea.

SEPTEMBER 28 WAS a blustery autumn day. As the Ottomans emerged to fight, the Christian fleet to seaward was badly strung out; the combination of the national flotillas and the mixture of galleys and sailing ships was badly coordinated. The Venetians, eager for battle, rowed forward with shouts of "Fight! Fight!" Doria unaccountably kept his squadron back. The lead ships were isolated. The Venetians had brought a heavily armed galleon in their fleet, which held its own against a swarm of Ottoman galleys. Other vessels were captured and sunk. When Doria turned toward the battle, he kept his ships well out to sea and engaged only in long-range cannonading. The great galleon held off the Ottoman fleet all day, but as night fell and the wind shifted, Doria abandoned the fight and withdrew, extinguishing his stern lanterns to foil pursuit. In the words of the Ottoman chroniclers, he "tore his beard and took to flight, all the smaller galleys following him."

Barbarossa claimed a famous victory and returned triumphant. "Such wonderful battles as those fought between forenoon and sunset of that day were never before seen at sea," wrote the later chronicler Katip Chelebi. When news was brought to Suleiman, "the proclamation of the victory was read, all present standing, and thanksgiving and praise were offered to the Divine Being. The Kapudan Pasha [Barbarossa] then received orders to make an advance of one hundred thousand pieces of money to the principal officers, to send proclamations of victory to all parts of the country, and to order public proclamations in all the towns."

In the scale of things the actual fighting had been quite light; the shattering collision of massed galleys had simply not occurred. The

Holy League lost perhaps twelve ships, a number dwarfed a few days later when seventy Ottoman ships were destroyed in a storm, but the psychological damage to the Holy League was immense. The Christians had been totally outmaneuvered. Of the Christian losses, most had fallen to the Venetians. Their ships had not been supported by Doria, and the Venetians were furious. They sensed treachery, malice, or cowardice by the Genoese admiral. Either Doria had been less than enthusiastic in the enterprise or he had been outmaneuvered by superior seamanship and had cut and run to limit the damage to his galleys. It seems highly likely that Barbarossa had gained the upper hand; safely tucked into the gulf of Preveza, he could choose the moment to strike when his opponents were at the mercy of the wind, but there were other factors that might have compromised the desire of either man to fight to the death.

What the Venetians did not know was that Charles, having failed to destroy Barbarossa at Tunis, had resorted to underhand methods. In 1537 he entered secret negotiations with the sultan's admiral to induce him to switch sides, and these talks were still taking place on the very eve of battle. On September 20, 1538, a Spanish messenger from Barbarossa held a meeting with Doria and the viceroy of Sicily. The terms could not be agreed—Barbarossa was said to have demanded the return of Tunis—but the negotiations suggested a certain complicity between the two admirals; both were hired hands whose reputations were at stake; both had reasons to be cautious. They had much more to lose than gain by a rash gamble on the state of the wind. The Spanish knowingly recalled the proverb that one crow does not peck out another's eyes. For Doria there were other business considerations: many of the galleys were his own property; he was certainly loath to lose them helping the detestable Venetians. It would take less experienced commanders to throw caution to the wind and risk everything in the same stretch of water thirty years later.

It is impossible to determine Barbarossa's sincerity in these maneuvers. Maybe the downfall of Ibrahim Pasha had illustrated the perils of high office in the sultan's service, or perhaps Charles had offered Barbarossa the chance to realize his dream of an independent kingdom in the Maghreb. More likely, Barbarossa's behavior was a way of playing Charles and Doria along, lulling his opponents into doubt and hesitation. Certainly, a French agent in Istanbul by the name of Dr. Romero had no doubts. "I can guarantee that [Barbarossa] is a better Muslim than Mohammed," he wrote. "The negotiations are a front."

If at first sight the immediate military consequences of Preveza seemed slight, the political and psychological ones were enormous. Only a unified Christian fleet could match the resources at the disposal of the Ottomans. In 1538 the idea of any coordinated Christian maritime response to the Turks had proved unworkable. The Holy League collapsed: in 1540 the Venetians signed a humiliating peace with the sultan. They paid a hefty ransom and acknowledged the loss of all their possessions taken by Barbarossa. They were virtually reduced to the status of vassals, though no one was using that term. The Venetians, the most experienced mariners in the whole sea, would not launch ships in anger for a quarter of a century, when distrust of the Doria clan would rise again. Preveza opened the door to Ottoman domination of the Mediterranean. All that the Venetians took away from the fight was the performance of their great galleon; they stored for future reference the value of stoutly built floating gun platforms.

CHARLES MADE ONE further personal attempt to break the stranglehold of Ottoman power in the western sea. Remembering the triumph of Tunis, he determined on a similar operation against Algiers. In the summer of 1541 Suleiman was in Hungary and Barbarossa was conducting naval operations up the Danube. It was an ideal moment to strike.

There was a streak of risk-taking in the emperor. By 1541 his treasury was under extreme pressure. To cut costs, he decided to descend on Algiers late in the year. It reduced the number of troops he had to pay, as he could be sure no fleet from Istanbul would come to oppose him on the wintering sea. Doria warned him about the gamble, but Charles was resolved to ride his luck.

The outcome was catastrophic. His substantial fleet sailed from Genoa in late September. Among the gentleman adventurers who accompanied the expedition was Hernando Cortez, the conqueror of Mexico, trying his fortune in the Old World. It was October 20 before all the units were gathered at Algiers, but the weather was fair. Only after the army had disembarked and was awaiting its supplies did Charles's luck run out. On the night of October 23 torrential rain started to fall; the men could not keep their powder dry, and suddenly found themselves at a disadvantage. Barbarossa had appointed an Italian renegade, Hasan, as governor of Algiers in his absence. Hasan acted with courage and determination. Sallying out of the city, he put Charles's army to flight. Only a small detachment of the Knights of Saint John prevented a total rout. Worse followed. Overnight the wind intensified; one by one the sailing ships riding offshore dragged their creaking anchors and rode onto the beach. As the survivors staggered through the pounding surf in the dark, they were massacred by the local population. Charles was forced to beat a ragged retreat twenty miles down the coast to a point where Doria's galleys could take him off. There were too few ships to re-embark the bulk of the army. With his galley bucking and heaving dangerously offshore, Charles threw his horses overboard and departed the Barbary Coast with the blasphemous screams of his abandoned army reaching him on the tempestuous wind. He had lost one hundred forty sailing ships, fifteen galleys, eight thousand men, and three hundred Spanish aristocrats. The sea had delivered a total humiliation. There was a glut of slaves in Algiers, so many that 1541 was said to be the year when Christians sold at an onion a head.

Charles viewed this catastrophe with a remarkable levelness of spirit. "We must thank God for all," he wrote to his brother Ferdinand, "and hope that after this disaster He will grant us of His great goodness, some great good fortune," and he refused to accept the inevitable conclusion that he had sailed too late. As regards the sudden storm, he wrote that "nobody could have guessed that beforehand. It was essential not so much to rise early, as to rise at the right time, and God alone could judge what time that should be." Any shrewd observer of the Maghreb coast would have begged to differ. Charles never went crusading at sea again. The following year he departed for the Netherlands to confront the intractable problems of the Protestant rebellion and another French war.

# The Turkish Sea

1543–1560

IT WAS CLEAR BY THE 1540S that Charles was losing the battle for the sea. The debacle at Preveza had slammed shut the possibility of effective Christian cooperation; the disaster at Algiers confirmed the city as the capital of Islamic corsairing, to which adventurers and converted renegades now flocked from all over the Mediterranean to plunder Christian coasts and shipping lanes.

In this atmosphere, nothing shocked and terrified Christian Europe as much as the extraordinary scenes along the French coast in 1543–1544. France and Charles were at war again, and Francis had moved to further strengthen his alliance with Suleiman. Barbarossa was invited to join forces with the French. Together they sacked Nice, a vassal city of Charles's; in the winter of 1543, to the scandal of Christendom, Barbarossa's lean predatory galleys were rocking safely at anchor in the French port of Toulon. There were thirty thousand Ottoman troops in the town; the cathedral had been converted into a mosque and its tombs desecrated. Ottoman coinage was imposed and the call to prayer rang out over the city five times a day. "To see Toulon, one might imagine oneself at Constantinople," one French eyewitness declared. It was as if the Orient had complicitly invaded the Christian shore. Francis, who styled himself the Most Christian King, had agreed to supply Barbarossa's fleet with food over the winter and to augment his forces—in return for the Ottoman fleet pillaging Charles's realms. In practice it was the people of Toulon who were obliged to foot the bill for their unwelcome visitors.

This strange cohabitation was soon soured by bad faith on both sides. Francis dithered and prevaricated in his wholehearted commitment to an alliance that shocked Europe. Barbarossa was contemptuous of his ally's faintheartedness, kidnapped the whole French fleet, and held it to ransom. The French began to feel that they had made a pact with the devil; Francis eventually had to pay Barbarossa eight hundred thousand gold ecus to depart, leaving the people of Toulon poverty-stricken but relieved.

As the Ottoman fleet sailed off to Istanbul in May 1544, they were accompanied by five French galleys on a diplomatic mission to Suleiman. Among those who went was a French priest, Jérome Maurand. The classically minded cleric volunteered for the voyage as chaplain; he was enthusiastic about the opportunity to see Constantinople and the great remains of the classical world along the way.

In his journal Maurand recorded the natural and man-made wonders of the Mediterranean from the deck of a galley. He witnessed the terrifying spectacle of lightning storms at sea and the eerie glow of Saint Elmo's fire shimmering from the mast; he saw the ruins of Roman villas still radiantly painted in blue and gold, and sailed past the volcano of Stromboli in the dark, "ceaselessly spewing out fire and enormous flames." He marveled at the sand of the island of Volcanello, "black as ink," and peered over the rim of its bubbling, sulfurous crater, which conjured up the gulf of hell. At the Ottoman port of Modon, in southern Greece, he inspected an obelisk constructed entirely of Christian bones and put ashore at the ancient site of Troy before finally reaching "the famous, imperial, and very great city of Constantinople" with a salute of gunfire as the galleys passed the sultan's palace. Along the way he was also an unwilling witness to the might of Ottoman sea power.

The imperial fleet with which Suleiman had provided Barbarossa— one hundred twenty galleys and support sailing vessels—rampaged down the west coast of Italy with unstoppable force. Charles's coastal defenses had no answer to such a heavily armed and mobile enemy. At word of Barbarossa's approach, people simply fled. Empty villages were burned to the ground; sometimes the invaders would follow the fleeing populace several miles inland. If the people retreated into a secure coastal fort, the galley captains turned their prows to the shore and pulverized the walls or dragged the cannon ashore and instigated a major siege for as long as it took. Barbarossa's men had no fear of counterattack. Only a few small detachments of Spanish soldiers guarded isolated towers. Out at sea, Doria's nephew, Giannetto, tracked the fleet with his twenty-five galleys but was forced to scurry back to Naples at any sign of an engagement.

Day after day Maurand watched the fleet at work. A combustible mixture of jihad, imperial warfare, personal plunder, and spiteful revenge fueled their rampage. The priest witnessed slave-taking on an enormous scale. From each assault, long lines of men, women, and children were led down to the shore in chains, where they risked the equal perils of the sea. Sometimes a coastal village would try to bargain part of its population in a cruel lottery. Port'Ercole offered eighty people, to be chosen by Barbarossa, in return for thirty going free. He accepted the bargain but torched their village anyway. Only one house was left standing. Fortifications were destroyed as a matter of course. Finding Giglio deserted, the seamen razed it, but the castle resisted and had to be blasted into submission and ruined. The 632 Christians who surrendered were enslaved, but their leaders and priest were beheaded in front of Barbarossa to discourage resistance. It was a calculated and effective means of breaking morale. "It's an extraordinary thing," Maurand testified, "how the very mention of the Turks is so horrifying and terrible to the Christians that it makes them lose not only their strength but also their wits." Barbarossa employed the exemplary brutality of Genghis Khan.

Some of his reprisals were acts of personal revenge, conducted even beyond the grave. Singling out the coastal town of Telamona, he had the body of the recently deceased Bartolome Peretti ripped from its tomb, ritually disemboweled, chopped into pieces, and burned in the public square, along with the corpses of Peretti's officers and servants. When Barbarossa left, the smell of burned flesh hung in the air. The terrified populace crept from their hiding places shaken and appalled. It was payback for Peretti's attack on Barbarossa's home island of Lesbos the previous year, when his father's house had been destroyed.

The Ottomans sailed on. The fleet burned several villages on the island of Ischia and took two thousand slaves. Naples crouched behind its shore guns as the fleet swept past like a black wing darkening the sun. Salerno, farther south, was saved only by a miracle. The galleys were closing in after dark, so near that Maurand could see the lights in the windows, when "God in his mercy" intervened. A sudden storm arose and there was "a cruel sea from the southwest and a blackness so thick that the galleys couldn't see one another, together with a rain falling without ceasing from the sky that was quite unbearable." The Christian slaves, huddling on the exposed deck like "drowned ducks,"

*Unloading slaves at Algiers*

were cruelly beaten. One galliot, overloaded with captives, foundered in the storm: "They all drowned, except for some Turks who escaped by swimming."

The last straw for the increasingly appalled French contingent came at Lipari, the largest of the volcanic islands off the coast of Sicily. The Lipariots had been warned of the approaching fleet. They strengthened their defenses but declined to evacuate the women and children and withdrew into their well-prepared fortress. Hayrettin landed five thousand men and sixteen cannon and settled down for a long siege. As he blasted away, the defenders tried to negotiate; when they offered fifteen thousand ducats, Barbarossa demanded thirty thousand and four hundred children. Eventually they thought they had brokered a deal with a payment to be made for each person. They gave up the keys to the castle, but he enslaved them all anyway, except for the richest families, who paid sizeable ransoms for their liberty. The ordinary people were ordered past the implacable pasha one by one. The old and useless were beaten with sticks and released. The rest were chained and marched down to their own harbor. A few of the most aged were found sheltering in the cathedral church. The corsairs seized them, stripped off their clothes, and cut them open while still alive, "out of spite." Maurand was totally unable to comprehend these actions. "When we asked these Turks why they treated the poor Christians with such cruelty, they replied that such behavior had very great virtue; that was the only answer we ever got." Nor could the priest understand why God permitted such sufferings; he could conclude only that it was because of Christian sin, in the case of the Lipariots because they were said to be "much given to sodomy."

Profoundly shaken, the French ransomed a few of the Lipariot captives at their own expense and watched the rest being led away, seeing "the tears, groans, and sobs of the pitiful Lipariots leaving their own city to be led away into slavery; fathers looking at their sons, mothers their daughters, were unable to hold back the tears in their sad eyes." Charles at Tunis, Hayrettin at Lipari: the battle for the Mediterranean had become a war waged against civilians. The castle, the cathedral, the tombs, and the houses were ransacked and burned. Lipari was a smoking ruin. While Barbarossa arranged a truce and offered to sell his new captives back in nearby Sicily, the French galleys made their excuses and sailed on alone.

In the summer of 1544 Barbarossa took some six thousand captives from the coasts of Italy and the surrounding seas. On his way home the boats were so dangerously overloaded with human cargo that the crews threw hundreds of the weaker captives overboard. He entered the harbor in triumph to the firing of cannon and nighttime fires illuminating the Horn. Thousands of people gathered on the shore to witness the triumphant return of "the king of the sea." It was to be his last great expedition. In the summer of 1546, at the age of eighty, he was carried off by a fever in his own palace in Istanbul to the universal mourning of the people. He was buried in a mausoleum on the shores of the Bosphorus that became an obligatory place of pilgrimage for all departing naval expeditions, saluted with "numerous salvoes from cannon and muskets to give him the honor due to a great saint." After so many decades of terror, Christians could scarcely believe that "the king of evil" was gone; so great was the superstitious dread attached to his name that legend persisted he could leave his tomb and walk the earth with the undead. Apparently it took a Greek magician to fix the problem: burying a black dog in the tomb appeased the restless spirit and returned it to Hades.

And in a real sense Barbarossa returned unceasingly to terrorize the Christian shore. A new generation of corsair captains sprang up in his wake; the greatest of whom—Turgut, Dragut to the Christians, born on the Anatolian coast—would replicate the career of his mentor, moving from enterprising freebooter on the shores of the Maghreb and battle experience at Preveza to imperial service under Suleiman during the twenty years after 1546. The king of evil had sowed dragon's teeth in the sea.

Barbarossa's last great raid of 1544 had shown that Muslim fleets could roam at will. These huge sweeps were campaigns in a full-scale Mediterranean war that the Ottomans were winning. Slave-taking was an instrument of imperial policy, and the damage was immense. In the four decades following the launch of Barbarossa's first imperial fleet in 1534, thousands of people were snatched from the coasts of Italy and Spain: eighteen hundred from Minorca in 1535, seven thousand from the Bay of Naples in 1544, five thousand from the island of Gozo off Malta in 1551, six thousand from Calabria in 1554, and four thousand from Granada in 1566. The Ottomans could apply sudden and overwhelming force at precise points; they could land at and destroy fair-size coastal towns with impunity and threaten even the major cities of Italy. When Andrea Doria's nephew trapped and captured Turgut on the Sardinian shore in 1540 and condemned him to the galleys, Barbarossa threatened to blockade Naples unless Turgut was ransomed; the Genoese thought it wisest to comply. Doria and Barbarossa met in person to agree the terms. The thirty-five hundred ducats would prove a bad bargain for the Christians: eleven years later Turgut would blockade Genoa himself. The Christians had no adequate naval presence to respond to such threats after Preveza. Charles was too busy attending to multiple other wars to frame—or pay for—a coherent maritime response. By now it was all that the Dorias could do to apply some counterpressure.

Nor was this assault conducted just through large fleet actions. War between Charles and Suleiman ebbed and flowed, depending on the timing of their conflicts, but when they signed a peace in 1547 so that the sultan could campaign in Persia, the big maritime expeditions were temporarily suspended; warfare continued anyway under another name. Enterprising corsairs from the Maghreb filled the vacuum and inflicted a different style of misery on Christian shores. Where the imperial fleets had brazenly smashed their way through local defenses, these lesser carnivores proceeded by ambush and stealth. It was a subtler kind of terror. Surprise replaced brute force.

The corsairs' tactics were soon horribly familiar. A few galliots might loiter offshore, below the rim of the horizon, sitting out the heat of the day. A captured fishing boat would be sent in to scout the coast, maybe with a local renegade to identify suitable targets. In the small hours of the morning the corsairs would make a move, the black, low-slung shapes of the vessels cutting the night sea beneath a sprinkle of stars. There were no lanterns; the Christian galley slaves were gagged with cork dummies to prevent them from calling out. When the prows touched the beach, the corsairs would hit the village at speed; doors were kicked in and the occupants dragged naked from their beds, the church bell rope slashed to forestall an alarm; a few screams and dog barks would echo in the square and a confused straggle of captives were marched down to their own beach and hustled aboard; then they would be gone. "They grabbed young women and children," recalled a Sicilian villager of one such raid, "they snatched goods and money, and in a flash, back aboard their galleys, they set their course and vanished." The terror lay in the surprise.

BY THE MID-CENTURY the Mediterranean was a sea of disappearances, a place where people working the coastal margins simply vanished: the lone fisherman setting out in his boat; a shepherd with his flock on the seashore; laborers harvesting corn or tending vines, sometimes several miles inland; sailors working a small tramp ship around the islands. Once seized they could be in the slave mart at Algiers in a couple of days—or they could be subjected to a lengthy cruise in pursuit of other prizes. Those who weakened or died en route would be dumped overboard.

In a particularly cruel twist, the captives might reappear at their home village a day or two later. The raiders would materialize offshore, hoist a flag of truce, and display the victims for ransom. The grieving relatives would be given a day to raise funds; the families might mortgage their fields and boats to the local moneylender and enter a spiral of inescapable debt. If they failed, the hostages would be gone forever. The illiterate peasantry too poor to be ransomed seldom saw their birthplace again.

The sudden terror of these visitations cast a profound dread over the Christian sea. Those who were taken, such as the Frenchman Du Chastelet, seized in the seventeenth century, never forgot the trauma of their capture. "As to me," he wrote, recalling the nightmarish moment, "I noticed a great Moor approaching me, his sleeves rolled up to his shoulders, holding a sabre in his large hand of four fingers; I was left without words. And the ugliness of this carbon face, animated by two ivory eyeballs, moving about hideously, terrified me a good deal more than were frightened the first humans at the sight of the flaming sword at the door of Eden."

This was a terror sharpened by racial difference; across the narrow sea two civilizations communicated through abrupt acts of violence and revenge. Europe was on the receiving end of the slavery it was starting to inflict on West Africa—though the numbers slaved to Islam far exceeded the black slaves taken in the sixteenth century, and where Atlantic slaving was a matter of cold business, in the Mediterranean it was heightened by mutual religious hatred. The Islamic raids were designed both to damage the material infrastructure of Spain and Italy and to undermine the spiritual and psychic basis of Christians' lives. The ransacking of tombs and the ritual desecration of churches that Jérome Maurand witnessed in 1544 were acts of profound intention. The Italian poet Curthio Mattei mourned "the outrage done to God"— the holy images skewered to the floor with daggers, the mocking of the sacraments and altars. Mattei was equally appalled by the disinterring of corpses and the destruction of generations of past people: "The bones of our dead are not secure underground . . . dozens of years after death." The corsairs entered Italian folklore as agents of hell, and what made it more difficult to bear was that as often as not Satan's emissaries were renegade Christians who had defected to Islam through circumstance or choice, and who were extremely well placed to maximize damage on their native lands.

IN THIS ATMOSPHERE, Charles's failure to retake Algiers in 1541 assumed a grave significance. The city, now protected by a breakwater and powerful defenses, became the center of piracy. It was a gold rush town, a place where a man might dream of becoming as rich as Barbarossa. Adventurers, freebooters, and outcasts came from across the impoverished sea and from both sides of the religious divide to try their luck at "Christian stealing." The city resembled in part a gaudy bazaar where humans and booty were bought and sold, in part a Soviet gulag. Thousands of prisoners were kept in slave pens—the dark, crowded, fetid converted bathhouses—from whence they would be taken daily in chains to work. Wealthy captives such as the Spanish writer Cervantes, held in Algiers for five years, might enjoy tolerable conditions, awaiting liberation through ransom. The poor would lug stones, fell timber, dig salt, build palaces and forts, or, worst of all, row galleys until disease, abuse, and malnourishment finished them off.

It is impossible to know how many slaves were being taken in the decades after 1540, but it was not a one-way trade. Both sides were engaged in "man-taking" throughout the whole length of the sea, and if Islam was in the ascendancy, there were small correctives. The Knights of Saint John were ruthless slavers, particularly La Valette, the French knight who had fought as a young man at Rhodes. Putting out a small force of heavily armed galleys from Malta, the knights returned to their old haunts in the Aegean, disrupting the Ottoman sea-lanes between Egypt and Istanbul. They could be as unscrupulous as any corsair on the high seas. Jérome Maurand reached the Venetian island of Tinos shortly after a visit by a knight with some ships. The islanders had greeted the visitors "as friends and Christians," until one morning, after most of the island men had left the town to work in the fields, "this Knight and his men, seeing that there were only a few men at the castle, killed them, sacked the castle, and took away the women, boys, and girls as slaves." This treacherous act soon got its own comeuppance; the knight was in turn seized by Turkish corsairs and taken off to Istanbul, where Maurand was in time to witness his execution. Changes of fortune could be abrupt.

The knights were not alone; any small-scale Christian pirate might try his hand at raiding the eastern sea; Livorno and Naples on the Italian coast had active slave markets. Muslims disappeared into the Malta slave pens or the pope's imperial galleys, but their numbers were far fewer than those taken to the Maghreb or Istanbul. There is a vast literature of Christian slave narratives; about the Muslims almost nothing. Occasional muffled accounts of personal suffering break the general silence. In the late 1550s Suleiman was bombarded by tearful requests from a woman called Huma for the restoration of her children, taken on a voyage to Mecca by the Knights of Saint John. The two daughters had been abducted to France, converted to Christianity, and married off. Distraught and persistent, Huma was a familiar figure in the Istanbul streets, trying to push a petition into the sultan's hand as he rode by. Twenty-four years after their disappearance, Sultan Murat III could still write that "the lady named Huma has time and again presented written petitions to our imperial stirrup." As far as we know the girls never came back; a further brother probably died at the oars of a Malta galley. There were countless thousands of such small tragedies on both sides of the religious divide, familiar tales of abduction and loss.

THE INSTRUMENT OF ALL this chaotic violence was the oared galley. These fast, fragile, low-slung racing craft were the war machines of the Mediterranean, bred by the conditions of the sea. They dictated absolutely how, where, and when wars could be fought. The advantages of a shallow draft allowed the vessels to be easily beached for amphibious operations; they could lurk in ambush close to the shore and spin on a sixpence around a lumbering sailing ship, whose powers of maneuver were limited by the sea's uncertain winds. At the same time, the galleys' extraordinarily poor seaworthiness and dependence on continuous supplies of fresh water for the rowing crews tied them umbilically to land. Galleys needed to put ashore every few days, which meant their range of operation was limited and their deployment strictly seasonal; winter storms ensured that warfare was suspended every year between October and April. Crucially, the dynamo of maritime war was human labor; in all the motivations for slaving in the sixteenth century, snatching men for the rowing benches assumed an important role.

In the heyday of Venetian sea power in the fifteenth century, galleys had been rowed by volunteers; by the sixteenth, the muscle power

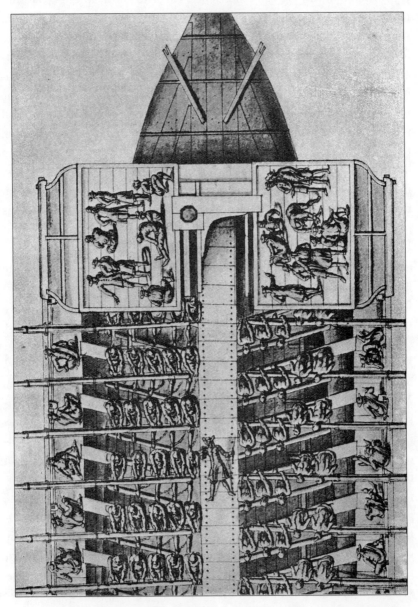

*Men at the rowing benches*

was generally conscripted. The Ottoman navy relied heavily on an annual levy of men from the provinces of Anatolia and Europe, and everyone employed chained labor—captured slaves, convicts, and, in the Christian ships, paupers so destitute they sold themselves to the galley captains. It was these wretches, chained three or four to a foot-wide bench, who made sea wars possible. Their sole function was to work themselves to death. Shackled hand and foot, excreting where they sat, fed on meagre quantities of black biscuits, and so thirsty they were sometimes driven to drink seawater, galley slaves led lives bitter and short. The men, naked apart from a pair of linen breeches, were flayed raw by the sun; sleep deprivation on the narrow bench propelled them toward lunacy; the stroke keeper's drum and the overseer's lash—a tarred rope or a dried bull's penis—whipped them beyond the point of exhaustion during long stretches of intensive effort when a ship was trying to capture or escape another vessel. The sight of a galley crew at full stretch was as brutal as any a man could wish to be spared. "That least tolerable and most to be dreaded employment of a man deprived of liberty," wrote the eighteenth-century English historian Joseph Morgan, conjuring up the vision of "ranks and files of half-naked, half-starved, half-tanned, meagre wretches, chained to a plank, from whence they remove not for months at a time . . . urged on, even beyond human strength, with cruel and repeated blows, on the bare flesh, to an incessant continuation of the most violent of all exercises." "God preserve you from the galleys of Tripoli," was a customary valediction to men putting to sea from a Christian port.

Disease could decimate a fleet in weeks. The galley was an amoebic death trap, a swilling sewer whose stench was so foul you could smell it two miles off—it was customary to sink the hulls at periodic intervals to cleanse them of shit and rats—but if the crew survived to enter a battle, the chained and unprotected rowers could only sit and wait to be killed by men of their own country and creed. The nominally free men who made up the bulk of the Ottoman rowing force fared little better. Levied by the sultan in large numbers from the empire's inland provinces, many had never seen the sea before. Inexperienced and inefficient as oarsmen, they succumbed in large numbers to the terrible conditions.

One way or another the oared galley consumed men like fuel. Each dying wretch dumped overboard had to be replaced—and there were never enough. Official Spanish and Italian memoranda report monotonously on the shortage of fodder for the benches, so that the supply of ships often outstripped the resources to power them, as in the case of a sudden disaster that overcame the galleys of the Knights of Saint John in 1555.

On the night of October 22, their four vessels were riding safely at anchor in their secure harbor in Malta. The commander of the galleys, Romegas—the Order's most experienced naval captain—was asleep at the rear of his ship when a freak whirlwind whipped across the sea, snapped the ships' masts, and flipped the galleys over. When dawn broke, all four galleys were floating upside down on the gray water. Rescuers put out in boats to hunt for signs of life and inspect the damage; when they heard a dull tapping coming from one of the ships, they smashed a hole in the hull and peered downward into the dark. Out promptly hopped the ship's monkey, followed by Romegas, who had spent the night up to his shoulders in water in an air pocket. It was only when the vessels were righted with the help of buoyant air barrels that the full horror of the event became clear; the corpses of three hundred drowned Muslim slaves still chained to the benches floated in the water like ghosts. Repair and replacement of the vessels was a manageable problem; it was securing new crews that was the real difficulty. The pope threw open the episcopal prison in Naples to supply some of the number; the knights then had to take some of their ships to snatch more slaves to fill the empty spaces. It was the same for both sides: much of the raiding was undertaken solely to make such raids possible. The violence was self-perpetuating. The galleys created their own need for war.

IT WAS CLEAR during the 1550s that inch by inch Charles was losing this contest. Plagued by trouble with Protestants in Germany and the Low Countries, interminable war with France, spiraling debts that even the bullion fleets from the Americas were now unable to control, the emperor was too busy sustaining the burden of his empire to attend coherently to the sea. Intermittent truce with Suleiman made little difference to the situation; when the Ottoman imperial fleet did not sail, the corsairs of the Maghreb still did. The plunder of the coasts of Italy, Sicily, the Balearic Islands, and Spain continued almost unchecked. Ruinous economic and demographic decline particularly affected Southern Italy. Sometimes the wholesale evacuation of a patch of coast was ordered by the local governor to save the population from an Ottoman raid, as on the Adriatic coast in 1566. Five hundred square miles of countryside were devastated anyway. Sea trade between Spain and Italy was intermittently on the brink of paralysis; the whole structure of Spain's Mediterranean empire seemed threatened by this merciless raiding. "Turgut," a French bishop wrote in 1561, "has held the kingdom of Naples in such a noose ... [that the galleys] of Malta, of Sicily, and other neighbouring ports are so harassed and confined by Turgut that not one of them can pass from one place to another." Rumors again spread across the western sea that these attacks were the prelude to a full-scale invasion of Italy. In Rome successive popes trembled and pleaded for concerted action. In the Maghreb, Spanish forts continued to fall one by one. Tripoli, held for Charles by the Knights of Saint John, went in 1551; henceforward it would mimic Algiers as a gold rush town for Islamic corsairs. Bugia went in 1555. Andrea Doria, now in his eighties, waged counterstrikes of varying effectiveness; he bottled up Turgut in the lagoon at Djerba, but the corsair slipped effortlessly through his fingers by dragging his ships overland. The following year, Turgut reappeared with Suleiman's imperial fleet and attacked Malta. Subsequent Spanish expeditions to the African shore met with disaster and death.

By the early 1550s Charles himself was a broken man, sunk under the weight of empire. His dutiful attempts to micromanage the Christian world in person had ended in nervous breakdown. Crippled by gout, his finances hocked to German bankers, he obsessively sought order in a miniaturized, private world: "He is seen for days on end in a dark humour," reported one eyewitness, "one hand paralyzed, one leg tucked under him, refusing to give audiences and spending his time taking clocks and watches apart and putting them together again." In 1556 Charles relinquished the Spanish crown to his son Philip and retired to a monastery to devote his soul to God. As well as religious books and the personal journals of his life, he took with him his maps of the world and the works of Julius Caesar. The final maritime disaster of his reign occurred in the summer of 1558: a Spanish expedition was annihilated in the Maghreb. When the news filtered back to Spain, Charles was on his deathbed. No one had the heart to tell him.

By this time Suleiman had already claimed to his own satisfaction to have won the contest with his great rival. In 1547 he had signed a truce with Charles and his brother Ferdinand; Ferdinand agreed to pay an annual sum for his Hungarian territories, which in Suleiman's eyes reduced him to the status of a vassal, while the document referred to Charles only as "king of Spain." Ferdinand and Charles signed in person. Suleiman, too elevated to treat with the infidel himself, had his imperial cipher appended, as usual, by an official. For the sultan, the titles, terms, and manner of the agreement assumed huge symbolic importance. Henceforward he considered himself to be "Emperor of the Romans"—Caesar.

A defining moment of triumph in the White Sea followed hard on the heels of Charles's death. When Philip II inherited the crown of Spain, the worsening situation on the shores of his domain made serious attention to the Mediterranean problem a pressing issue: North African corsairs were now venturing into the Atlantic and disrupting the galleon traffic with the Indies. A further break in the interminable fighting with France in 1559 seemed to offer the decisive moment to tackle the Maghreb again.

A plan was developed to retake the strategic port of Tripoli and regain control of the axis of the sea. The preparations, like all Spanish naval ventures, were laborious and somehow inhibited by Philip. The new king was not like his father: where Charles had been a risk taker, Philip was cautious—destined to go down in history as the Prudent King; where Charles led his own armies, Philip fought by proxy, attempting to control his commanders by a string of orders issued distantly from the royal palace in Madrid. The choice of commander was controversial. Even the apparently indestructible Andrea Doria at ninety-three was finally too old to take part; the baton passed to his great-nephew Gian'Andrea, an inexperienced twenty-one-year-old. The results were disastrous.

The fleet did not sail until December of 1559, with fifty galleys and six thousand soldiers. It dithered about its objective and finally settled on Turgut's pirate lair at Djerba. The island was easily overrun in the spring of 1560 and a fort constructed and garrisoned. But the corsairs had hurried word to Istanbul, and an Ottoman fleet of eighty-six galleys under their commander Piyale Pasha hastened to sail. They made the journey to Djerba in a record twenty days. Gian'Andrea's fleet was caught in total surprise when the Ottoman sails loomed on the horizon. There was an indecent haste to embark, then no attempt to form a line of battle. Piyale just picked off the ships one by one. Gian'Andrea slipped away from the scene with his privately owned galleys and vague promises of relief for the stricken fort. None came; Philip acted with an ambivalence that would soon become customary: He hastened the preparations for the relief fleet, then forbade it from sailing, fearing at the last minute to risk more ships. He abandoned the men to their fate. Besieged, then cut off from a water source, the doomed fort fell. All five thousand men inside were either killed in the fighting or put to death; only the aristocratic commanders were spared. They were sent as trophies with the captured galleys to Suleiman. On Djerba the Muslims built a pyramid out of the bones of the dead; the "fortress of skulls" was still there in the nineteenth century.

The catastrophe for Spain was far more serious than the simple tally of lost ships and men; it was not the thirty galleys, the five thousand soldiers, and the six thousand four hundred oarsmen—difficult though they would be to replace—that were truly significant. It was the six hundred experienced mariners, the two thousand naval arquebusiers, the seasoned commanders—a whole generation of men skilled in galley warfare whose expertise, acquired with years of practical experience, could not be replaced with any quantity of Inca gold. The debacle at Djerba left Spain and Italy more exposed than ever.

On October 1, 1560, Piyale Pasha's victorious fleet rounded Seraglio Point below the sultan's palace and pulled into the Golden Horn to a tumultuous welcome. The Flemish diplomat Busbecq was there to witness a spectacle "as pleasing to Turkish eyes as it was grievous and lamentable to Christians." Suleiman went to the tiled kiosk at the end of the palace gardens, "in order that he might see at closer range the armada as it entered and the Christian commanders who were on display." The procession of ships had been arranged to demonstrate the supremacy of Ottoman sea power. The Ottoman galleys were vividly painted in red and green; the captured Christian ones had been stripped of masts, rigging, and oars "so that they might appear small, shapeless, and contemptible when compared with the Turkish galleys." On the poop of Piyale's flagship, resplendent with banners and noise, the Christian commanders were paraded as an object lesson in humiliation.

Ottoman naval power was at its apogee. If ever there was a moment when one side might be said to control the uncontrollable sea, it was now. Yet those who closely observed the sultan on that early autumn day could see no hint of joy or triumph in his face. His manner was grave, severe, implacable.

In Genoa, Andrea Doria, four days short of his ninety-fourth birthday, turned his face to the wall and died.

# Part Two

## EPICENTER: THE BATTLE FOR MALTA

1560-1565

# CHAPTER 7

# Nest of Vipers

1560–1565

NEWS OF THE DJERBA DEFEAT passed along the Christian shore with a convulsive shudder. It was clear that the situation in the central Mediterranean was now critical. On July 9, 1560, the viceroy of Sicily, who had planned—and survived—the ill-fated venture, wrote starkly to Philip: "We must draw strength from our weaknesses; let Your Majesty sell us all, and myself first, if only he can become lord of the seas. Only thus will he have peace and tranquility and will his subjects be defended, but if he does not, then all will go ill with us."

Invasion fears stalked Spain and Italy; people braced themselves for the new sailing season. There seemed now to be no counterforce capable of resisting Ottoman maritime aggression: it was only a matter of time before Suleiman struck again and in force. The Mediterranean became a sea of rumors: every spring confidential dispatches from Istanbul suggested the imminent departure of a substantial fleet, yet nothing happened. Even to close watchers of the Turkish scene, the explanation was obscure. Suleiman had other priorities and problems. There was rumbling civil war between his sons, trouble with Persia, power struggles among his viziers, plague, and food shortages. An atmosphere of phony war hung over the sea. Every year the coastal defenses of Philip's realms were prepared, then stood down; and in the meantime Philip, starkly aware of Spain's vulnerability at sea, set about building galleys. The French watched him closely: "for two months now," read a report to the French king in 1561, "the said King of Spain has had the shipyards of Barcelona working diligently to finish several galleys and other seagoing vessels." Philip was playing catch-up against the inevitable moment.

The storm finally broke over the central Mediterranean in 1564. That summer the Knights of Saint John triggered a series of events whose reverberations were felt within the tiled kiosks of Suleiman's palace—and unwittingly unleashed a decisive contest for the heart of the sea.

AFTER THEIR ARRIVAL ON MALTA in 1530, the galleys of the Order set sail almost every year to conduct their personal maritime crusade, sweeping the seas for Islamic plunder and slaves in the name of religion. When Jean Parisot de La Valette was elected grand master of the Order in 1557, this activity intensified. La Valette had witnessed the siege of Rhodes as a young knight and pursued sea warfare with zeal. The line between crusading and lucrative piracy was wafer-thin; for the Venetians, the knights were merely "corsairs parading crosses," indistinguishable from their Muslim counterparts, and their activities provoked endless trouble. Foremost among these corsairs was Romegas, who had survived the tornado of 1555. His nervous system had been permanently damaged by the long hours trapped in the water under the hull—it was said that ever after, his hands shook so much that he could not drink from a glass without spilling the contents—but Romegas maintained a fearsome reputation for seamanship, courage, and violence. Muslim mothers invoked him as a bogeyman to frighten their children to bed; to demoralized Christians he was a source of hope. Rumors of his sudden appearances on the coasts of Greece brought the local populace thronging to the beach with gifts of fruit and poultry.

His raids were comparatively small-scale affairs. The knights could put to sea only a miniature fleet of five heavily armed galleys, but their reach stretched as far as the shores of Palestine, and their impact could be dramatic. In the summer of 1564, Romegas's activities suddenly became very dramatic indeed.

On June 4, cruising off the west coast of Greece with the Order's squadron, Romegas came upon a huge galleon accompanied by a posse of Ottoman galleys. Sensing a rich prize, the knights advanced into battle and captured the ship after a fierce fight. It proved to be a valuable trophy; the ship was a business venture of the chief eunuch, an important personage at the sultan's court, laden with eighty thousand ducats worth of oriental merchandise bound for Venice. The galleon was sailed back to Malta, where it was soon to become a potent symbol of injured Ottoman pride. Meanwhile Romegas set out again with orders from La Valette to wreak havoc on the sultan's shipping. He chose

*Galley of the Knights of Saint John*

his targets unerringly. Off the coast of Anatolia, he used his cannon to hole a large armed merchantman and captured its high-ranking passengers as they abandoned ship. He scooped up the governor of Cairo and the 107-year-old former nurse of Suleiman's daughter Mihrimah, returning from the Mecca pilgrimage. Three days later he took the governor of Alexandria, on his way to Istanbul on the sultan's orders. These notables were worth considerable ransom. As Romegas sailed back to Malta with his galley laden with three hundred extra captives, word of each successive outrage filtered back to Istanbul. Howls of indignation and rage from Mihrimah and the court echoed in Suleiman's ears. The abduction of the old lady, dearly loved by his daughter and destined to die on Malta, was particularly lamented. There were loud demands; insults to the Lord of Two Seas and the Protector of the Faithful could not go unpunished.

The Suleiman who listened to these tears and lamentations was very different from the energetic young sultan whose splendid array and chivalrous actions had so impressed Christian hostages at Rhodes in 1522. He was seventy years old and had ruled the greatest empire on earth for almost half a century. He had led a dozen extensive campaigns to east and west against his great imperial rivals and had outlived all except Ivan the Terrible. Suleiman was the most feared potentate in the whole arena of empires. He had been almost as ruthless as his great-grandfather Mehmet the Conqueror, as magnificent in his shows of splendor as Charles V, and like his great rival he had been used up in the process.

European prints of the elderly sultan show a haggard figure, haunted and hollow-eyed. He had much to be sorrowful for. In addition to the ceaseless wars against the infidels to the west and his Muslim rival, the shah of Persia, to the east, he had struggled against the internal problems of the Ottoman system: the murmurings of his janissary troops, the corruption and ambition of his ministers, civil wars by his sons, revolts by dissident ethnic groups, inflation, outbreaks of religious heresy, plague, and famine. His personal life had been marked by acts of weakness, bad judgment, and tragedy. Unique among sultans, he had married for love his favorite slave girl, Roxelana, renamed Hurrem, but the cruel logic of Ottoman succession, whereby only one son could survive and rule, had torn his family apart. There had been heartbreaking moments. He had personally witnessed the strangulation of his favorite son, Mustapha, for supposedly plotting against him. Only later did he come to see that the accusations were false. Another son,

*The elderly Suleiman*

Beyazit, had been put to death with all his young children. By the 1560s only the least capable of his sons, Selim, survived to succeed him. Where the early years had seen extravagant shows of worldly splendor in competition with the potentates of Europe, Suleiman's reign became marked by increasing piety and sobriety, as he sought to emphasize his position as guardian of the caliphate and leader of Orthodox Islam. An austere gloom fell on the court. Hurrem died and Suleiman retreated from the world. He was rarely seen in public and watched meetings of the divan—the council of state—silently from behind a grille. He drank only water and ate off clay plates. He smashed his musical instruments, forbade the sale of alcohol, and gave his energy to the building of mosques and charitable foundations. He was crippled by gout, and rumors of his failing health circulated across Europe. Year after year in the late 1550s and early 1560s, reports of his imminent death surfaced in the obsessively attentive courts of Europe: "The Turk is still alive but his death is imminent," it was confidently reported in faraway England in 1562. Increasingly he was held to be under the influence of his devout daughter Mihrimah and pious figures in the court circle.

It was against this background that the violations of the Knights of Saint John reached his ears in the late summer of 1564. It became the belief of Christian chroniclers that the ailing and henpecked sultan was goaded into the invasion of Malta by the personal grievances of the harem circle—the loss of the chief eunuch's ship, the abduction of Mihrimah's former nurse, the governors of Alexandria and Cairo held to ransom—but the inner workings of Ottoman strategy were largely hidden from foreign eyes. Romegas's brazen raids were not the reactive cause of Suleiman's decision to wipe the knights off the face of the earth. They were simply the last straw.

There was certainly hurt pride for the pious sultan if the emperor of the White Sea was unable to guarantee the safety of pilgrims to Mecca; Mihrimah never ceased to present the capture of the infidel rock as a pious duty for the sultan, but there were far deeper reasons why Malta had to be taken, and taken now. The certainty of a strike on the island had been predicted by every Christian naval strategist for years. Barbarossa had dreamed its capture in 1534. Turgut went to plead for it before the sultan in person in 1551: "You will do no good," he told the sultan, "until you have smoked out this nest of vipers." Malta was simply too central, too strategic, and too troublesome to be ignored indefinitely. It represented both an opportunity to control the heart of the sea and a permanent threat to Suleiman's hold on his North African possessions; year after year the knights whom the sultan had imagined to have sailed away from Rhodes into dusty oblivion mocked his power more tauntingly. Spies informed the sultan that the knights had plans for massive new fortifications within the secure harbor. Suleiman's previous experience at Rhodes taught him that once they had become firmly established in their new home, the knights might prove impossible to dislodge.

There were large strategic issues at stake on both sides in the summer of 1564. The Ottomans had failed to capitalize on the success at Djerba; the unexpected breathing space had allowed Spain to regroup. Philip's eyes were now firmly fixed on the Mediterranean as the crucial theatre of war. He was building galleys as fast as he could. In February 1564 he appointed a wise and experienced seaman, Don Garcia de Toledo, as his captain general of the sea. In September, while Istanbul was digesting news of Romegas's latest raids, Don Garcia crossed the straits from southern Spain and seized back a fortified corsair base on the African shore, Peñón de Vélez. This small victory was talked up by the Spanish across Europe, to the fury of Suleiman. Behind the claims and counterclaims to imperial prerogative in the great sea, it was clear that Philip and Suleiman were blindly groping toward some definitive contest.

Both sides grasped that Malta was the key to the central Mediterranean. In the autumn of 1564, Don Garcia wrote to Philip analyzing the Ottoman maritime threat to every Spanish base in the sea. Malta was at the top of his list. Held, it would enable Spain to secure the southern shores of Europe and ultimately exclude the Ottomans from the western seas. Lost, it "would redound to the harm of Christendom." Malta would become the launchpad for deeper and deeper strikes into the belly of Europe; Sicily, the shores of Italy, the coasts of Spain, Rome itself would be vulnerable to the Ottoman advance.

At a meeting of the divan on October 6, 1564, Suleiman made the decision to go for Malta; in the words of the Christian chroniclers, "to enlarge the empire, and to reduce the power of the king of Spain, his rival. . . . With his fleet or at least a large squadron of galleys in this most secure position, all the surrounding kingdoms in both Africa and

Italy would be forced to pay him tribute, as well as all Christian shipping both commercial and private." It was to be a strike at the heart.

A month later, the sultan named his commanders and gave more
explicitly religious reasons for this operation: "I intend to conquer the
island of Malta and I have appointed Mustapha Pasha as commander of
this campaign. The island of Malta is a headquarters for infidels. The
Maltese have already blocked the route utilized by Muslim pilgrims
and merchants in the Eastern part of the White Sea, on their way to
Egypt. I have ordered Piyale Pasha to take part in the campaign with
the Imperial Navy." The Ottoman war machine started to swing into
action. The phony war was over.

SULEIMAN WAS ABOUT TO COMMIT the resources of his empire to
the most ambitious maritime venture in the Mediterranean since the
early Crusades. It was a long-range operation of enormous complexity
with lengthy supply lines. Malta is not Rhodes. Where Rhodes hugged
Suleiman's own lands, Malta lay eight hundred miles west, close
enough to be visible from Christian Sicily, at the outer strike range of a
large galley fleet. Rhodes was fertile and well watered, large enough to
support an invading army and worth the risk of an extended campaign
over the winter. Malta offered nothing. Lying in the channel between
Africa and Italy, flogged by the wind and the unforgiving sun, the island and its smaller neighbor Gozo are the barren remnants of eroded
mountaintops, separated from Sicily and the Italian peninsula by cata-
clysmic flooding at the end of the Ice Age. It is a terrain of neolithic
severity—a bleak, parched, stony place of immense antiquity. There are
no rivers and few trees. The winter rain had to be collected in rock-cut
cisterns; wood was so scarce it was sold by the pound weight. The
summer climate is intense; humid winds pick up water vapor from the
sea and envelop the island in an equatorial heat ferocious enough to kill
a man in armor. The miniature size of the place—only twenty miles
long and twelve wide—increases the difficulties. There are few landing
places: the western side is defended by high cliffs, leaving a handful of
small bays on the eastern flank in which to land troops, and one magnificent deep-water harbor, unequaled throughout the whole sea, that
the knights commanded. An invading army must take everything with
it for the whole duration of its stay: food, shelter, timber, siege materi-

als. Though the Ottomans could rely on limited support from the corsairs of North Africa, they were materially dependent on a long and fragile supply line. Timing was critical: they must neither sail too early nor stay too long. The window of opportunity was just a few months.

Nor could they expect any support from the indigenous population. The Maltese are the Basques of the Mediterranean, a unique micropeople formed by the particular position of their island at the center of every invasion, migration, and trading enterprise in the history of the sea. They comprise a genetic summary of the sea's past. Grafted onto an ancient rootstock, successive waves of Phoenicians, Carthaginians, Romans, Byzantines, Arabs, Normans, and Sicilians had shaped a people of original identity—"a Sicilian character with a mixture of African," a French visitor simplistically called them in 1536. The Maltese had strong affinities with the Islamic world and spoke an Arab dialect, in which the word for God was "Alla," but they were fervent in their Catholic faith, proudly traced back to the biblical shipwreck of Saint Paul and the early conversion of the islands. These hardy people, scratching an impoverished living from the thin soil, endured a life as destitute as any in the Mediterranean, but the likelihood that they could be detached from the ruling knights had been severely reduced by the Muslim corsairs who kept the island in a state of unrelieved wretchedness. Turgut, who gloried in the honorific title "the Drawn Sword of Islam," was particularly feared. His raid of 1551 enslaved five thousand people and completely depopulated Gozo. The knights seemed the best protection against such terror.

All this the Ottomans were largely aware of. No Ottoman campaign was undertaken without thorough preparation. Despite the promptings of the harem, the invasion of Malta was not a snap decision. It came off the back of years of reconnaissance and espionage. Malta had been mapped and described by the Ottoman cartographer Piri Reis in *The Book of Navigation*, and Turgut's detailed knowledge of the islands from a dozen raids was widely shared. Shortly before the siege, Ottoman engineers, disguised as fishermen, visited Malta; using their fishing rods to measure the walls, they returned with reliable plans of the fortifications. Suleiman was said to possess accurate models of the forts. The Ottoman high command knew where the water sources and secure anchorages were, the strengths and weaknesses of the defenses. In Istanbul they tailor-made a strategy based on this information: a secure harbor was a first priority to protect the all-important fleet, then control of wells; the knights wore stout armor so a good number of arquebusiers—musketeers—were essential. The shortage of wood meant that all the timber for siege works would have to be imported by ship. As for the siege itself, the limestone terrain was too rocky for successful mining; they would have to blast their way in, so emphasis must be placed on cannon. It was hoped that heavy bombardment might rupture the knights' water cisterns and force a quick surrender in the summer heat.

The task of collecting and coordinating men and materials required sophisticated planning and logistical support, but in the backroom organization of campaigns, the centralized Ottoman administration was unsurpassed. Peremptory orders went out across the empire. Soldiers were detailed to present themselves at collection points around Istanbul and in southern Greece. There is an insistence in the campaign registers that emphasizes the sheer scale of the task, an anxiety too in the litany of curt orders to provincial administrators and governors: "The question of grain is very important. . . . There is a shortage of gunpowder. . . . If because of your neglect, cannon shells, gunstocks and black gunpowder do not reach us very quickly, by God's name you will not save yourself . . . you should not even lose a minute. . . . Whatever kind of fruit and other types of food are to be found there, you should assist the traders to bring them to the fleet. . . . When my command arrives have the ship's biscuit baked urgently, have it loaded carefully and send it . . . beware of any neglect. . . . You must muster volunteer captains in the area who are willing to participate in the Malta campaign." The whole empire was abuzz with activity.

Within Istanbul itself, foreign agents and spies were soon aware that the Turk was at last stirring himself for war. The evidence was literally in front of their eyes. All foreigners were barred from living in the main city. Instead they resided within the small walled town of Galata across the Golden Horn, the narrow creek that provided Istanbul's deepwater harbor. Situated on a steep hillside above the bay, Galata afforded commanding views of the comings and goings in the basin below and overlooked, just three hundred yards upstream, the complex of wooden hangars and slipways clustered around a small bay that comprised the city's arsenal.

Shipbuilding is a slow, noisy, labor-intensive activity, and observers

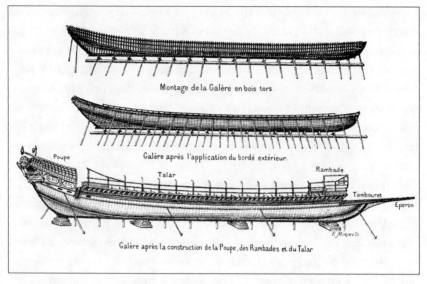

Montage de la Galère en bois tors

Galère après l'application du bordé extérieur.

Poupe

Talar

Rambade

Tambouret

Eperon

E. Morieu Sc.

Galère après la construction de la Poupe, des Rambades et du Talar

*The stages in constructing a galley*

could scarcely miss the telltale signs of a major military enterprise: lumbering sailing barges rounded the point into the harbor with bulky cargoes of timber from the forests of the Black Sea, with rope, sail-cloth, pitch, and cannonballs. Vats of tallow for greasing galley hulls rumbled down the rutty tracks on oxcarts. Hundreds of temporary workers flocked through the arsenal gates to swell the core teams of carpenters, caulkers, oar makers, and blacksmiths. During the winter of 1564–1565, the air rang with the incessant rasping of saws, the ringing of hammers, the blows of axes, the battering of iron on anvils. Smoke rose from the cauldrons of bubbling pitch, mingled with the odor of rancid animal fat and sawdust.

In the arsenal, hulls were growing on the slipways from the keel up; carpenters were installing decks and masts and planing oars; riggers were fitting sails. The logistics of the operation spread throughout the city and far beyond. In foundries and smithies, weapons—cannon, swords, javelins, and gun stocks—were being cast or forged, ovens were turning out batches of double-baked biscuits, imperial agents were crisscrossing the provinces to enforce the manpower levy. In due course gangs of men would arrive in Istanbul and Gallipoli, skilled sailors from the coastal plains, and sturdy peasant boys from the Balkans or Anatolia who had never glimpsed the sea, to provide raw muscle power for the oars. Christian slaves waited in the pens to be chained to the oars again.

The work hurtled forward with a bristling urgency, "furiously," a Spanish observer reported in February. Turgut had stressed the need to sail early to catch the spring wind. The Venetians reported that the sultan was personally inspecting the ships; he "wanted more than once to go . . . around the arsenal to see with his own eyes how his affairs are getting along, and he has been urging on the expedition with much insistence." The cost was phenomenal—perhaps 30 percent of the treasury income—and military aid was denied to other campaigns. Yet no European observer could be sure of the objective. Malta was guessed at, but so too was a strike against Sicily. The Spanish feared for La Goletta, their strategic toehold near Tunis. Even neutral Venice prepared to strengthen Cyprus. The Turks held their cards characteristically close to their chest and kept building.

In December, Suleiman decided on the command structure. He would not go himself; he would be represented in proxy by Mustapha Pasha, a veteran of campaigns in Persia and Hungary, who had fought the knights at Rhodes as a young man. The pasha was an experienced general but possessed an explosive temper and a streak of cruelty— and a particular hatred of Christians. Assisting him, with responsibility for the fleet, was the hero of Djerba, Piyale Pasha; according to the Christian chroniclers, Suleiman commanded Mustapha "that he should treat Piyale like his own son; and ordered Piyale to honor and revere Mustapha like his father." Also summoned to Malta from Tripoli was Turgut, who with his firsthand knowledge of the island was given a watching brief to help and advise both men. "I am relying on you because of your military experience," the sultan wrote to the old corsair. "You must help Mustapha Pasha at sea and you should protect our navy against the enemy's navy, which could set out from other countries to help Malta." This division of power between the three men would later be held by Christian chroniclers to be the source of great trouble for the campaign, though it seems clear that Mustapha was the overall commander.

During March, the galleys, galliots, and barges were launched and loaded. Everything that was required for the siege had to be anticipated: sixty-two cannon were lugged aboard, including two giant basilisks that fired enormous stone shot; one hundred thousand cannonballs; two thousand tons of gunpowder; arquebuses and musket balls; arrows and helmets; tools for trenching and mining; "lead, rope, spades, picks, shovels, iron bars, wood"; preformed wooden frames to serve as breastworks to defend the men; "large numbers of hides, woollen sacks, old tents and old sails for making defences"; prodigious quantities of double-baked biscuits and other food, tents, gun carriages, wheels—all the paraphernalia of a major campaign, listed, checked, and counted by imperial bean counters who formed the backbone to any venture.

ON THE DAY OF DEPARTURE, March 30, in one of those displays of imperial theatre at which the Ottomans excelled, Mustapha Pasha received his standard and general's sword and stepped aboard his galley, the *Sultana*, in a tumult of noise. The vessel was a personal gift of the sultan, constructed out of fig wood, with twenty-eight benches of oarsmen rowing four or five to the oar, flying a red-and-white standard. Piyale, as admiral, had his own flagship, a vessel of great beauty, whose stern was marked out by the symbols of maritime authority—three stern lanterns, a green silk banner, and a beaten-silver plaque ten feet square, crested by a crescent moon and a golden ball trailing the horsehair plume of imperial power. The sultan himself was also there in proxy, represented by a third flagship—the imperial galley, whose stern was decorated with moons and verses from the Koran in gold lettering "and different pictures in the Turkish style." It was by all accounts an extraordinary spectacle. The armada set sail after morning prayers. Multicolored banners bearing verses from the Koran, crescent moons, and pictures of scimitars fluttered in the breeze. Oars dashed the still waters of the Golden Horn. Cannon fire thundered from the shore forts; cymbals and pipes crashed and brayed. The soldiers sat upright in the boats, still as stones—janissaries in white headdresses topped by flickering ostrich plumes, holy men in green turbans, levied men in white. To the murmuring of prayers from the assembled imams and the timekeeping drums of the galley masters, the huge armada pulled away under the lee of the palace point, west toward the White Sea. The greatest amphibious venture in Ottoman history departed, according to one account, "in an atmosphere of triumph."

And yet there were uneasy notes. Despite deep planning, the expedition had been hastily assembled to catch the spring wind. Had the Ottomans properly calculated the risk? Had they marshaled enough men? Had it all been too rushed? Within a few days some of the vessels had to be recaulked and their keels greased again. One huge ship foundered off the coast of Greece with the loss of several hundred men and valuable supplies of gunpowder. There had been the usual difficulties making up the full complement of oarsmen.

Nor was the venture universally popular. The soldiers, particularly the dismounted cavalry, disliked long sea voyages, and the rumor was that the fight would be tough; some paid to be excused. Criminals had to be pardoned to make up the numbers. All this was summed up in a remark attributed to the grand vizier, Ali, staying complacently at home beside the sultan, that hinted at both the risk and the fault lines in the command structure. Watching Mustapha and Piyale step aboard their ships, he quipped ironically, "Here are two good-humored men, always ready to take coffee and opium, about to take a pleasure trip around the islands together." In its haste to depart, the fleet had also omitted an important ritual. It had failed to make the customary visit to the tomb of Barbarossa on the shores of the Bosphorus, the talisman of naval success.

# CHAPTER 8

# Invasion Fleet

March 29 to May 18, 1565

PROFESSIONAL TURK WATCHERS within the city dispatched hurried memoranda west on a daily basis. "On the morning of March 29 the admiral of the fleet and Mustapha the overall commander went to kiss the sultan's hand and to receive their authorization," read the breathless dispatches from the banking house of Fugger. "It's not yet known where the fleet is heading but the word is it will go to besiege Malta." Eight hundred miles away in Malta, muffled news of this activity had reached La Valette before the end of 1564—the knights had their own sources of information in all the key listening posts of the sea. In January the grand master gradually stirred into action.

Whether it was because of the years of phony war—there was hardly a spring when the Ottoman fleet did not threaten an expedition west—or the possibility that the Muslims might be aiming for La Goletta, or a shortage of cash, or La Valette's personal indecisiveness, is unclear, but everything necessary for the island's defense was happening almost too late.

In the spring of 1565 the grand master was seventy years old. Behind him lay a lifetime's unbroken service to the Order. Unique among knights, from the time he had donned the Order's surcoat at the age of twenty, he had never returned to his family home in France. He had given everything to warfare in the name of Christ—he had been badly wounded in a fight with Barbary corsairs, been captured and spent a year as a galley slave, served as captain general of galleys, and as governor of Tripoli. As a man born in the fifteenth century, La Valette harked back to the feudal crusading spirit: stern, unyielding, fiery, imbued with a sense of Christian mission that deeply irritated the Venetians. "He is tall and well made," wrote the Italian soldier Francisco Balbi, "of commanding presence, and he carries well his dignity of Grand Master. His disposition is rather sad, but, for his age, he is very

*La Valette*

robust . . . he is very devout, has a good memory, wisdom, intelligence, and has gained much experience from his career on land and sea. He is moderate and patient and knows many languages." Despite Balbi's observations, there were indications that La Valette was no longer a young man: his large, shaky signature suggests someone at least short-sighted—and he gave signs of particular cautiousness with regard to expensive preparations for an uncertain war. Now, almost too late, panicky work was put in hand for Malta's defense. The security of the island rested, as at Rhodes, on the implacable defense of fortified places, but in early 1565 these defenses left something to be desired.

The key to Malta was the extraordinary natural harbor on the eastern side of the island, a complex series of inlets and small peninsulas that cut their way four miles back into the island and provided a series of magnificent sheltered anchorages. Here on two small adjacent promontories, jutting out into the great harbor like stone galleys tethered to the shore, the knights had established their strongholds. The first of these, Birgu (the town), was the knights' own fortress, encircled in familiar style with bastioned walls and a deep ditch. It was a small site, a thousand yards long, that tapered to a point, where a stout inner castle, Fort Saint Angelo, commanded the water. The second promontory, Senglea, separated from Birgu by a strip of water three hundred yards wide, was less developed but was similarly guarded by a fort, Saint Michael, at the landward end. As a defensive system these tongues of land were interdependent. The creek between provided a secure harbor where the knights kept their galleys; in the spring of 1565 this harbor also held the chief eunuch's prized galleon. Its mouth could be closed by a chain at its seaward end and the two settlements connected across the creek by a pontoon bridge. The problem in the spring of 1565 was that neither Birgu nor Senglea had complete fortifications on their landward side.

Worse still the terrain was unfavorable. Both settlements were commanded not only by higher land behind them but by the heights of a much higher peninsula across the water, called Mount Sciberras, which was the strategic key to the whole harbor. Sciberras overlooked both Birgu and Senglea on one side and a symmetrical deepwater harbor, Marsamxett, on the other. Over the years a succession of visiting Italian military engineers had strongly recommended that the knights should build a new stronghold and capital on Sciberras; it afforded total control of the only secure anchorages on the island and would render the knights virtually invulnerable to attack. No move had been made to act on this advice; all that had been done was the hasty construction of a small star-shaped fort, Saint Elmo, at the tip of the peninsula to provide some security for the harbors.

As La Valette surveyed his defenses, it was clear that all three strongholds—Birgu, Senglea, and Saint Elmo—were unfinished and needed urgent attention if they were to provide any kind of contest for the experienced Ottoman siege gunners. In the early months of 1565, the knights swung slowly into action. There was much to do.

THE TOTAL NUMBER of military knights in the Order was about six hundred—few more than at Rhodes half a century earlier—and many of these were scattered across Europe. On February 10, the grand master issued a summons for all knights to report to the island; about five hundred made it before the siege began. In times of war, the knights traditionally relied on paid troops and levies of local men as an extra source of manpower. In January, La Valette set about the arrangements for hiring soldiers; these were to be Spanish and Italian contingents released by the king of Spain, as well as mercenaries, but the process of assembling and transporting these troops from the Italian mainland and Sicily was a slow process, and in the end few of them arrived in time. The third component of his force, the Maltese militia, La Valette had little regard for. "A people of little courage and with little love for the Faith," he called them, "a people that as soon as they see the enemy are terrified just by the shots from the arquebus—how much greater their terror will be at the cannon balls that will kill their women and children." As it turned out these slighting comments were wholly un-justified. The Maltese would provide the majority of the fighting men and they would prove to be totally reliable.

At the same time the search for provisions intensified. Within the island, huge quantities of water were transported to Birgu and Senglea in clay bottles, and ships were dispatched to Italy to buy food. It was not easy: there was famine in the Mediterranean and grain was short. Romegas took to detaining luckless cargo ships in the Malta channel and requisitioning their contents. There was a forcible evacuation of noncombatants: women and children, the elderly, freed Muslims, and prostitutes were carried away to Sicily, though many of the civilian Maltese successfully petitioned to be allowed to stay. Siege materials, armaments, and food were shipped back: "hoes, picks, shovels, hard-ware, baskets, ... bread, grain, medicines, wine, salted meat, and other provisions." Grain was poured into cavernous underground chambers and sealed with stone plugs. A trickle of soldiers arrived: Spanish and Italian infantry, volunteer brigades assembled by enterprising adven-turers called to the cause of Christendom, paid mercenaries recruited by the Order's functionaries in Italy. The straits between Malta and Sicily were busy with shipping. Work was started to complete the wall encircling Senglea and to strengthen the bastions on Birgu, but it pro-ceeded slowly. Materials had to be imported from Italy and labor was in short supply. La Valette levied the services of the Maltese, both men and women, and the knights themselves, including the grand master, put in a couple of hours a day to set a suitable example. At the same time La Valette wrote to the king of Spain, his temporal overlord, and the pope, his spiritual one, requesting men and money.

EVERY STATE IN THE Christian Mediterranean watched the progress of the Turkish armada with bated breath. Messenger boats sped across the sea with news. For Philip it was clear that this was war against

Spain by proxy: "The Turkish fleet will be coming with more galleys than in past years," he wrote on April 7. The arsenals of Barcelona were working at full stretch and, in a tide of rising panic, he ordered an inventory of private ships as a last-ditch defense. The Ottoman fleet was moving fast to strike early in the year, beating a path around Greece to take on board food, water, and men at prearranged collection points. On April 23 the fleet was at Athens, on May 6 at Modon in southern Greece, on May 17 the local commander at Syracuse in Sicily dispatched a posthaste messenger to the viceroy: "At one in the morning, the guard at Casibile fired thirty salvoes. For them to fire so many it must, I fear, be the Turkish fleet."

There was a rising tide of panic throughout the sea. Everyone understood the importance of Malta, if Malta it were to be. The diplomatic exchanges resounded with the knowledge of a supreme crisis, but Europe rang to the same old drumbeat: disunity and mutual suspicion. The possibility of a united response to the infidel was as remote in 1565 as it had been at Rhodes in 1521 and Preveza in 1537. Pope Pius IV thundered for a Holy League against the infidel and was bitterly disappointed by the response. He gifted large sums of money to Philip to build galleys, yet nothing seemed to be forthcoming. The king of Spain "has withdrawn into the woods," the pope complained, "and France, England and Scotland [are] ruled by women and boys." The danger was huge and the support minimal. He saw that the sultan "must be coming to do harm to us or to the Catholic King [Philip II], that the armada was powerful, and the Turks valiant men, who fight for glory, for empire, and also for their false religion." They had nothing to fear, "considering our small resources and the division of Christendom." In the meantime he promised what help to the knights that he could.

Yet Philip, despite a crippling natural caution, had not been inactive. The Spanish were running hard to rebuild their fleet after the disaster at Djerba. In October 1564 he appointed his captain general of the sea, Don Garcia de Toledo, as viceroy of Sicily. This gave him oversight of the whole central Mediterranean and the defense of Malta. Don Garcia, a man "serious, of good judgement and experience," had a sound strategic grasp of the issues, but was shackled by insuperable difficulties. He lacked the coordinating resources and central bureaucracy of the Ottoman state. The Spanish fleet was a coalition of four squadrons—those of Naples, Spain, Sicily, and Genoa—and still reliant in part on private galley contractors such as the Dorias. The task of bringing these forces together in one place with their full complement of rowers and soldiers, munitions and stores, was a daunting one— while at the same time these squadrons were needed to protect Spain and Southern Italy from random corsair attacks. While the Ottomans sailed on a calm sea, the gathering Spanish squadrons had to contend with much more taxing winds in the Western Mediterranean. By June 1565, a month into the siege, Don Garcia had still managed to assemble only 25 galleys; the Ottomans came with 165. Philip's man was bound to be careful; the annihilation of his nascent fleet could have disastrous consequences for Christendom. However, he started to gather men and resources on Sicily against the eventuality of an Ottoman attack.

On April 9, Don Garcia, with thirty galleys, made the short thirty-mile voyage from Sicily to confer with La Valette. The two commanders toured the defenses of Birgu and Senglea together. Then Don Garcia demanded an inspection of the star fort of Saint Elmo on the tip of Sciberras. The shrewd old Spaniard immediately pinpointed the strategic importance of this small fortification. In his opinion it was the key to the whole defense. The enemy would be sure to target it early in order to secure a safe anchorage for their fleet and to bar seaborne relief for Birgu and Senglea. It was the pivot "on which the salvation of all the other fortresses on the island depended." It was essential "to make every effort to protect and conserve it for as long as possible" in order to wear down the enemy and allow sufficient time for a serious relief force to be assembled. Yet the whole structure was deficient: it was too small to accommodate many men and guns; it was poorly built and lacked suitable parapets. Don Garcia studied the terrain in microscopic detail and identified a specific weakness. On the western side, above the sea, one flank was patently vulnerable to attack: "The enemy could get in here without any difficulty." He recommended the urgent construction of a further flanking fortification—in the language of the siege engineers, a ravelin—a triangular-shaped external fortification to protect that section of wall, and detailed his military engineer to oversee the work.

The next day he sailed off to see to the security of the port of La Goletta at Tunis, but not before he had promised to send a thousand

Spanish soldiers and left his son as surety of his good faith. La Valette was disappointed that the viceroy had brought no reinforcements, but Don Garcia was himself scouring the sea for resources to repel the Turks. Eyeing the Order's five galleys and the two owned by La Valette personally, he requested their loan. They were sure to be bottled up uselessly in the harbor if the Turks came. Almost as valuable was the Order's detachment of a thousand Muslim slaves to row the vessels, who might be a security threat as much as a resource during a siege. La Valette politely refused: the galleys were still being used to transport materials, and the slave labor force was at work on the walls. As the two men parted, Don Garcia offered three pieces of advice: the grand master should restrict his war council to just a few trusted men to ensure decisions could be taken secretly and quickly; he should forbid his hotheaded knights from glamorous but foolhardy skirmishing outside the walls—lives would be too precious to waste; last, he should not risk his own person in battle, "because experience has shown that in war the death of the leader often leads to disaster and defeat." Then he was gone.

On the island, preparations became more urgent but La Valette was probably still unaware how fast the enemy was moving and how little time was left. Frenetic efforts were undertaken to construct the ravelin—in effect little more than a stone-faced earthwork—to add some security to Saint Elmo. On May 7, a chain was paid out by galley across the mouth of the harbor between Senglea and Birgu to seal the inner water; companies of Spanish troops and mercenaries arrived on May 10 to hearten the defenders. Musters of men and equipment were undertaken; rudimentary firearms training was given to the Maltese militias—"each man was required to fire three musket shots at a target, with a prize for the best"—gunpowder mills churned out powder, masons cut stone for the walls; in the knights' armory, blacksmiths' hammers rang, repairing helmets and breastplates. Overall responsibility for sectors of the defense and resources—water, gunpowder, slaves— was assigned to particular knights. Plans were laid for fire signals and cannon shots to warn of the enemy's approach, for the poisoning of wells and water sources in the open countryside, for the local population to retire to fortified refuges, for the gathering in of crops and the rounding up of cattle—everything to ensure that the Turks would be greeted by a barren and inhospitable terrain. The knights carried out

morale-raising parades, splendid in their steel bascinets and red surcoats.

Beyond the harbor there were two other strategic positions of immense importance to Malta. One was the small fort on the adjacent island of Gozo; the other, the fortified citadel of Mdina in the center of
Malta. The Old City, as it was known among the inhabitants, was the
island's original capital. This dense medieval citadel of narrow lanes
and tortuous thoroughfares, encircled within impressive ramparts,
commanded the central heights of the island. Its position afforded a
panoramic view over the island far down toward the harbor nine miles
away. Mdina was the traditional place of refuge for the Maltese during
raids, yet in reality its fortifications were old-fashioned and vulnerable
to cannon. La Valette appointed a Portuguese knight, Pedro Mezquita,
as commander of the town and the rest of the island. To reassure the
nervy local population, who were frightened that all defensive resources would be concentrated on the harbor, detachments of soldiers
were dispatched to both Gozo and Mdina; the knights' cavalry was also
concentrated in Mdina, from where it might carry out sorties.

And yet despite all these preparations, the island was taken by surprise. On the morning of May 18, when lookouts on Saint Angelo and
Saint Elmo caught sight of sails pricking the horizon thirty miles out
to the southeast in the clear dawn light, crops and cattle still stood in
the fields, arrangements for sheltering civilians were still unclarified,
allocation of the knights to their posts was still to be finalized, fortifications were still incomplete, houses built against the fortress walls
that could shelter the enemy remained undemolished. The speed, effi-
ciency, and logistical skill of the Ottoman war machine had taken the
whole of the central Mediterranean by surprise.

As fort guns fired their three warning shots, drums and trumpets
sounded and the watchtower fires sped the news across the island.
There was panic among the civilian population. People streamed toward
Mdina; those closer to the harbor crowded into the tiny fort at Saint
Elmo or toward Birgu, "bringing with them their children, their cattle
and their goods." So many converged on the town gates that La Valette
ordered out a detachment of knights to divert part of the human stream
toward the adjacent peninsula of Senglea.

By midday the defenders could understand how vast the Ottoman
fleet was. By all accounts it was an extraordinary sight: "At fifteen or

twenty miles from Malta the Turkish armada was clearly visible, all in sail, so that white cotton sails covered half the horizon to the east," recorded Giacomo Bosio, the Order's historian. The spectacle took the breath away: hundreds of ships in a vast crescent drawing forward across the calm sea—one hundred thirty galleys, thirty galliots, nine transport barges, ten large galleons, two hundred smaller transport vessels, thirty thousand men. As the invasion fleet filled the whole field of view, the three colorful flagships became clearly visible, their standards fluttering in the breeze. Each was rowed "five to a bench and was superbly decorated; that of the sultan with twenty-eight benches had red-and-white sails; that of Mustapha flying the general's flag given to him by Suleiman with his own hands, sailed by the general himself, with his two sons with him, and that of Piyale sporting three lanterns— all three had poops carved with crescent moons and intricate gilded Turkish lettering and were individually and richly adorned with silken ornings and sumptuous brocades."

There were men watching from the battlements of Saint Angelo, and others sitting upright in the galleys, for whom this moment framed their lives. Forty-four years before, a world and a lifetime back, La Valette had stood on the ramparts of Rhodes and seen this sight, and there were old Greeks with him on Malta who could remember the young Suleiman's invasion fleet rowing in from the Asian shore with the rising sun. Mustapha Pasha too had been at Rhodes and had watched the knights sail away on a winter's morning. For nearly half a century the battle for the Mediterranean had been pushing west; now it had reached its literal center. On a fine May morning the turbaned warriors in the gently rocking galleys stared up at the limestone heights of the harbor; the knights in their steel armor and red surcoats stared back. It was a climactic moment in the long rhythm of this contest, as organic and inevitable as the winds that pushed ships around the sea in preordained patterns according to the seasons of the year.

The planners and leaders of this conflict were astonishingly old by the standards of the time. The contest for Malta brought together the collective experience of an enduring generation of potentates, admirals, and generals, literally hundreds of man-years of voyages, raids, and wars. Suleiman, La Valette, Don Garcia, and Mustapha Pasha were all in their seventies; Turgut, preparing to sail from Tripoli, was reckoned to be eighty. Their lives stretched back into the fifteenth century. It was as if all the experience and all the wars in the trackless sea had shrunk to a single spot. The fates of the protagonists were interwoven like the wakes of ships crisscrossing in the water; they shared common experiences and memories of victory and defeat, capture and ransom. La Valette and Turgut had met before, when the corsair, captured by Andrea Doria's nephew, was serving in the Christian galleys awaiting ransom; and Piyale, triumphant at Djerba, would again be confronted by its defeated Spanish commander, Don Alvare Sande. For Turgut especially, Malta was a place of destiny. He had raided the island seven times, and his brother had been killed on Gozo; failure to obtain release of the body from the island commander had led to Turgut's extraordinary act of vengeance, enslaving the whole population. A fortune-teller had once told him that he would also die on Malta.

La Valette dispatched a fast cutter to Don Garcia in Sicily and called a council of war. The galleon of the chief eunuch, captured by Romegas the previous summer, lay at anchor in the knights' inner harbor like a taunt.

# CHAPTER 9

# The Post of Death

May 18 to June 2, 1565

As the ottoman fleet swung south around the island, its progress was tracked from point to point by warning shots and fire signals along the chain of watchtowers. A force of a thousand men was dispatched from Birgu to shadow its progress toward the bay the Maltese called Marsaxlokk—the harbor of the south wind—a wide anchorage ideal for landing. However, the sight of the Christian troops drawn up on the shore dissuaded Piyale from the attempt and the fleet pressed on around the western side of the island under the sheer limestone cliffs. By nightfall the fleet had dropped anchor in the translucent waters off a series of small bays. Sentries on the headland watched all night as the boats rocked ominously at anchor. In the darkness men started to come ashore.

The next morning before dawn a detachment of cavalry was dispatched from Mdina under a French knight, La Rivière; their mission was to ambush the intruders and take prisoners. The exercise went disastrously wrong. La Riviere and a few men were well hidden, watching the advance guard and biding their time, when another knight broke cover and galloped toward him. Confused, La Riviere emerged from his hiding place and was spotted by the Turks. With all surprise gone, the Frenchman had no option but to charge the enemy, but his horse was shot down and he was seized and dragged off to the galleys; the defenders knew the implications. In war, all useful captives were tortured for information. It was a bad start.

It was a Sunday morning; the Christian population was hurrying to church in the fortified settlements to pray for deliverance when the Ottoman fleet sailed quietly back to Marsaxlokk and started to land in force. For those watching distantly from the shore, it was quite an extraordinary sight, by turns terrifying, magnificent, and alien—as if all the flamboyant spectacle of Asia had erupted onto the European shore.

*Janissary with arquebus*

There were unfamiliar clothes, brilliant colors, outlandish hats: impressively mustachioed janissaries in trousers and long coats, cavalrymen in light mail, religious zealots in white, pashas in robes of apricot and green and gold, semi-naked dervishes in animal skins; enormous turbans, helmets shaped like onions, conical caps in duck-egg blue, white janissary headdresses with flickering ostrich plumes—and an array of equipment. The janissaries carried long arquebuses inlaid with arabesques of ivory. There were circular shields of wicker and gilt brass; pointed shields from Hungary; curved scimitars and pliant bows from the Asian steppes; flags of shot silk decorated with evil eyes, scorpions, and crescent moons; devices in flowing Arabic; bell tents; music; and noise.

By the following day the Ottoman fleet had unloaded the majority of their stores and heavy guns and pushed forward to establish a camp above the knights' forts at Birgu and Senglea. The spectacle filled the Italian Francisco Balbi with eerie wonder. "A well-ordered camp was now set up on the heights of Santa Margarita, and was bright with flags and banners. The sight of it aroused great wonder amongst us, as did the sound of all their musical instruments, for—as is their custom—they brought with them many bugles, trumpets, drums, bagpipes, and other musical instruments."

The tumultuous throng probably numbered between twenty-two thousand and twenty-four thousand fighting men supported by eight thousand noncombatants, though the knights' chroniclers would always put the figure much higher. The core troops were the six thousand janissaries—the sultan's own men—each armed with the long-barreled Ottoman arquebus, unfamiliar to Europeans and slower to load but more accurate, designed for sniping and capable of penetrating medium-weight plate armor. With the janissaries came a large consignment of sipahis, cavalrymen largely fighting on foot, volunteers attracted by the lure of booty, marines, and adventurers. There was a gunnery corps, and the support resources: armorers, engineers, sappers, standard-bearers, carpenters, cooks, and hangers-on, including, apparently, Jewish merchants hoping to acquire Christian slaves. These men were drawn from across the Ottoman Empire. There were riflemen from Egypt; cavalrymen from Anatolia, the Balkans, Salonika, and the Peloponnese; many were renegades, converted Greeks, Spaniards, and Italians, freed Christian slaves taken in battle, or mercenaries attracted by the opportunities under the crescent banners of Islam. Some were not Muslims at all. The Ottoman Empire was a melting pot of loyalties and motives. Some had come to fight for Islam, others out of compulsion or hope of gain.

Within the knights' citadel at Birgu, religious fervor engulfed the population. The grand master and the archbishop of Malta organized a penitent procession through the narrow streets, with the priests and the people "devoutly imploring divine aid against the furious attack of the barbarians." Robert of Eboli, a Capuchin friar who had once been a slave of the corsairs at Tripoli, astonished and inspired the people with a fervent oration, standing before the altar of the conventual church dispensing the sacraments for forty hours.

It was a situation to arouse the deepest crusading instincts of the knights. For nearly five hundred years they had been hunkering down behind stout bastions they could defend to the death against Islam. This was the chivalric myth they had made for themselves at Crac des Chevaliers, Hattin, Acre, Rhodes—the glorious last-ditch stand against impossible odds, massacre, martyrdom, and death. The existence of the Order was justified by this roll call of defeats in the cause of Christendom. For La Valette, however, it was clear that Malta was the last redoubt. Defeat would not only expose the heart of Christian Europe; it would also sweep the Order of Saint John away forever.

There were somewhere between six thousand and eight thousand fighting men on Malta. Of these the aristocratic knights of Europe in their stout plate armor and peaked helmets, who looked like conquistadors and wore the red surcoat marked with a white cross as a pledge to Christ—and which was useful as a target for enemy snipers—accounted for just five hundred at most. Alongside them were the professional Spanish and Italian companies sent by Don Garcia. These were the king of Spain's men, well armed and motivated, but they had not come to Malta for glory. They had the expectations common to most soldiers; they fought for pay and rewards and to live for another day. In this respect they were little different from many of their Muslim counterparts. Among those who enrolled was the Italian Francisco Balbi, sixty years old and down on his luck, who fought as an arquebusier and survived to write a firsthand account of the siege.

Over and beyond the professionals there was a handful of gentleman adventurers who had come to the defense of Malta for the glory of the thing, some Greeks from Rhodes, released convicts, galley slaves, and unreliable converts from Islam. The conflict at Malta brought all the diverse peoples of the Mediterranean to a central point. It was a trading place of destinies and motives, where loyalties might suddenly reverse; both sides were to be bedeviled by defectors motivated by a desire to escape slavery, to revert to the faith of birth, to hedge bets against the final outcome, or to vie for better rewards. But the bedrock of the Christian defense rested on three thousand irreducible Maltese militiamen in their crude helmets and padded cotton tunics. Alongside the knights, they would prove to be unflinchingly loyal to Christ's cause; ardent in their Catholic faith, the Maltese population would fight to the last child for their homes and stony fields.

On May 20 the Ottomans started to push inland from the harbor at Marsaxlokk, toward the grand harbor. As they did so, La Valette sent out skirmishing parties to ambush them in the broken landscape of walled fields and dusty lanes. The temper of the conflict was set down in these early exchanges. The young knights, fired with dreams of glory, played hide-and-seek with the trudging army on its way to collect water. They returned to Birgu like Apache braves with staring heads swinging from their saddlebows, and banners and jewelry hacked from the dead. One brought in a finger with a gold ring; another stripped an engraved gold bracelet from the richly dressed corpse of an officer that read "I do not come to Malta for wealth or honor but to save my soul." Any hope that the local population might be detached from the aristocrats' cause was also quickly dispelled. The Maltese set about preparing contemptuous ambushes. Having killed one Turk, they found a pig nearby and slaughtered it, then arranged the dead man at a convenient spot with the animal's snout inserted into his mouth. Then they retired behind a wall. When fellow Muslims saw the body, they rushed forward with cries of horror and rage to rescue their fallen comrade from this final indignity—and were shot down.

Despite these local successes, the weighty advance of the army was unstoppable. Camps were established and guarded; flags fluttered from pickets and tents; guns and supplies were dragged up by oxen the Maltese had left in the fields, small-scale Christian operations pushed back. Mustapha set up his headquarters on the heights overlooking the grand harbor and seized the watering holes at Marsa, which the defenders had attempted to poison with bitter herbs and excrement.

Within a few days the whole of the south of the island was in the hands of the invaders and on fire. Having gathered all the usable materials they could glean from the landscape—food, cattle, brushwood—the Ottomans torched the fields, so that from the ramparts of Birgu and Senglea, "that part of the island seemed to be completely in smoke and fire."

After setting up camp, Mustapha had La Rivière, the French knight taken in the first encounter, brought out onto the hill overlooking Birgu. He had probably already been tortured. The Frenchman was asked to show Mustapha the weak sectors of the defenses and promised his liberty in return. La Rivière indicated two positions: the posts of Auvergne and Castile. The pasha determined to test the knights' defenses.

On the morning of May 21, the whole army rolled forward. From the ramparts, the spectacle assumed an unearthly beauty: "The Turkish army covered the whole countryside in one complete formation arranged like a crescent moon; seen from Birgu it was a quite spectacular sight, with men in splendidly rich and ostentatious clothes. Besides their shining armaments and principal standards and banners, they carried other triangular flags in a rainbow of colors, which glimpsed from a distance looked like an immense shimmering field of flowers, that delighted the ear as much as the eye because one could hear them playing various strange musical instruments." Up close, these impressions were drowned out for the onlookers by "the horrible explosions of our guns—and theirs—and the rattle of our muskets."

As the Turks drew near, the defenders beat their drums and unfurled the red-and-white standard of Saint John. La Valette saw that his men were straining to get at the invaders, and determined to test their morale. Waiting until the enemy was in range of his fortress guns, he unleashed seven hundred arquebusiers from the gates with drums battering and flags unfurled, and a detachment of cavalry. He had to stand lance in hand to prevent the reserves from joining in the fray; had he not done so "not one man would have remained in the Birgu, so great was their ardour to fight the Turks." After five hours of fierce fighting, the Christians withdrew into the gates, having killed a hundred and lost ten, according to their own accounts. It was a sign of redoubtable intent from the defenders. And from the posts of Castile and Auvergne there was such a torrent of fire that Mustapha's own life was in danger.

The pasha concluded that La Rivière had lied. He was marched off to a galley and beaten to death with excruciating and exquisite skill in full view of the Christian slaves.

The next day, May 22, the Ottomans mounted a similar reconnaissance in force against the adjacent peninsula of Senglea. This time, La Valette, remembering Don Garcia's advice, forbade any skirmishing beyond the walls. (Another injunction—to guard his own person—the grand master had already ignored; standing on the battlements of Birgu, bullets whistling around him, he had seen two men drop at his side.) Henceforth the defenders would put their faith in fortifications. Despite the impression left by La Rivière's disinformation, the defenses were perilously weak. According to Francisco Balbi, the scarp of the ditch "was so low at one point that it presented no obstacle to the enemy." Men worked round the clock to shore it up.

Meanwhile, in the newly established camp at the Marsa, the Ottoman high command was considering its options. Even for experienced campaigners, Malta posed a problem, or rather a set of interlocking problems with many variables. There was much to contemplate: the conundrum of the intricate harbor complex, the unfamiliar Maltese winds, the barrenness of the terrain, the demands for water, the length of the supply chain from fleet to camp. It was not that the invaders were confronted by one impregnable fortress as at Rhodes; rather they had to consider a variety of weaker but dispersed objectives, all of which required attention.

There were the two linked promontories of Birgu and Senglea that made up the nucleus of Christian resistance, but these were interlinked with the fortress of Saint Elmo across the water on Mount Sciberras that provided the key to the best harbor. The main Ottoman camp at Marsa was six miles from the fleet anchored at Marsaxlokk, and the early skirmishes had revealed the need to guard the supply chain from ambush along its entire length. There were also the two forts in the hinterland to consider, that at Mdina and the other on Gozo, which provided potential centers of guerrilla warfare and rallying points if left unattended. One of these targets had to be chosen first; the others had to be managed. It would be necessary to split the army into sections. Perhaps twenty-two thousand fighting men was not so large a force after all.

Other things were concerning the commanders too. Piyale was

edgy about the winds, less predictable in summer than those in the eastern half of the White Sea. The imperative to keep the fleet safe was his absolute priority. Shipwreck or a daring raid by enemy fire ships would commit the expedition to lingering but certain collective death at the hands of an enemy with reinforcements uncomfortably close at hand. Malta, lying under the eagle wing of Christian Sicily, was the king of Spain's domain; sooner or later a counterattack was certain. The long lines of communication, the finite time frame, the inability to remain on Malta over the winter—all these things were weighed in the balance.

Relations between Mustapha and Piyale were tense as the options were discussed on May 22. The admiral and the general had issues about priorities and seniority; both were aware of Suleiman looking over their shoulders; he was there by proxy in his banners and flagship, more directly in the presence of his personal heralds—the *chaushes*— who reported back to him directly. Both Piyale and Mustapha were wellconnected within the Ottoman court; both were eager for glory and to avoid disgrace. The two were united only in their jealousy of Turgut, the third player in the sultan's triangle of command, expected any day from Tripoli. Christian accounts provide vivid and probably highly imaginative accounts of the wrangles, the choices, the votes cast on the day—it is highly unlikely that any Christian slave was present in the pasha's ornate tent—as they lobbied for their tactics.

In the end they chose the objective that Don Garcia had predicted they would: the little fort of Saint Elmo, "the key to all the other fortresses of Malta." This decision had probably been taken months ago in Istanbul, well before departure, at a divan meeting on December 5, 1564, when engineers laid plans and models of Saint Elmo before the sultan, explaining that they had found it to be "on a very narrow site and easy to attack." At the time Spanish spies in the city had filed a report back to Madrid that was eerily prophetic in all but one respect: "Their plan is to take the castle of St Elmo first so that they can get control of the harbour and put most of their ships there to overwinter and then capture the castle of St Angelo by siege." Now Mustapha's engineers studied the site again and were confident it would be an easy task, "four of five days" was the estimate; "losing St Elmo, the enemy would lose all hope of rescue." But if they were confident of taking the fort quickly, there was also a note of defensiveness, even fear, in this decision. Saint Elmo would "secure the fleet, in which lay their safety, by drawing it inside the harbor of Marsamxett, out of all danger from prevailing winds and maritime disasters and all possibility of enemy attack ... [and] ... of all dying on the island without being able to escape." Even at the outset they were pondering the implications of operating so far from home. For Piyale particularly, preserving the fleet was the key to everything. The commanders decided not to wait for Turgut to confirm this decision; time was pressing. They set to work straightaway.

Time was critical for La Valette too. When he learned of the Ottoman plan from escaped renegades, he was said to have given thanks to God; the attempt on Saint Elmo would buy a breathing space to repair the defenses of Senglea and Birgu and time to dispatch pleas to Don Garcia, Philip, and the pope for a rescue fleet. Work continued on the fortifications day and night; obstacles outside the walls that could provide sheltering positions for the enemy—trees, houses, and stables—were demolished; the whole population was engaged in hauling vast quantities of earth inside the settlements for running repairs to walls damaged by gunfire. All that the grand master had to do was persuade the garrison over on Saint Elmo to sell their lives as dearly as possible.

On May 23, the Ottomans started to transport heavy wheeled guns from the fleet to the Sciberras Peninsula. It was an immensely difficult journey over seven miles of rocky ground, involving large numbers of animals and men. The landscape echoed to the grinding of the iron wheels, the bellowing of the oxen, the shouts of exhausted men. Balbi watched the guns from Senglea: "We could see ten or twelve bullocks harnessed to each piece, with many men pulling the ropes."

The defenders made their own preparations. As the Turks established their positions on the peninsula, the only safe way out of Saint Elmo was by boat from the rocky foreshore across the harbor to Birgu, a distance of five hundred yards. La Valette ordered the evacuation of some women and children who had taken refuge there, and he sent back supplies and a hundred fighting men under Colonel Mas, sixty released galley slaves, food, and ammunition. In all there were about seven hundred fifty men in Saint Elmo, the majority of whom were Spanish troops under their commander, Juan de la Cerda.

From the landward side, where the Turks were establishing their

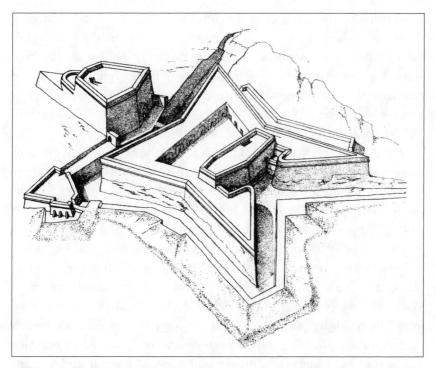

*Saint Elmo, showing the blockhouse and central parade ground, the cavalier at the rear, the ravelin on the left (Courtesy of Dr. Stephen Spiteri)*

gun platforms, Saint Elmo presented a long low raked profile, like a stone submarine floating on the end of the rocky ridge. Two of the four points of its star faced the hill on which the Turks were establishing their position. The fort was protected at the front by a stone-cut ditch, and at the back on the seaward side by a detached keep, a cavalier, which reared up above the whole fort like the submarine's conning tower. Hidden in the heart of the fort were a central parade ground— protected in front by a blockhouse—a cistern for water, and a small chapel to provide for the men's spiritual needs. The hastily constructed triangular ravelin was outside the fort and linked to it by a bridge; it provided some protection from a flank attack, but to an experienced siege engineer looking down from the heights of Mount Sciberras, Saint Elmo looked small and vulnerable. There were numerous short-comings; the fort's design was poorly thought out and badly executed. It had low parapets and no embrasures to protect the men, so that no defender could shoot without making himself a clear target; its small size precluded the siting of many guns on the ramparts; it lacked sally ports from which troops could safely exit to clear the ditch of enemy infill or launch counterattacks. Worst of all, the angles of the stars were so sharp that there were large areas of dead ground beneath the ramparts upon which defenders were unable to fire. The Ottoman engineers' assessment of the task ahead seemed reasonable. To all intents and purposes, Saint Elmo was a stone death trap.

No army in the world could match the Ottomans for their grasp of siege craft, their practical engineering skills, their deployment of huge quantities of human labor for precise objectives, their ability to plan meticulously but to improvise ingeniously. Armies that had reduced castles in Persia and frontier forts on the plains of Hungary, who had dug trenches at Rhodes with such astonishing speed, who had, their enemies acknowledged, "no equal in the world at earthworks," went about their task with dreadful skill. From the fort itself, and from across the water on Birgu and Senglea, the defenders watched with awe. The rocky terrain and the lack of topsoil and wood made trench cutting difficult, but the sappers pushed forward their spidery network of trenches "with marvelous diligence and speed." Careful angles of approach shielded the work from the fort for a considerable time. Earth was transported from a mile away to construct gun platforms. Hundreds of men marched in long columns up the slopes of the hill with sacks of earth and planks of wood. The deep planning of this operation was astonishing; they had brought the materials and components for their gun batteries ready-made from Istanbul. The trenches advanced with sinister intent. Within a couple of days the Ottomans were entrenched at little more than six hundred paces from Saint Elmo's ditch. Soon the Turks' front lines had reached the edge of the ditch itself. They created two lines of raised earth platforms to mount their guns, and protected them with triangular wooden battlements filled with earth. Flags fluttered brightly from their forward positions; the guns were hauled painstakingly up the bare hill to their emplacements at the summit; other positions were established to bombard Birgu across the water. At night, transport barges rowed silently into the harbor of Marsamxett below Saint Elmo with bundles of brushwood for filling up the castle ditch. Across the water La Valette watched this activity with alarm and dispatched urgent messages to Don Garcia in Sicily.

By Monday, May 28, the Ottoman guns were starting to bombard

Saint Elmo from the heights; by Thursday, Ascension Day in the Christian calendar, the Turks had twenty-four guns positioned in two tiers, wheeled guns that fired penetrating iron balls, and giant bombards, one a veteran of Rhodes, firing enormous stone ones. The initial bombardment was preceded by a rattling barrage of musket fire to prevent any defender from showing his head over the parapet, then the cannon opened up. The Ottomans started to pulverize the two star points facing outward toward the ditch and the weak flank toward the ravelin. From Birgu, La Valette did his best to disrupt this cannonade by mounting four cannon of his own on the end of Saint Angelo and pummeling the platforms that were visible on the ridge across the water. He was not without success; as early as May 27, Piyale was slightly wounded by a stone splinter; but the cost in gunpowder was too great to be sustained.

From the start the omens were not good for the defense. The men could hardly raise their heads over the parapet without being ready targets, clear against the summer sky. The janissary snipers with their long-barreled arquebuses waited in the trenches below for any sign of life. Their patience was extraordinary; they watched, concealed and motionless, for five, six hours at a time, sighting down the barrel, finger on the trigger, waiting like hunters for the prey. They shot thirty men dead in a single day. The defenders did their best to erect makeshift protecting parapets; at the same time they worked to reconstruct crumbling walls out of earth and whatever other materials came to hand. Within a few days, morale started to collapse: whenever the defenders risked a sighter at the Ottoman guns looming on the hill above, they were in danger of being picked off. The proximity of the trenches, the crash of cannonballs, and the patent shortcomings of the fort made it obvious that their position was not sustainable. As early as May 26 the defenders slipped a man across the harbor in the dark. Juan de la Cerda was one of Philip's Spanish commanders and owed no allegiance to the knights. He gave La Valette and his council a blunt, uncomfortable, and public assessment of what the grand master already knew: the fort was weak, small, and without flanking defenses, "a consumptive body in continuous need of medicine to keep it alive." It could hold out without reinforcements for eight days at the most. More resources must be committed.

This was not what the grand master wanted to hear. Everything in his calculations depended on Saint Elmo buying time for Birgu and Senglea to strengthen their defenses and for Don Garcia, thirty miles away in Sicily, to send a relief fleet. He ironically thanked the Spaniard for his advice and appealed to the defenders' honor. At the same time he promised to send what was required: one hundred twenty men were ferried across under the command of Captain Medrano, who was now to be in charge of all the rebellious Spanish troops, as well as extra food and munitions. Wounded men made the journey back to the knights' hospital at Birgu. The defenders' morale was bolstered by these prompt actions but their underlying predicament remained unchanged. Smoldering dissatisfaction would soon break out again.

A regular interchange of small boats, apparently able to break the Ottoman naval blockade with impunity, carried messages to and fro between La Valette and Don Garcia in Sicily. The viceroy's news was profoundly discouraging. There were innumerable delays in gathering ships and men. The logistics of assembling a task force were proving immensely complicated. Some galleys were still being fitted out in Barcelona; in Genoa, Gian'Andrea Doria had been waiting for soldiers from Lombardy; then it rained heavily and the sea was too rough to risk moving his ships. In Sicily, Don Garcia had five thousand men but only thirty galleys, and the Ottomans knew this. They could afford to disarm many of their own galleys and send the crews ashore to work, leaving seventy to patrol the coast. They pressed forward with the bombardment. La Valette confined this information to his small council.

The days were heating up; nights were lit by brilliant moons, but the Ottoman sappers worked around the clock, snaking their trenches closer and closer to the walls, building protective embankments from earth carried up the stony slopes of Sciberras. "In truth it was a remarkable thing," declared Giacomo Bosio, "to see, in a barren landscape, the speed with which the Turks could make mountains of earth appear almost in a flash, from which they created bastions and platforms to bombard Saint Elmo, and the urgency with which they advanced their trenches and covered ways." Medrano mounted unexpected sorties to disrupt the work and kill the laborers; but during one of these sallies on May 29, the janissaries counterattacked and planted their flags on the counterscarp, hard up against the outer defenses and close to the ravelin. On Ascension Day, May 31, the Ottoman gunners opened up again on an even larger scale with twenty-four cannon, determined to blast Saint Elmo's fortifications back to the living rock. The bombardment continued unabated all night; so unceasing was the firing that the defenders calculated that the guns were not being cleaned out or allowed to cool between rounds—a highly risky practice for guns and gunners alike. The following morning at dawn, a shot knocked down Saint Elmo's flagstaff and flag. A great cry went up from the Turkish troops; it was taken as a sign of impending victory.

However, across the water in Birgu and Senglea, the time being bought by the small fort was put to good use. The soldiers and inhabitants worked feverishly, raising walls, building parapets and fighting positions for the day when Saint Elmo would fall and the guns would be turned on their fortifications. At night the sound of gunfire set the dogs in the towns barking; La Valette had them all killed—including his own hunting dogs—and dispatched a continuous stream of small boats to the fort. By now, however, the Turks were starting to think about this loophole. They set up two small artillery pieces and some arquebusiers on the shore to try to disrupt the lifeline to Birgu.

On the morning of June 2, it all took a further turn for the worse. At daybreak, lookouts on the cavalier of Saint Elmo spotted sails to the southeast. There were brief hopes that these were the outriders of Don Garcia's rescue fleet, but the truth was grimmer. It was Turgut, coming up from Algiers with his corsairs—some thirteen galleys and thirty other vessels, fifteen hundred Islamic fighters under the most experienced and resourceful commander in the whole sea. The circumstances of his welcome perhaps highlighted the gulf in ability between Turgut and the commanders already in place. Piyale, determined to make an impression, sailed his own galleys out "in superb order" to greet the newcomer. Passing Saint Elmo, they fired off a volley of gunfire at the fort. Their shots whistled overhead and killed some of their own men in the trenches, while return fire from the fort holed one galley amidships, so that it had to be towed quickly off to prevent its total loss.

Suleiman had perhaps placed his ultimate confidence in Turgut, "a wise and experienced warrior"—and Mustapha and Piyale were aware of this. "The Drawn Sword of Islam" knew Malta better than anyone; he was not only an expert seaman, but also a highly experienced gunner and siege specialist. Once ashore, the old corsair was quickly apprised of the situation. He pursed his lips with displeasure. He probably disliked the whole venture and would have preferred an easy attempt on the Spanish enclave at La Goletta, an irritant to his own personal North African fiefdom. He may or may not have disagreed about the decision to go for Saint Elmo first—all Christian accounts of the matter have the ring of invention—but since the siege was under way, it would be best if it were concluded as quickly as possible. He wasted no time in going up to the front line to reanalyze the terrain and the disposition of the artillery. He saw that speed was essential: more guns must be brought up and they must be brought nearer. A second heavy bombard was hauled forward, and four cannon were placed on the northern shore to bombard Saint Elmo's weakest flank. He was determined to pulverize the fort as heavily as possible. To this end he set up a battery of guns on a point across the Marsamxett harbor that could rain shot onto the ravelin and cavalier; in due course he established another battery on the opposite headland. Saint Elmo was now under fire from a hundred and eighty degrees; so heavy was the shot, Bosio declared, "that it was extraordinary that the tiny, straightened fort was not reduced to ashes."

Turgut's final suggestion was to take the ravelin as quickly as possible, "even at the cost of many good soldiers."

# CHAPTER 10

# The Ravelin of Europe

June 3–16, 1565

Iɴ ᴛʜᴇ ʟᴇᴛᴛᴇʀꜱ ᴛʜᴀᴛ ʟᴀ ᴠᴀʟᴇᴛᴛᴇ ᴅɪꜱᴘᴀᴛᴄʜᴇᴅ day after day to Sicily and the Italian mainland, he never failed to stress the strategic importance of Malta. Its loss would leave Christian Europe as "a fortress without a ravelin." The metaphor was not wasted on his audience. Since the fall of Constantinople, the technical language of Italian fortress engineering had been constantly on the lips of Christian potentates and churchmen. They conceived the whole of the Christian Mediterranean as a vast system of concentric defenses, at the center of which sat Rome, God's keep, constantly under attack from the barbarian horde. One after another, the outer works had crumbled. In the years after 1453, Venice had been the outer wall of Europe; the Ottomans had neutralized it in just fifty years. Then Rhodes was the shield of Christendom. It had fallen. With each retrenchment, the Turk was a step closer. Now Malta had become the ravelin of Europe. Everyone realized the significance of this—the pope in Rome, the Catholic King high up in his palace in Madrid, Don Garcia across the water in Sicily—for when the ravelin fell, the end of a fortress was nigh. In late May and early June 1565, concern for the defenses of Christendom focused on a single point. For if the key to Europe was Malta, the key to Malta was Saint Elmo; and the fortress, in its turn, was dependent on the small makeshift triangular ravelin that protected its vulnerable side. Turgut understood this as clearly as La Valette. And he was determined to act.

By the morning of June 3, following a night of intense bombardment, Ottoman troops had established sheltering positions close to the ditch and only tens of yards from the ravelin's protecting walls. It was, by irony, the saint's day of Saint Elmo—the patron saint of seamen.

Ottoman engineers, intent on assessing the effect of the night's barrage, slipped into the ditch in front of the fort and approached the ravelin. There was silence from the position—no challenge, no shots from a lookout. They got up to the foot of the fortification unnoticed. In all likelihood, the assigned sentry had been silently felled by a single arquebus shot, and lay on his stomach on the parapet looking "as if he were still alive." His comrades, only forty in all, assumed he was still on guard. Other versions give a more cowardly version of the sentries' behavior.

The engineers stole away and informed Mustapha. A force of janissaries with scaling ladders crept forward and stealthily climbed the parapet. They burst into the small fortress with ululating cries and shot to death the first men they saw. The remainder turned and fled, too panic stricken to raise the drawbridge into the main fort behind them. Only a determined sally by a small group of knights stopped the rush of the janissaries into Saint Elmo. A spirited counterattack was mounted to force the intruders out of the ravelin; two or three times they seemed to have succeeded, but more men were flooding the ditch, and the defenders were forced to withdraw. With lightning speed the Turks seemed able to consolidate their position in the ravelin, bundling in sacks of wool and earth and brushwood to construct a rampart against counterattack from the fort. Flags—the critical markers of possession—started to flutter from the makeshift defenses. It was just the prelude to a berserk, impromptu assault by the men in the ditch, who propped ladders against the walls with the hope of finally storming Saint Elmo. They felt certain of success, but the attempt was suicidal. The defenders hurled down rocks and liquid fire on the Turks' unprotected heads. The din of the battle was extraordinary; according to the Christian chroniclers, "with the roar of the artillery and the arquebuses, the hair-raising screams, the smoke and fire and flame, it seemed that the whole world was at the point of exploding." After five hours of havoc, the Turks were forced to withdraw, leaving five hundred crack troops dead in the ditch. The defenders claimed to have lost sixty soldiers and twenty knights, including the French knight La Gardampe, who crawled away into the fortress chapel and died at the foot of the altar. Despite the huge Ottoman losses, the ravelin was now in enemy hands.

The serious consequences of the loss were felt almost at once. The Ottomans worked furiously to consolidate their command of the ravelin, using goatskins filled with earth to raise the platform until it was level with the wall. They now occupied an offensive position within yards of the fort; they were soon able to bombard its very heart with two captured guns. In the ditch below, men could work their way up to the base of the walls without being attacked.

Toward dawn on June 4, while the Turks were still fortifying the ravelin, a small boat was seen approaching the rocky promontory below the fort; the sentries on the rampart tensed themselves, ready to fire, when a cry rang out in the dark: "Salvago!" It was a Spanish knight, Raffael Salvago. He had been dropped by galley from Sicily with messages from Don Garcia, and had run the blockade around the harbor. With him was an experienced captain, Miranda. The two men clambered ashore and briefly inspected the fort in the dark, then climbed back on board. By now the crossing between Saint Elmo and Birgu was under threat from sharpshooters. Boats could no longer make the journey in broad daylight; even night crossings were fraught with danger. As they rowed quietly across the harbor, a volley of shot struck the boat and killed one of the crew.

La Valette listened to their report in gloomy silence. It was devastating to have lost the ravelin so negligently. Hardly more reassuring was the news from Sicily: Don Garcia was struggling to gather forces but he hoped for relief by June 20. The question was simply how long Saint Elmo could be kept alive. Miranda was dispatched back again to make a more detailed appraisal of the defenses and the men's morale. His second report was emphatic: "The fort could not be held for long if the Turks were persistent, because the lack of traverses meant that the defenders' fire had little effect. Furthermore, there was no strongpoint to which the defenders could retire." Yet again La Valette wanted to test this information. Another commission was dispatched specifically to study the feasibility of retaking the ravelin, with the same conclusion: "It was impossible to get the ravelin back; they should shore up the defenses for as long as they could." From now on Saint Elmo was living on borrowed time. A nightly transfusion of men and materials slipped across the harbor, dodging the enemy guns, keeping the doomed fort alive. It was on life support.

IN THE WAKE OF THE LOSS, La Valette was desperate to sustain the fort's morale; with this in mind he appointed Miranda as de facto commander of Saint Elmo. The Spaniard was not an aristocratic knight, but an experienced and practical field commander who understood his men. It was not the consolations of religion that would stiffen their resolve but tangible rewards. He asked for money, "for nothing pleases soldiers more than money," and barrels of wine. He paid the men and set up gaming tables and a bar in the covered arcades around the parade ground. In the short run it was effective.

The Ottomans, however, felt that the end must be near. They kept raising the ravelin to overtop the fort and peppered the interior with shot. The men worked furiously to fill up the ditch with brushwood, earth, and bales of wood. At the same time, the Ottomans hauled up masts from some of the galleys and constructed a scaffolding bridge across the ditch and adjacent to the ravelin, from which the workers were protected by arquebusiers: any defender who showed his head above the parapet was immediately shot down. A second bridge was built farther down the wall. The bridge building, however, provoked a furious response: a sortie was mounted to burn the first bridge with only partial success—and "by Vespers they had repaired it again." Bridge work continued: a causeway was laid, wide enough for five men to walk abreast, and covered with earth to proof it against incendiaries. The defenders were compelled to crouch beneath the parapet, so that it was impossible to hinder this operation; the whole fortress was being probed by gunfire so that "there was not a safe place in St Elmo." Seeing the hopelessness of their situation and the likelihood of another assault, morale in the fortress snapped again.

The whole body of men, including the Knights of Saint John and Captain Miranda, agreed to dispatch another captain, Medrano, to Birgu to put the case to La Valette and his council. It was a unified response. Medrano declared that the fort could not be held much longer; "because their defences had been levelled, the enemy's bridge was nearly completed, and that, owing to the height of the ravelin, which commanded the whole fort, whence the Turks were bombarding them, it was not possible to defend themselves." La Valette somehow persuaded the concerned Spaniard to return to the fort with vaguely reassuring words, but they failed to assuage the growing panic inside. While the bridge building continued apace, the chink of pickaxes working at the foot of walls convinced the garrison that the Turks were about to plant mines. Meanwhile the bombardment went on night and day without stopping, "so that it seemed as though they wanted to reduce the fort to dust." It was clear an all-out assault was near. On June 8 the council on Birgu received a second letter from Saint Elmo: the end was nigh, they were expecting to be blown sky high at any moment, they had withdrawn to the church in the center of the fort and would prefer to sally out and die straightaway. This letter was signed by fifty knights.

La Valette's response was again to play for time: he sent across another commission. When the three knights arrived, they found the fort in uproar. The defenders' nerves were in shreds. Panicky preparations were being made to abandon the fort; cannonballs and trenching equipment were being thrown down wells; work was in hand to blow up the fort from within. When the commissioners declared that Saint Elmo was still defensible—and that it was impossible to mine a fortress built on solid rock—rage boiled over. An open mutiny erupted in the parade ground; they taunted the commissioners to show them exactly how the fort could be held. The gates were closed to detain the visitors inside. Only when someone had the wit to sound the alarm bell did the men disperse back to their posts, and the commissioners slipped back across the water. On Birgu the council met to discuss the matter; the rebellious garrison dispatched a swimmer across the harbor in quick time to reiterate their fears. In camera, the council was deeply undecided about how to proceed; some wanted withdrawal to preserve the men, others were for holding out, but in practice there was no choice; it would be impossible safely to evacuate such a large body of men now that the harbor was monitored by Ottoman guns. The defenders had to be persuaded to go on buying time.

A combination of promises and blackmail eventually quelled the mutiny. Don Constantino, one of the knights' commissioners, offered to raise volunteers to go to Saint Elmo. In Birgu's main square drums summoned recruits to the standard. The council then calmly informed the mutineers at Saint Elmo that they could return if they wished: "For every one who came back, there were four begging and imploring to take their place." Meanwhile La Valette wrote to the knights in the fort, reminding them of their vows to Christ and their Order. A new commander was appointed, Melchior de Monserrat; there was an upsurge of zeal; the Christians were impressed that two converted Jews volunteered for the cause, and the inspirational preacher Robert of Eboli went across. Captain Miranda made a stirring speech to the men

*The attack on Saint Elmo (E); Mount Sciberras (Y); Mustapha Pasha's tent, in the foreground (Q); Turgut's gun battery (O); Senglea (D); Birgu (B); the fort of Saint Michael (A)*

"in the language that soldiers understand" to the effect that "they should fight bravely and sell their lives to the barbarians as dearly as possible." A second swimmer came back from the fort, announcing that "all said with one voice they did not wish to leave the fort, but that reinforcements and munitions should be sent to them; that they all wished to die in St Elmo." The nightly transfusions of men and materials continued; a hundred men were ferried over with a great number of banners to plant on the ramparts to give the impression of a large relief force. There was no more talk of dissent.

The battle that raged day after day over the small fort was being conducted with all the evolving weapons of the age of gunpowder. The Ottomans certainly had—and used—deadly companies of archers, but it was the sound of explosions echoing around the stricken fort that gave the impression of Armageddon. From a distance it was a conflict of sniper fire and artillery bombardment; a man could be smartly felled by a single bullet or dismembered by an iron ball, but in the close-quarters struggle for the walls, an ingenious range of small-scale incendiary devices came into play. The Christians had primitive hand grenades and flamethrowers, pots of Greek fire and barrels of pitch, as well as swivel guns and heavier arquebuses that fired stones the size of pigeons' eggs and chain shot for slaughtering close-packed charging men. The Ottomans responded in kind with bursting grenades that hurled clinging fire at the heavily armored defenders. All these weapons were crude, experimental, and unstable. The risks in using them were considerable. Accounts of the siege ring with the accidental deaths of the weapons' handlers: barrels of gunpowder exploded; grenades ignited the stock around them before they could be thrown; men were regularly maimed and burned to death by their own weapons. When these weapons worked, they could be devastating.

In this laboratory of flame warfare, the Christians decided to test a new device. On June 10, La Valette sent over a stock of fire hoops, an innovation said to have been invented by the knight Ramon Fortuyn. "These consisted of barrel hoops well covered with caulking tow and well steeped in a cauldron of boiling tar. They were again covered with tow and once more immersed in tar. This process was repeated until they became as thick as a man's leg." The aim was to hurl them over the parapet into a mass of charging men.

They were soon pressed into service. On that day the Ottomans launched another fierce attack; the janissaries in their loose robes poured over the bridges and set ladders to the walls. As the charging, scrabbling men pressed forward, torches were set to the hoops; they were levered over the parapet with iron tongs and set bouncing and spinning down the slope like demented circles of fire. The effect was devastating. The clothes of two or three soldiers at a time would get entrapped by the giant wheels. Balls of flame now, the men would turn and run, robes and turbans alight, scattering terror and fire in their wake as they headed for the sea. The psychological impact of the wheels was profound. The janissaries pulled back, but only for a while. Mustapha was determined to finish off the fort. After dark the men came again. The whole sky was illuminated by the flash of cannon and the flare of incendiaries—fire hoops, flamethrowers, and pots of Greek fire rained over the walls; the onrushing Muslims hurled back exploding fire grenades that burst on the parapets and illuminated the defenders in an incredible and ghastly light. There was no darkness; from across the water Saint Elmo looked like a volcano of fire. It was bright enough for the gunners on Birgu, trying to disrupt the Turks with cross fire, to prepare their guns without torches. The screams and shouts, the explosions and the violence of the light, convinced the grand master that Saint Elmo had fallen. Yet somehow it held. Again the Turks drew back.

By now it was dawn; the early sun was rising; the defenders were exhausted, dead on their feet, and Mustapha knew it. He called for one more frenzied attack. Fresh men surged forward again with ropes and grappling hooks, which they attached to the barrels of earth and makeshift barricades on the parapets that screened the defenders from rifle fire. Hauling themselves up, they managed to establish a position on top and plant their flags. Sensing the danger, the commander of the bastion, Colonel Mas, loaded a light gun and blasted the janissaries off the wall with a enormous crash "and hurled them into the ditch again, with great terror to the others." The attack collapsed. The Turks withdrew with great losses. Silence fell over the battlefield. The Muslims spent the day collecting and burying their dead in mass graves. But the defenders were also hemorrhaging men at an unacceptable rate. La Valette ferried across another one hundred fifty men together with ammunition and "baskets, mattresses and unravelled rope" for building barricades. The four-day siege was now in its fourteenth day.

Bad news was starting to leak out of the Ottoman camp. Christian deserters and captured Turks drip-fed encouraging scraps of information about the assault on Saint Elmo to La Valette and the army council in Birgu. Ottoman losses the previous night had been considerable; many seasoned troops had been killed. There was disease in the camp and the wounded were dying; rationing had been instituted—laborers were limited to ten ounces of biscuits a day. There was ill will between the pashas and the janissaries: "The pashas were reproaching the janissaries for calling themselves the Sons of the Sultan and for their many other brave boasts, yet still they had not got the spirit to take a small, weak and ruined fort, against which a bridge had already been laid." At the same time an atmosphere of intense competition between Mustapha and Piyale, between the army and the navy, was further straining the morale of the camp. Two opposing forces propelled Mustapha forward: the fear of disgrace and a desire for glory. Whispers reached the pashas that Don Garcia was gathering ships and men in Sicily; Piyale dispatched a fleet of galleys daily to patrol the Malta channel.

However, if morale inside Saint Elmo had been raised, it was by no means rock solid; and on June 13, Mustapha received information that seemed to promise a final solution. An Italian soldier, no doubt reckoning that the end was nigh, slipped over the walls and presented himself in the Ottoman camp. He told Mustapha to raise the ravelin even higher, to prevent any movement around the fort and to cut off all relief from Birgu. One last assault would then finish off the few remaining men. The following day the defenders could hear a voice calling to them in Italian. Mustapha was making them an offer, "on the promise of his head." The pasha would give them free passage out of the fort to wherever they wanted to go. The alternative was a horrible death. The voice was promptly answered by a volley of arquebus fire and a succession of spinning fire hoops. The defenders were resolved to fight to the last. They prepared themselves for one more attack.

Mustapha began what he hoped would be the final preparations with the time-honored Ottoman tactics: continuous bombardment day and night, skirmishes, localized attacks, and innumerable false alarms—all designed to leave the defenders sleepless and exhausted ahead of the last push. Labor corps worked incessantly, trying to fill in the ditches with earth and bundles of brushwood, while arquebus fire rattled the parapets. The defenders hampered these attempts as best they could. They set fire to the brushwood and shot dead the brilliantly attired aga (commander) of the janissaries, which caused great disturbance in the Ottoman camp. The night of June 15 saw another thumping artillery barrage under a bright moon. Then silence.

IN THE PREDAWN of June 16, a lone voice broke the stillness. The mullahs summoned the men to prayers; for two hours the priests called and the men responded in a gathering rhythmic crescendo to psych them up to fight and die. The defenders crouched behind their makeshift barricades, listening to the eerie chants rising and falling in the darkness beyond. La Valette had sent further reinforcements across, and the defenders, if already weary, were well ordered. Each man had his duty and his post. They were grouped in threes: one arquebusier to two pike men. There were men assigned to drag away the dead and three mobile troops to reinforce wherever the need was greatest. Large quantities of fire weapons had been stockpiled, rocks gathered, and quantities of bread soaked in wine. Barrels of water stood behind the parapets into which men torched by adhesive fire could hurl themselves.

As the sun rose, there was a further searching barrage of fire "so that the earth and the air shook," and then Mustapha signaled the advance along a huge crescent. Suleiman's imperial standard was unfurled; a turban was hoisted on a spear; farther down the line there was an answering puff of smoke. An incredible array of banners and shields was visible surging forward, "painted with extraordinary designs; some with devices of different birds, some with scorpions and with Arab lettering." In the front rank, men dressed in leopard skins with eagle headdresses ran wildly toward the walls, calling out the name of Allah in a crescendo of shouts. From the battlements came the Christian countercalls: Jesus, Mary, Saint Michael, Saint James, and Saint George—"according to the devotion of each man." There was a furious push toward the bridge; scaling ladders were put to the walls and battle was joined. The whole front was a struggling mass of humanity fighting hand to hand. Men were thrown back from the ladders and hurled off the bridge. In the tumult men shot their own side and the enemy simultaneously. The westerly wind blew the smoke from their guns back into the defenders' faces so that they were temporarily blinded; then a stock of unstable incendiaries caught light and burned many men to death.

On Birgu they watched the unfolding battle, "with our minds split, wondering how we could help our men in such grave peril." Individual details stood out. Balbi glimpsed an individual soldier silhouetted against the skyline, "fighting like one inspired, with a flamethrower in his hands." They could also make out a small colorful band of Turks hurling themselves forward in a mass; in the competition between the army and navy, thirty leading galley captains had sworn "to enter the fort or die together." With scaling ladders they climbed up onto the cavalier at the rear of the fort. La Valette ordered his gunners at Saint Angelo to aim at the intruders. The shot was misdirected and killed eight defenders. Calmly the others on the cavalier signaled to the gunners across the water to redirect their fire. The second attempt landed in the middle of the raiding party, killing twenty of them: "Those who remained were dispatched with fire and steel and their bodies thrown below; not one of them escaped," recorded Balbi. Mustapha and Turgut were plainly visible in their brilliant robes, urging the men on, but the furious assault on the cavalier failed. Fire hoops tore through the Ottoman ranks, "so that the enemy seemed to be crowned and encircled with fire"; men were pitched off the wall; the ditch started to fill with the dead. The brightly colored Ottoman banners planted on the parapets were ripped down. Captain Medrano seized one; a moment later he was shot through the head, but two of the iconic standards were torn to pieces. The sultan's personal banner was captured. Miranda was wounded but had himself hauled into a chair by the parapet with his sword in his hands. After seven hours of heavy fighting, the attack started to falter; the Ottomans withdrew their men. Triumphant shouting carried across the water: "Victory and the Christian faith!" The day belonged to the exhausted garrison. Hardly able to stand, they watched as the enemy withdrew. It was a victory of sorts, though at a high price: one hundred fifty men dead, a third of the garrison. And the final riposte to their triumphant cries was a voice calling out in Italian: "Keep quiet. If not today, tomorrow will be your last."

The Italian renegade who had instigated this attack did not live to enjoy his escape. A few days later, wearing Turkish dress, he was caught in the countryside by Maltese from Mdina, tied to a horse's tail, and beaten to death by children with sticks. Each day made the conflict uglier.

# CHAPTER 11

# The Last Swimmers

June 17–23, 1565

It WAS A CHASTENED ARMY COMMAND that met at Mustapha's tent on June 17 to reanalyze the intractable problem of Saint Elmo. Turgut again pointed out the Ottoman blind spot in the whole operation: their failure to close the supply route across the harbor to Birgu had allowed the fort to be continuously resupplied. The Turks started a new trench down the shoreline to the point below the fort where boats from Birgu were accustomed to land. And they strengthened the battery pummeling the cavalier. With this initiative, it became apparent that the end must be near. When the grand master heard of this work, he is said to have given thanks to God that the Turks had been so slow to cut the fort's lifeline. Twelve knights volunteered to assist the fort, but La Valette refused. It was pointless to lose more men in a vain cause. He dispatched two boats with desperate letters to Don Garcia and the pope, begging for help. One was taken by the enemy, but to Mustapha's fury, he could find no renegades in his army who could break the code. In Birgu and Senglea they pressed on with the fortifications.

The next day brought a brief moment of cheer. Accounts of what happened differ. The Ottoman army command was in the trenches down by the water supervising a gun battery. Most likely, the cannon were firing too high and Turgut ordered the aim to be lowered. Because the cannon were still aiming too high, he instructed a further adjustment. The third shot was too low. It failed to clear the trench above and struck the wall; stone splinters were hurled across the gun platform. One caught Turgut beneath the ear. Another hit Soli Aga, the master general of the army, killing him outright. Turgut, protected by his turban, fell to the ground badly wounded. The old corsair lay there, unable to speak, his tongue hanging out of his mouth, blood spurting from his head. Mustapha, unperturbed by the devastation around him, had Turgut covered up and carried away secretly to his tent in an attempt to preserve morale, but word quickly got out. Renegades soon reached Birgu with news of the accident. Turgut lingered on, unconscious, neither dead nor alive.

The Ottomans pressed forward. The following day the pummeling of one of the bastions was so intense that a breach had been opened sufficient to permit easy scaling of the walls; repairs were becoming almost impossible. The men could not sally out to gather earth without being shot dead; they filled the breaches as best they could with blankets and old sails, and crouched below the parapet. During the night a massive explosion rocked the whole harbor basin; a powder mill accidentally exploded on Birgu. The Turkish troops cried with joy. La Valette fired half a dozen cannon shots across the water to quell their enthusiasm, but the news for the defenders was unremittingly bad. On June 20, the new Ottoman gun platform guarding the harbor was finished; it was no longer possible to get boats across from Birgu even at night. A last boat had made the journey on the night of June 19; it was quickly spotted. One man was decapitated by a cannonball on the way over; another was killed by arquebus fire on return. Miranda relayed a last message to the effect that it was cruelty to send more men to die. Henceforth only Maltese swimmers, slipping silently into the night sea, could make the crossing. La Valette reluctantly agreed that nothing more could be done.

JUNE 21 WAS THE FEAST of Corpus Christi, a signal day in the Christian calendar. "We, for our part, did not fail to honour this great and noble day as best and devoutly as we could," Balbi recorded in his diary of the observances on Birgu. There was a procession, in which the grand master participated, though the route had to be carefully chosen to avoid enemy fire across the harbor. The garrison of Saint Elmo was at its last gasp. Now a dozen of the best Ottoman snipers had established positions high up in the side of the cavalier from which they could probe the heart of the fort. Even the parade ground could be hit. Yet the defenders kept trying to set fire to the brushwood filling up the ditch; one man, the Italian Pedro de Forli, lowered himself over the wall on a rope with a flamethrower strapped to his back to attempt to destroy the threatening bridge. He failed—the bridge was too well covered with earth; it is not known if he made it back alive. And the bombardment went on. All night Ottoman guns pummeled the shattered walls; regular false alarms kept the weary men blinking out into the darkness. Now they could go only on all fours beneath the parapet; it was impossible to leave their posts. The priests crawled up to them with the sacraments.

At dawn on June 22, Mustapha resolved to finish the job off with another general assault. He ensured that Saint Elmo was completely surrounded; Piyale brought up his galleys and bombarded the stricken fort from the sea. Small boats crammed with arquebusiers guarded the crossing from Birgu. Again the janissaries surged over the bridge; the complete circumference of the fort was throttled by thousands of men raising ladders against the wall. It was hand-to-hand fighting on the parapets with the Muslims trying to plant their banners, the Christians hurling rocks and pots of fire onto their unprotected heads. The defenders were now being shot in the back by snipers lodged on the cavalier, who picked off the knights in their ostentatious armor. Montserrat, the fort commander, was beheaded by a cannonball. According to Giacomo Bosio, "the sun was like a living fire." The Christians roasted in their helmets and plate armor but fought on hour after hour. From Birgu, the knights watched in terror and confusion. They heard the cries, the thump of the guns, saw the doomed fort "covered in flames and fire." And then after six hours of confused tumult, the sound of voices could be heard drifting across the water, shouting in Italian and Spanish: "Victory! Victory!" The attack faltered; the Ottomans drew back. Somehow Saint Elmo had held out.

Under the afternoon sun, the survivors crawled across the ruined fort. Many of the commanders were now dead; others—Eguerras, Miranda, Mas—were too wounded to stand. Bodies sprawled across the parapet and lay dead in the parade ground where they fell. It was no longer possible to bury or even move the corpses. The walls had been breached in many places; there were no materials to make repairs. In the atomizing summer heat, the smell of stone dust and gunpowder, the buzz of flies, the stench of the dead. It was the twenty-sixth day of the siege.

Those who could still stand gathered in the small church. Here, in the words of the chroniclers, "everyone resolved with one accord to finish life and the human pilgrimage." They decided to make a final appeal for help. A swimmer slipped into the sea and a last boat also put out. It was attacked by twelve Turkish barges but somehow made it across. Both boat and swimmer delivered the same message: they were at their last gasp. There were very few men left alive and most of these were wounded; they had no more incendiaries and little powder. They had no hope of relief.

La Valette listened to these words with a stony face. He had willed these men to resist to the very last, and that moment had now come. "God knows what the grand master felt," Balbi wrote in his diary. He refused all requests to send more volunteers; it was simply a waste of precious resources, but relented to the extent of permitting a small flotilla of boats to attempt to run the blockade with supplies. Five captains, including Romegas, put to sea in the dark. The attempt was futile; they were spattered with fire from the shoreline and then ran into eighty of Piyale's galleys lurking off the point.

When the defenders saw this attempt had failed, they "made themselves ready to die in the service of Jesus Christ." They were unable to leave their posts, so "like men to whom the next day was to be their last on earth, confessed to each other and implored Our Lord to have mercy on their souls." In anticipation of acts of desecration, the priests buried the Christian utensils under the floor of the chapel; the tapestries, pictures, and wooden furniture they took outside and burned. The Ottoman guns kept hammering the fort. All night La Valette watched from his window; he could see the fort vividly illuminated by flashes of gunfire.

Saturday, June 23, Balbi wrote in his diary: "At sunrise . . . being the eve of the feast of Saint John Baptist, the name-saint and protector of this Order, the Turks began their last assault." Piyale's ships closed on the stricken fortress, with their bow guns forward, and started to bombard. The army massed at the walls. Inside there were only seventy or a hundred men left alive. All were exhausted; many were wounded. They searched the corpses of their fallen comrades for the last few grains of gunpowder to prime their arquebuses. Miranda and Eguerras, unable to stand, were placed in chairs with their swords in their hands. For four hours the men held the line. Two hours before midday, there was a visible pause in the assault. When the janissaries and sipahis lined up to attack again, there was no answering fire. The gunpowder was all gone. Six hundred men lay dead in the square and at the walls. The surviving defenders grasped swords and pikes and stood their ground but the arquebusiers no longer hid. Sensing that resistance was at an end, hundreds of men poured over the bridge and climbed the parapets unopposed, slaughtering all they met. Others disembarked from the boats. Miranda and Eguerras were shot dead in their chairs. Those who could still run fell back on the square to make a last stand. Someone tried to call a parley by the beating of a drum, but it was far too late. After the humiliations of the previous weeks, Mustapha had ordered that no one should be left alive; he would buy the head of every defender from his men. The janissaries converged on the square, shouting, "Kill! Kill!" Hemmed in, some of the defenders made for the church, hoping that they might surrender, "but as soon as they saw the Turks were pitilessly butchering those who had surrendered, they rushed out into the centre and sold their lives dearly."

Those on Birgu caught some last glimpses of the fort in its death throes: a lone figure could be seen on the ruined summit of the cavalier laying about him with a two-handed sword; smoke from a signal fire—an agreed signal for the imminent loss of the fort—was lit by the Italian knight Francesco Lanfreducci; then the flag on the cavalier was torn down and the Ottoman flag raised, "which made our hair stand on end on Birgu."

In the parade square the fort lived its last ghastly moments. Under the watchful eye of Mustapha, men were being lined up against the wall for target practice and shot full of arrows; the wounded who made it to the church were killed inside; the knights were the targets of particular hatred. They were hung upside down from iron rings in the arched colonnades and had their heads split, their chests ripped open, and their hearts torn out. A frenzy of bloodshed and madness came upon the janissaries whose pride had been so badly dented. A few of the surviving professional Spanish and Italian troops fell on their knees and cried out that they were not knights and begged "by your god" to be saved. It made no difference. One unfortunate, seeing the slaughter, ran to hide in a chest. Two renegades found the weighty item and were carrying it away in the hope of profitable loot when they were stopped by Mustapha, who demanded the chest be opened in front of him. The dumbfounded man inside was hauled away and killed. No one was to survive.

Now that the last obstacle had been dismantled, the whole of Piyale's fleet, with banners flying and guns booming, entered the harbor of Marsamxett. Lying safely at anchor, they could look up at the Ottoman banners fluttering from the castle walls.

Mustapha had thought to kill every living thing in Saint Elmo, but he failed. Some men, fleeing from the fort down toward the sea, were not taken by the vengeful Ottoman army but surrendered to Turgut's corsairs and were spirited away as ransomable booty. Some of these, including Francesco Lanfreducci, would reappear, as if from the dead, years later. And four or five Maltese, unencumbered by armor, slipped out of the gates down to the water facing Birgu and hid in some caves on the shore. After dark, these men slid into the night sea and swam silently across to Birgu to deliver a firsthand account of everything they had seen.

IF THE PEOPLE OF BIRGU were appalled by what they had heard, they received a further demonstration the following day. The heads of the principal commanders were displayed on lances in full view of the harbor. Mustapha then had some of the bodies of the knights and a Maltese priest—"some mutilated, some without heads, some with their bellies ripped open"—dressed in their distinctive red-and-white surcoats and nailed to wooden crosses in parody of the crucifixion. The bodies were launched into the water off Saint Elmo's point, where the current washed them across to Birgu. This gruesome flotsam was intended to terrify the inhabitants out of further resistance; it had quite the opposite effect. La Valette was determined not to take a step back: he would give the enemy no comfort. He delivered a ringing speech to the people and forbade any public displays of grief. He had the bodies buried with honor. The feast of the patron saint, Saint John, was celebrated in the usual manner and the grand master then conceived an act of immediate retaliation. All the Turkish prisoners were taken out of the dungeons and slaughtered on the ramparts. He sent a messenger to the commander of the garrison at Mdina with orders to kill all his prisoners, but slowly, one a day, every day. Later that day the guns of Saint Angelo opened up. A volley of human heads bombarded the Ottoman camp across the water. There would be no repeat of the chivalrous truce at Rhodes.

IT IS SAID that when Piyale entered the fort and surveyed the horrific scene, he was overcome by repulsion. He asked Mustapha why such cruelty had been necesssary. It was the question, said or unsaid, that hovered repeatedly in the Mediterranean air throughout all the decades of this war. Mustapha replied that it was the sultan's orders: no grown man must be taken alive. He promptly dispatched ships to Istanbul with news of the victory and captured war trophies. When they heard about the capture of Saint Elmo, the Venetians, with shriveling cynicism, celebrated in the streets—or the authorities might have organized this expression of spontaneous joy to satisfy Ottoman spies that the republic was still loyal to the sultan.

Two hours after Saint Elmo's fall, Turgut "drank the sherbet of martyrdom and forgot this vain world."

# CHAPTER 12

# Payback

O N  T H E  A F T E R N O O N  O F  J U N E  24—the feast day of Saint John—from their fortified positions on Birgu and Senglea, the defenders could look gloomily across the water at the Ottoman flags fluttering from the ruined walls of Saint Elmo. After dark the Turkish camp was brilliant with fires and celebrations. "It grieved us all," sighed Francisco Balbi in his diary, "because this celebration was not such as the Knights used to make on this day in honour of their patron saint."

But La Valette was not the only commander to be troubled. Mustapha had lost valuable time—a rigid coordinate in the whole plan—and at least four thousand men, conservatively a sixth of his whole force, including a large part of his crack janissaries. He had fired eighteen thousand cannon shots, and no matter how ample the military planning had been in Istanbul, gunpowder was not inexhaustible. The death of Turgut was another blow. Mustapha ordered the corsairs to transport his body to Tripoli and to return with all the gunpowder they could find. He also hurried a galliot off to Istanbul with some cannon from the fort as trophies; it was a wise move. Instinctively he could sense that lack of positive news was starting to make Suleiman frown with displeasure. It was essential that Mustapha move the final assault forward. In Istanbul meanwhile, a bloodless revolution was taking place in the imperial administration. On June 27, the chief vizier died. He was replaced by the second vizier, the Bosnian-born Sokollu Mehmet Pasha, who would prove to be one of the ablest of Ottoman viziers and a statesman worthy of his great master. It was Sokollu who would largely steer the Ottoman ship in the years ahead.

O N  B I R G U, La Valette was confronting the consequences of defending Saint Elmo to the last. Proportionately, the fifteen hundred dead Christians were an even heavier loss—about a quarter of all his fighting men—but the lives had at least bought time to strengthen the flimsy defenses on the two peninsulas. However, behind the resolute public face, there was something approaching despair. A string of urgent letters was dispatched to Mdina in the center of the island, then on by small boat to the wider world. To Philip in Spain he wrote immediately, "I had put all our forces to defend St Elmo ... We are now so few we can't hold out for long." To Don Garcia, the man on the spot in Sicily, he begged repeatedly for an immediate full-scale rescue fleet, "without which we're dead."

Both the grand master and the pasha had fought at Rhodes as young men, and the lessons of that encounter had not been forgotten. Even as Ottoman engineers surveyed the harbor, mapping angles of fire and siting gun platforms for the inevitable bombardment of Birgu and Senglea, Mustapha decided to try to cut the knot of his difficulties. On June 29, "at the hour of vespers," a small posse of horsemen approached the walls of Senglea, carrying a white flag. The leader, richly dressed in a brilliantly colored caftan, fired a gun in the air indicating that he wanted to parley. He was answered by a blast of cannon fire, which forced him to dodge smartly behind a rock. A single man was pushed forward and ran blindly for the walls, hoping not to be shot dead; this unfortunate was an old Spaniard who had been an Ottoman slave for thirty-two years and spoke Turkish. The knights took the man, blindfolded him, and led him to the grand master. He had been sent to repeat the offer made by Suleiman forty years earlier—that they could avoid inevitable death by accepting the offer of free passage to Sicily, "with all your people, your property and your artillery." La Valette promptly replied "in a terrible and severe voice," "Hang him!" The old man fell on his knees in terror, "saying that he was only a slave and that he had been forced to come with this message." La Valette let the wretched man go, with a word to the pashas that he would accept no envoys; the next man would be killed.

Behind this lay a clear lesson from Rhodes. La Valette understood that the low morale of the townspeople had been a crucial factor in the outcome in 1522. Any hint of negotiation could undermine resolve. Defeatist talk would be met by death. When a Maltese renegade started to call over the wall to his compatriots a few days later, La Valette forbade any response. There would be only silence and gunfire. In any event, Mustapha had already lost any last chance of detaching the sympathies of the Maltese at Saint Elmo, with the decapitated and crucified body of their priest floating in the bay. The whole civilian population, down to the women and children, was ready to tear their prisoners to bits.

Having failed to achieve a quick win, Mustapha pressed urgently forward. A decision was taken to seal off both peninsulas but to tackle Senglea first, the weaker of the two, then to crack the knights' main stronghold on Birgu. Senglea consisted of a fort at its landward end, Saint Michael, that defended the peninsula from the land and sheltered a small town. The promontory beyond was barren; there was a hill with two windmills on it, and where it tapered to a point in the harbor, there was a beaked fighting platform, called the Spur. Almost all of Senglea's defenses were unsatisfactory; the Saint Michael bastion with its unfinished rock-cut ditch was as deficient as Saint Elmo in the finer points of fortress design. The western, seaward side of the promontory around to the Spur at the end, which could easily be bombarded from the shore, contained no serious fortifications; only the eastern side was reasonably secure. It faced into the inner harbor and was protected by Birgu on the other side; the mouth of the harbor between Senglea and Birgu was sealed by a massive chain. But if Mustapha could find a seaborne way of attacking the westward side, the peninsula's doom would quickly be sealed.

IN FACT THE PASHA had conceived a bold strategy for taking Senglea, called by the Turks the Fortress of the Mill. Unfortunately, details of the plan were quickly leaked by a curious defection. The Ottoman forces contained a substantial number of Christian renegades—either voluntary or forcible converts—and the durable loyalty of these men, in such close proximity to their coreligionists, was to prove a continual problem. On the morning of Saturday June 30, Francisco Balbi, looking from the Spur on the end of Senglea across the harbor, saw a lone figure in cavalry armor waving furtively from the foreshore opposite. He indicated that he wanted a boat to come and collect him. No vessel could easily be dispatched without attracting attention; he was gestured to swim across. The man stripped off his armor, tied his shirt around his head, and struck out inexpertly across the water. Three sailors dived into the water from the Spur to help him across. They reached the exhausted man at the same moment that the Turks raised the alarm and ran down onto the beach. Covering fire from the

Christian side pinned the Turks back until the fugitive was dragged from the water, more dead than alive.

The defection was something of an intelligence coup—and a serious blow to Mustapha. The man's name was Mehmet Ben Davud but he had been born Philip Lascaris, the son of a noble Greek family from the Peloponnese. He was fifty-five years old and had been taken as a child by the Ottomans and converted to Islam; now, seeing the heroic defence of Saint Elmo, "his heart touched by the Holy Spirit," according to the pious chroniclers, he was resolved "to return to the Catholic Faith." Mehmet had been a soldier of some standing in the Ottoman camp and party to the pasha's innermost councils. He unfolded the details of Mustapha's plan to La Valette, point by point. In order to attack the westward flank of Senglea without having to sail ships into the harbor past the Christian guns, the pasha was planning to have his smaller boats dragged overland across the base of Mount Sciberras into the top of the creek beyond Senglea. This was invaluable information; the defenders set about planning energetic countermeasures. And while Mustapha was busy preparing his gun platforms for a furious bombardment of Senglea, he suffered a further indignity.

On the night of July 3, a long column of dark figures was making its way furtively across the Maltese landscape. They moved through the warm summer night without talking; just the occasional snort of a horse, muffled footsteps, the faint clink of armor; they picked their way through the maze of dusty lanes behind the Ottoman camp.

These seven hundred armed men were a small relief force dispatched in four galleys from Sicily by Don Garcia and put ashore secretly on the north of the island a few days earlier. The operation had been carefully planned with an elaborate system of fire signals and messages conveyed by Maltese runners dressed as Turks. In thick fog the force had been conducted to Mdina and secreted in the walled city. Their presence was successfully kept from the enemy, but only through lucky chance. A child looking out of a window on the ramparts spied a ghostly figure slipping away through the fog, and called out "Turks! Turks!" Horsemen hunted down the fleeing figure and dragged him back; a Greek slave, hoping to win his freedom, had set out to the Ottoman camp with the news. He was chopped to pieces.

The relief column reached the coast beyond Birgu before dawn for a prearranged rendezvous with boats sent by the grand master. The

*The assault on the walls of Saint Michael (I) and Senglea. The windmills are at the end (G);*
*into the harbor (X); the pontoon bridge (L) connecting Senglea to Birgu (B); the chief eunuch's*
*and M closing the inner harbor*

*the spur is just to the left of them. Also shown: Saint Elmo (H); the boats being hauled galley (K); just to the left, the hidden gun battery; Fort Saint Angelo (A); chains at E*

twenty-mile march had entailed a huge semicircular detour to avoid the Ottoman lines, but passed almost without mishap. Only one knight, Girolamo of Gravina, "heavily armed and very fat," had got detached from the party, along with a dozen soldiers laden with baggage. They were captured and hauled before Mustapha. The rest made a triumphant entry into Birgu by boat. It was a cheering moment for La Valette; the new contingent consisted mainly of professional soldiers from the garrison of Sicily under their commander Marshal de Robles. Among those who also came were La Valette's own nephew, and two English adventurers, the exiled Catholics John Smith and Edward Stanley.

When Mustapha learned the truth from Gravina, he was both stunned and furious. A row broke out with Piyale over culpability for this humiliating relief right under their noses. Mustapha thought it prudent to get his explanation to Suleiman in first; another ship was dispatched to Istanbul on July 4. The army was put to frantic work, finally sealing off Birgu and Senglea from all contact with the outside world. Henceforward the dispatch of messages became a risky business; Maltese swimmers slipped into the night sea with coded letters scrolled into cows' horns and stoppered with wax.

Meanwhile the inhabitants of Senglea were being subjected to all the measures they had witnessed at Saint Elmo. Wooden gun platforms were established in an arc around the two promontories; the guns were laboriously dragged back around from the high ground above Saint Elmo by teams of men and oxen, and were then sited and prepared to fire. The cannon fire that opened up in earnest on July 4 pounded the land walls of the Saint Michael fort and the exposed western shoreline; it was accompanied by sniper fire from the arquebusiers designed to pick off soldiers and laborers working to strengthen defenses against the coming attack. The bombardment was ceaseless. La Valette countered by sending the Muslim slaves out to work in exposed positions, chained together in pairs. It made no difference; Mustapha pressed on regardless—felling the reluctant workers from the heights above. Balbi found their plight pitiful. "These poor creatures became so exhausted by sheer fatigue from the continual toil that they could hardly stand. They cut off their own ears and even preferred getting killed to working any longer." A few days later a pair of chained slaves, caught in the firing line, called out in Turkish to their comrades over the walls to stop firing out of pity for their plight. The intent of their words was misunderstood by the Maltese, who guessed they were directing the gunners to the weak sections of wall. A mob of yelling women fell on the slaves, dragged them through the city streets, and stoned them to death.

On Friday, July 6, the intelligence of Philip Lascaris was proved correct. As if from nowhere, six boats appeared in the upper reaches of the harbor: they had been dragged the one thousand yards across the peninsula of Mount Sciberras on greased rollers by ox teams and floated into the upper basin. The next day there were six more. By July 10 there were sixty; by July 14 there were eighty. Mysteriously the boats in the bay also seemed to be getting bigger: somehow the sides were being built up to provide a protective superstructure against arquebus fire.

Both sides were engaged in ceaseless preparations: the Ottoman bombardment and skirmishing were unceasing—with just an eerie lull on July 8 for the Sacrifice Festival. On July 10 Mustapha's undue haste resulted in a spectacular accident. The barrels of the guns were not allowed to cool sufficiently between rounds. One of the guns cracked; a tongue of fire set the gunpowder store alight. "With an enormous flash and smoke, it blasted forty Turks into the air, and killed them."

In the workshops and smithies of Senglea and Birgu furious countermeasures were in process. Smiths and carpenters were busy making small shot and fuses for arquebuses, repairing guns, forging nails, constructing wooden defensive structures. Forewarned by Lascaris of the coming attack, La Valette had instigated two major engineering projects. A pontoon bridge of airtight barrels was assembled, ready to be floated into position in the inner harbor between Birgu and Senglea; it would connect the two settlements and allow troops to be quickly transferred from one to the other. Meanwhile Maltese shipwrights had come up with an ingenious defense for the vulnerable shoreline against shipborne attack. Wading out into the warm sea in the dark—the only safe time to work—they drove a long line of stakes constructed from ships' masts into the seabed about a dozen paces from the shore. Iron rings were attached to each stake and a chain passed through them to form a sturdy defensive barrier stretching the entire western shore of Senglea as far as the Spur, with the aim of stopping boats from riding up onto the beach.

This device instantly irritated the Ottoman high command, and the next day it became the focus of an extraordinary contest. At dawn four men armed with hatchets walked into the sea from the Ottoman shore, and swam underwater to the boom. Climbing up the poles, they managed to balance on top and started to hack away at the chain. At the same time, arquebuses put up a blanket of fire to prevent the defenders from shooting down the swimmers. The situation called for a swift response. A band of Maltese soldiers and sailors, stimulated by the promise of rewards, stripped off their clothes and struck out into the water. They were naked apart from their helmets and carried short swords clenched between their teeth. A furious swimming battle ensued; the naked men inefficiently thrashing and jabbing at each other, paddling with one hand and trying to land blows with the other. The blue water began to run pink with blood. One of the intruders was killed; the others retired wounded to the opposite shore. Another batch of swimmers returned that night to try a different strategy. They attached ships' cables to the stakes, which were run back to capstans on the shore. Teams of men strained to tighten the capstans and drag the stakes out of the water; again Maltese sailors swam out and chopped the cables.

Impatient and frustrated, Mustapha decided to press ahead with a final assault. The impetus had been accelerated by the arrival of Hasan, Turgut's son-in-law, the governor of Algiers, with twenty-eight ships and two thousand men thirsting for the fight and contemptuous of the army's efforts. The gunfire continued all day and all night, opening breaches in the land walls. La Valette had the pontoon swung into position between Senglea and Birgu; despite furious attempts, Ottoman gunfire failed to destroy it. Ammunition and incendiaries were distributed to the men waiting at their posts. There was no surprise about the impending assault. Mustapha's explicit plan was simply to mount a simultaneous attack by land and sea to overwhelm the defense—though the plan contained hidden details. Deserters from the Ottoman camp had also conveyed to the Christians Mustapha's intention to kill them all; only La Valette was to live. He would be delivered to Suleiman in chains. The grand master's response was a public vow never to be taken alive.

It was an uneasy night for the defenders, tensed at their posts. The moon shone brightly; Balbi waited with other men at the Spur with his arquebus. Across the harbor, he could hear the voices of the imams, rising and falling in the darkness, endlessly chanting the names of God.

SUNDAY, JULY 15, an hour and a half before dawn. A fire was lit on the hill behind Senglea; another answered from Saint Elmo across the water. The Algerians massed in the ditch beyond the land walls; Ottoman arquebusiers filed into trenches on the shore facing Senglea and sighted their guns; the artillery crews primed their cannon. Marshal de Robles and the fresh consignment from Sicily mustered on the walls. At the Spur, Francisco Balbi and his colleagues, commanded by the Spanish captain Francisco de Sanoguera, crouched behind their low earthworks ready to repel a seaborne attack. Over the bay in the dark, men were clambering noisily into invisible boats. The name of Allah rang out three times. Oars dipped and splashed as the small armada pushed off from the shore.

As dawn broke, the defenders on the shore could see the mass of ships moving slowly forward across the calm water. The low morning sun lit an extraordinary sight: hundreds of men packed into the boats bulwarked with bales of cotton and wool—janissaries with tall headdresses and flickering plumes, splendidly dressed Algerians in scarlet robes, "in cloth of gold and silver and scarlet damask," wearing exotic turbans and armed with "fine muskets of Fez, scimitars of Alexandria and Damascus, and magnificent bows." In the vanguard came three boatloads of turbaned holy men, "strangely dressed" according to the Christian accounts, "wearing green caps on their heads and many holding open books and chanting imprecations." They were reciting verses from the Koran to inspire the men to battle. The boats were adorned with a huge number of multicolored pennants and flags fluttering in the morning breeze; the sounds of castanets, horns, and tambourines floated ahead across the water. The whole incredible effect was being directed by the Greek corsair Candelissa, seated high up in a small caïque, waving a small flag like the leader of an orchestra. To the defenders it was an extraordinary sight, a scene of unearthly beauty, "if it had not been so dangerous."

As the Turks neared, the chanting stopped and the religious boats dropped back. The shore guns opened up and ripped through the fleet, killing many; "yet in spite of this they came on to the attack with immense courage and determination," with shouts and the crackle of arquebus fire. The rowers labored harder at the oars, picking up speed. At the Spur Balbi and his comrades awaited the shattering impact of the boats against the palisade.

Meanwhile, at the land walls, Hasan led the Algerians forward in a furious charge. Breaking from the ditch, they hurled themselves at the ramparts with their scaling ladders, eager to prove their courage. The defenders riddled them with shot; they were caught in a further hail of bullets from Spanish arquebusiers in flanking positions; hundreds were mown down, but by sheer weight of numbers they pressed on and managed to gain a foothold on the parapets. The whole front was in uproar. "I don't know if the image of hell can describe the appalling battle," wrote the chronicler Giacomo Bosio, "the fire, the heat, the continuous flames from the flamethrowers and fire hoops; the thick smoke, the stench, the disemboweled and mutilated corpses, the clash of arms, the groans, shouts, and cries, the roar of the guns ... men wounding, killing, scrabbling, throwing one another back, falling and firing." All the people of the sea struggling in confused combinations; shouts in Maltese, Spanish, Turkish, Italian, Arabic, Serbian, and Greek; flashes of fire and thick smoke; momentary drifting glimpses of individuals— the Franciscan friar, Brother Eboli, crucifix in one hand, sword in the other, going from post to post; an enraged janissary jumping up on the parapet and shooting a French knight in the head at point-blank range; Algerians encircled in hoops of fire running screaming into the sea. But the attackers were hindered by the narrowness of the terrain, and, despite their ardor, Hasan eventually withdrew his men. Without a pause, the aga of the janissaries ordered forward the regular troops. A second wave hurled itself at the walls.

Back on the seashore, the boats were gathering speed and crashed into the fence; it withstood the shock and the men were forced into the water, wading in their robes toward the beach, shouting and firing. The defenders were ready for this moment; they had prepared and loaded two mortars to sweep the beach, but so rapid was the Ottoman advance that the mortars were never fired. Unopposed, the attackers made for the Spur at the end of the promontory, whose only protection was a low embankment.

The captain of the Spur, Sanoguera, had just rallied his men to push the intruders back "with pikes, swords, shields, and stones," when their defense was thrown into sudden confusion. A sailor mishandled a lit incendiary; it exploded in his hand, and set fire to the whole stock, burning men to death around him. In the smoke and confusion, the Turks scrambled up and planted their flags on the parapet. Sanoguera ran in person to stem the tide; balancing on the parapet in a suit of rich armor, he made a tempting target against the sky. A bullet pinged harmlessly off his breastplate; then a janissary, "wearing a large black headdress with gold ornaments on it, knelt at the foot of the battery, aimed upwards at him and shot him in the groin." The captain fell dead on the spot. Both sides ran forward to try to seize the corpse—from below they had him by the legs, above by the arms. After a grimly ludicrous tussle, the defenders secured the prize and dragged the body back. The Turks reluctantly abandoned their prize, "but before giving up they removed the shoes from his feet." The enemy was so close and so numerous that Balbi and his colleagues dropped their guns and started to bombard the intruders with rocks.

It was at this moment, while the defenders were heavily engaged by land and sea, that Mustapha played his trump card. He had kept back ten large boats and about a thousand crack troops—janissaries and marines. Almost unnoticed, these boats, crammed with men, pushed off from the other side, heading around the tip of the Spur to the small part of the promontory outside the chain that was not protected by the palisade. Here there were no defenses; the ramparts were extremely low; a landing would be easy. These men had come to do or die; to increase their appetite for battle, they had been selected from those unable to swim. The boats passed quietly beyond the furious carnage on the beach, ready to turn in to the shore. Two hundred yards beyond their objective lay the end of the tip of the second peninsula of Birgu.

However, in planning this diversionary attack, the high command had missed a crucial detail. At the tip of the peninsula of Birgu, opposite the intended Ottoman landing spot, the defenders had positioned a concealed gun battery, almost at water level. As the boats came on, the commander of the post realized to his surprise that the intruders had no idea he was there. Stealthily he loaded his five cannon with a lethal mixture of grapeshot: bags of stones, pieces of chain, and spiked iron balls—unblocked his gun ports, and waited with bated breath. Incredulously, the boats had still not seen him. He held his fire until they were sitting ducks, impossible to miss, then put the taper to the cannon. A murderous hail of bullets ripped across the surface of the water and shredded the boats. Totally surprised, the men were either massacred by the blizzard of fire or tipped into the sea. Nine of the ten boats shattered and sank immediately; those who were not killed outright drowned off the point. The tenth boat somehow limped home. At a stroke, hundreds of crack troops were floating dead in the water.

The fighting went on fiercely at the wall and the beach. Candelissa the Greek, offshore, spurred his men on with news that Hasan's men had breached the land wall; it was not true, but the position there was still critical. Anxiously, La Valette called up reinforcements over the bridge from Birgu. Half went to turn the tide at the land wall; seeing these fresh men on the ramparts, the aga of the janissaries started to withdraw his troops. The Turks retreated, carrying their dead with them and launching a last furious cannonade that felled a number of knights. The rest of La Valette's reinforcements went to prop up the situation on the seashore. Among them was the son of Don Garcia de Toledo, the viceroy of Sicily, against La Valette's orders. He was killed almost immediately by a musket shot.

The first the men on the beach knew about the Ottoman retreat from the land walls was the arrival of a crowd of young Maltese hurling stones at the boats from slingshots, and crying out "Relief! Victory!" The seaborne attack force suddenly realized that the tide had turned against them. Worse, they had been deceived by Candelissa. Howling curses at "the Greek traitor," they turned to run to the water's edge. Panic broke out, confusion, horror, fear, disorder. There was a furious scramble to re-embark; the few boats close to the shore were overturned by the scrabbling horde; those who could not swim, sank, entrapped in their robes. Worse still, the majority of boats had withdrawn from the beach. The landing party was now cut off. They signaled frantically for the rescue fleet to return.

Sensing the moment, the defenders burst onto the beach, stabbing and jabbing at the Muslims flailing in the shallows. Balbi and his comrades calmly stood back and shot the wretched men one after another. Some, preferring to drown, threw themselves despairingly into the water; others dropped their weapons, fell to the ground, and begged for mercy. It was not given; with the memory of Saint Elmo still vivid, the Christians streamed forward, howling "Kill! Kill! Pay for Saint Elmo, you bastards!" Among them, the enraged Federico Sangorgio, too young to be bearded, hacked and slashed without remorse, remembering the mutilated corpse of his brother. "And so, without any pity, they dispatched them."

Offshore, the boats still hung back, hesitant and uncertain what to do, receiving contradictory orders. Piyale was fearful for his ships. He climbed onto his horse and galloped down, ordering them not to move—but he was sprawled in the dust by a passing cannonball, which blew off his turban and left him deafened. Mustapha, the land general, watching the ghastly slaughter unfold, countermanded. He ordered the boats back to rescue his soldiers, but they were hit by the battery at the point of Birgu and quickly withdrew again.

To the Christian chroniclers, the scene in the water resembled carnage on a biblical scale, "like the Red Sea with Pharaoh's army overwhelmed by the waves": a brilliantly colored viscid mass of military paraphernalia—flags, banners, tents, shields, spears, and quivers floated on the surface so densely that it seemed more "like a field where a battle had been fought"—and here and there, wriggling like fish on a market slab, the living and half-living, the writhing and bloody, the maimed and dying.

The Maltese waded into this ghastly soup finishing off the survivors and stripping the corpses. They plundered extraordinary garments from the dead, and beautiful weapons. They grabbed inlaid scimitars and finely worked arquebuses chased with gold and silver that gleamed brightly in the sun—and other things that signaled the intentions to capture and occupy the place: large quantities of food, ropes for binding prisoners, even prepared letters to send to Istanbul announcing the victory. Mustapha had been supremely confident. The looters also recovered a sizeable quantity of money—for each man carried his wealth about his person—and "a great deal of hashish."

Only four men were taken alive. They were brought before the grand master for interrogation, then turned over to the people. Cries of "Saint Elmo's pay!" rang through the narrow streets as they were dragged away. Four thousand dead lay sprawled at the walls and drifted gently in the sea. Bodies washed up on the shore for days.

# CHAPTER 13

# Trench Wars

July 16 to August 25, 1565

T HE FOLLOWING DAY Suleiman dispatched an order to Mustapha:

> I sent you over to Malta a long time ago in order to conquer
> it. But I have not received any message from you. I have decreed
> that as soon as my order reaches you, you should inform me
> about the siege of Malta. Has Turgut, the governor of Tripoli,
> arrived there and has he been any help to you? What about the
> enemy navy? Have you managed to conquer any part of Malta?
> You should write to me telling me everything.

Suleiman sent a copy of this letter to the doge of Venice with the
peremptory demand to "make sure that it reaches Mustapha Pasha
without delay. And you should send me news as to what has happened
there."

The sultan was not the only one anxious about Malta. Christian
eyes were focusing on the island's plight with ever-increasing apprehension. The Western Mediterranean was busy with messenger ships
tracking to and fro with rumors, news, advice, warnings, and plans.
From his headquarters on Birgu, La Valette kept up a steady flow of
correspondence with Don Garcia de Toledo on Sicily, but after the fall
of Saint Elmo, it became increasingly difficult to get messengers
through. Maltese swimmers, dressed as Turks, crossed the harbor and
slipped through the enemy lines to Mdina, then traveled by small boat
via Gozo to Sicily. It became dangerous work; sometimes La Valette
dispatched four copies of the same letter in the hope that one would get
through. Piyale's ships patrolled the straits, running these vessels
down. The messengers threw their letters into the sea and gave themselves up to death; even when the messages were taken, Mustapha re-

mained unable to break the codes, and the lines of communication, though parlous, were kept open.

There was live terror down the coasts of Italy as the news worsened and Saint Elmo fell. No one was more clear-eyed about the consequences of defeat than Pope Pius IV. "We realise," he wrote, "in how great peril the well-being of Sicily and Italy will be put, and what great calamities threaten the Christian people, if (which God forbid!) the island ... should come under the domination of the impious enemy." Rome was acknowledged to be the ultimate target of Ottoman warfare. In Pius's fevered imagination the Turk was almost at the gates. He gave orders that he should be woken at any hour of the night to hear dispatches from Sicily; he had already resolved to die in the city rather than flee.

As comprehension of the stakes at Malta spread across Europe, a trickle of adventurers and Knights of Saint John from the Order's farther outposts headed for Sicily to join the rescue attempt. Europe held its collective breath and watched with apprehension. Even Protestant England said prayers for Catholic Malta.

But the bid to relieve the island was progressing at a snail's pace. La Valette wrote with frosty politeness and increasing urgency to Don Garcia—and cursed him under his breath. Why was there no follow-up to the small detachment sent at the end of June? The morale of the civilians was at breaking point and a relief would be simple; only ten thousand men would be sufficient to shatter the Turks who were "mostly a rabble and a wholly inexperienced soldiery." Don Garcia, as King Philip's man on the spot, was being accused of hesitation and overcaution; he would become, in time, the target of round condemnation for the island's prolonged suffering.

It was unjustified. The problem lay not in Sicily but in Madrid. Don Garcia was an immensely experienced and shrewd campaigner with a keen grasp of the issues. He had framed the problem of Malta early on and laid the issues before Philip with exceptional clarity. Malta was a challenge to Spain's mastery of the whole sea; it was essential to act— and to act decisively. He begged for men and resources to do so. "If Malta is not helped," he wrote on May 31, "I consider it lost." He urged Philip to confront the issue now. Don Garcia was no casual bystander to the fate of Malta. He had given a son to the siege, who was dead before Don Garcia received a reply. Philip's responses were cautious. The king was haunted by the memory of Djerba and frightened by the size of the Ottoman fleet. His own fleet had been rebuilt at great cost after Djerba—Philip had no intention of losing it a second time. He gave explicit orders to Don Garcia that no risk was to be taken with his ships and that nothing should be done without his say-so. Don Garcia was charged with conserving the king's fleet as carefully as Piyale guarded the sultan's: "Its loss would be greater than the loss of Malta. ... If Malta was lost, which God forbid, there would be other means to return and recover it." It was not a view widely shared at the center of the sea. The Prudent King gave permission for the collection of troops but no permission to use them.

All the divisions of Christendom were once again being cruelly exposed. Pope Pius was beside himself with indignation at Philip's response. The king's fleet had been, in large part, paid for by papal subsidies; it was intended for the defense of all Christendom. The pope got the Spanish cardinals to remind Philip that "if he had not aided your Majesty with the subsidy for the galleys, today you would not have an oar at sea which might defend us against the Turks." The king remained evasive and cautious; Don Garcia could help the island, as long as he risked no danger to the fleet. Forward progress was not helped by the lengthy response times: it took, at best, six weeks for a letter from Sicily to reach Madrid and for a reply to be received. Meanwhile the viceroy pressed forward with the collection of men and ships and kept up the lobbying of officials in Philip's court. By early August Don Garcia was ready to mount an expedition, but he still did not have permission to use his ships, and every day the situation was becoming more parlous.

Despite the catastrophe at the Spur on July 15, Mustapha pursued the siege vigorously, as if he could sense the sultan's distant displeasure. He abandoned any other attempt on the fortress of Malta by sea. Henceforward he would pursue an attritional siege in the style of Saint Elmo—heavy bombardment, relentless trenching, and surprise attacks to catch the defenders off guard—and he would concentrate his resources on the short land fronts of both Birgu and Senglea simultaneously.

It was the first time that Birgu had come under heavy attack. This second peninsula was the urban heart of the island and the knights' ul-

timate stronghold. The landward side was protected by substantial fortifications in the shape of the two weighty protruding bastions of Saint
John and Saint James—the protecting saints of the Order and of Spain.
The promontory that lay behind this bulwark was a densely packed
town, a warren of narrow streets that tapered to a point in the separate
fortress of Saint Angelo. This stout little castle, separated from the
mainland by a sea moat and drawbridge, was designed as a fallback position in the event of a last stand.

By July 22 Mustapha had all his cannon concentrated in batteries
on the heights above the harbor. At dawn of that day, sixty-four guns in
fourteen batteries started to hit the defenses of Birgu and Senglea.
These delivered "a bombardment so continuous and extraordinary that
it was both astounding and frightening." To Balbi it seemed like the
end of the world. The people of Sicily needed no reminding that war had
reached their doorstep. They could hear the rumble of gunfire in Syracuse and Catania, a hundred and twenty miles to the north. The weight
and penetration of this bombardment was extraordinary; the guns
could search the whole of Birgu, destroying houses, killing the people
within, reducing the fortifications to rubble. Men were blown away behind the apparent security of a twenty-one-foot-thick earth rampart.
The bombardment continued for five days and nights without ceasing.
Ottoman engineers had quickly identified the weakest point in Birgu's
land defenses—the post of Castile, the section of wall at the eastern
end down to the sea, that could not easily be defended by cross fire.
They singled it out for special treatment in preparation for a major
attack.

During the hot days of July a furious contest developed along the
land defenses of Birgu and Senglea between two well-matched opponents. Mustapha could draw on a lifetime's experience of capturing
fortresses and all the practical engineering skills and human resources
of Ottoman warfare. La Valette, the stern disciplinarian who gave no
quarter, brought a matching understanding of defense against impossible odds. The old man knew that he was making a last stand—not just
for himself but for the Order to which he had given his life. Mustapha
Pasha could feel Suleiman's gaze bearing down; the tiled kiosks of Istanbul seemed close indeed. The sultan's banner fluttered in the camp;
Suleiman's own men, the *chaushes*, sent back their reports to the sultan.
Neither leader could afford to lose; both were personally prepared to

*The bombardment of Birgu (B); a troop of janissaries in their plumed headdresses (O);*
*Mustapha (L) and Piyale (N) watching from horseback*

risk their lives in the front line. The contest between the two was as much a test of mental strength as military skill.

Despite the capability to reduce the fortifications to mountains of rubble, Mustapha was beset by difficulties, not least by the miniature scale of the battlefield. The front at Birgu was one thousand yards wide; that at Senglea less. No matter how many thousand men he had, only a fraction could be deployed at any one time. A small number of defenders, well armored and protected by makeshift walls and ramparts, could fight at no particular disadvantage. He was worried too by muffled reports from spies and captives of the buildup of men and ships thirty miles away in Sicily. And by the height of summer, he had sickness in the camp. No army of the time took such care with the hygiene and organization of its encampments as the Ottomans, but Malta was unfavorable terrain. The army had had to camp in low-lying marshy land around the available water sources, which the knights had taken care to contaminate. In the sweltering summer heat, in a landscape strewn with unburied corpses, the men started to succumb to typhoid and dysentery. Time was pressing down on the Ottoman commanders.

Mustapha proceeded with all speed to try to break the defense. In the first few days after defeat at the Spur, attempts were made to cross Senglea's ditch with a bridge of masts. The defenders made several attempts to burn it—the grand master's nephew, hideously visible in rich armor, was shot dead in one incautious assault—but ultimately they were successful. Undeterred, Mustapha put his miners to work tunneling through the solid rock to lay explosives charges, covering the noise of the work with gunfire. Only luck saved Senglea; on July 28 "by the will of God," the miners were probing with a spear to see how close they were to the surface, when the men on the wall spotted the spear tip protruding from the ground. They dug countermines and burst into the tunnel, hurling incendiaries and chasing the miners out. The shaft was blocked up. Mustapha was visibly discouraged by this failure—it had represented a huge effort, but the battle of wits went on. When the Ottomans bombarded the streets, La Valette had stone walls built across them. When the arquebusiers started to pick off laborers repairing the ramparts, Marshal de Robles screened his men with ships' sails that forced the marksmen to shoot blind. Attempts to fill in the ditches were countered by night sorties to clear them out. As the outer defenses collapsed under cannon fire, the defenders responded by constructing retrenchments—makeshift fallback barriers of earth and stone—to staunch the crumbling front line, demolishing houses for building materials. In the rubble-strewn wasteland each side attempted to maintain positions of cross fire and to build barriers to protect their own men. Siege warfare required huge quantities of human labor, but the Ottomans had the resources to work on an immense scale: digging tunnels, erecting walls, snaking forward covered trenches, moving earth, and repositioning cannon. And Mustapha drew on a wide vocabulary of stratagems: he moved his guns from place to place, mounted sudden attacks at mealtimes or in the dead of night, inflicted nerveshredding bombardments in irregular patterns, sometimes targeting precise sectors of wall, sometimes randomly shelling the town behind to frighten the civilian population, repeatedly attempting to distract or undermine morale with requests to parley.

There seemed no limit to these variations. When the Ottomans launched a concerted attack on August 2 it was accompanied by a heavy bombardment. While the defenders were forced to keep their heads down, the enemy troops mysteriously advanced unhindered by their own gunfire and started to climb the walls. It took some time for the hard-pressed defenders to realize that the guns were firing only blanks. They regrouped and repulsed the assault.

La Valette maintained an iron grip on the organization of the defense. Determined not to be surprised, he instructed the morning Angelus bell to be rung two hours before sunrise, rather than the usual one; men were summoned by drumbeat and stood down by the ringing of bells; stockpiles of ammunition were maintained at all critical points; ad hoc incendiaries—sacks coated with pitch and filled with cotton and gunpowder—were kept at hand; sacks of earth were gathered for making running repairs, pots of pitch kept bubbling. The grand master was seen everywhere, accompanied by two pages carrying his helmet and pike, and by a jester whose duties included informing him of what was happening at various posts and "trying to amuse him with his quips— although there was little enough to laugh about."

For both sides it was critical to maintain morale. The Ottomans ran all their campaigns on a well-understood system of rewards and punishments. The naval registers for the Malta campaign clearly documented the bravery of the men and their rewards: "Omer has performed outstanding service by capturing one of the infidels of the Mdina fortress during the night. . . . Mehmet Ben Mustapha captured the banner of the infidels in the battle of the St Elmo fortress and chopped off some heads. . . . Pir Mehmet has rendered outstanding service by cutting off many heads. . . . It has been decreed that a post should be given to him." The knights gave prizes in a more ad hoc way for acts of courage. Andreas Muñatones, who had led the charge down the tunnel to repel the miners, was rewarded with a gold chain; three arquebusiers who had distinguished themselves during the attack on August 2 were granted an extra ten scudi above their pay; Romegas offered a hefty hundred scudi out of his own pocket for any man who could capture a Turk alive out of the trenches.

Man-taking was critical; gathering intelligence was an endless preoccupation for both sides. Under torture, a captured Turk revealed on July 18 that there was now genuine apprehension in the Ottoman camp about the gradual buildup on Sicily. A few days later Piyale slipped a light sailing vessel into Syracuse manned by Italian renegades to try to confirm the story. Discord broke out between the two Ottoman commanders about how to proceed. Piyale, renouncing responsibility for the land siege, put the fleet to sea to scour the approaches for signs of a gathering armada; this caused a ripple of fear among the army that they were being abandoned. It was several days before the differences were patched up. Piyale returned to the siege at Birgu in an increasingly competitive atmosphere; it became a question of honor among the two pashas who could breach the walls first. Behind this lay a long catalogue of mutual grievances about personal honor, tactics, and use of the fleet. Piyale considered himself to have been snubbed while Turgut was alive, and held the general to favor his own troops over the fleet when it came to rewards. Niggling disputes affected group morale, according to the chronicler Pechevi: "When the admiral was firing his cannon, his gunners were told, 'Don't fire now, the general's having his siesta.'" The sailors' response was to shrug. How much care and effort should they bother to put in? They blamed Mustapha for creating these disagreements.

The news of these ruptures and the faltering Ottoman morale was extremely valuable to La Valette, but he had problems of his own. The people had been reassured that help was on its way; it was widely believed that relief would come on July 25, the feast day of Saint James, the patron saint of Spain. When nothing materialized, La Valette felt compelled to make a ringing speech to the people, urging everyone to put their faith in God. He had worries about water supplies too; there were riots in the streets. His letters to Don Garcia had by now taken a more pessimistic turn: "He doubted that the water would hold out, they were being led to ultimate and irreducible ruin." As it transpired, the water shortage was providentially solved; a flowing spring was discovered in the cellar of a house in Birgu that met the needs of a large part of the populace. The grand master gave his public thanks to God, as he did for every successful skirmish or battle won, but the constant bombardment, "like a moving earthquake," was taking its relentless toll. In this atmosphere the two pashas redoubled their furious assaults; the defenders continued to retrench and snipe.

Outside the beleaguered forts, there was a second, guerrilla war in play. Daily a small band of cavalry rode out from Mdina to ambush stragglers and spy on the Ottoman camp. The leader of this tiny force was an Italian knight called Vincenzo Anastagi, a man of intelligence and enterprise, destined to a small immortality after the siege in a portrait by El Greco—and a violent end, murdered twenty years later by two of his fellow knights. Anastagi snatched up stragglers from the camp for interrogation and planted Turkish-speaking spies inside it. From a distance he studied the daily activities of the huge tented encampment and came to the conclusion that it possessed no defenses in its rear. "These we found in the same condition as have been described many times," he wrote in a letter to Sicily, "that is, built only to defend themselves from the gunshots of our forts, without trenches behind them or at the sides, and that they sleep without sentinels." At the same time he realized by late July that the Ottomans were planning a final massive assault to end the siege. For seven nights in a row, the Mdina cavalry holed up in a dry valley a mile from the camp and watched. On the eighth night, August 6, they could hear a large body of men leaving the camp in the dark. Anastagi's men reined in their horses and waited.

MONDAY, AUGUST 6, had not been a good day for La Valette. During the dinner hour, when all was relatively quiet on the Birgu ramparts, a Spanish soldier called Francisco de Aguilar sidled up to the post of Aragon, close to the sea. He was wearing the plumed upturned steel casque of an arquebusier and carried his gun over his shoulder. He had come, he said, to snipe at the enemy. He lit the slow-match of the weapon and studied the terrain for targets in the trenches below. "I can't see any of these dogs!" he called back to the sentry. Then, while no one was watching, he suddenly jumped down into the ditch and started to run at full speed for the Ottoman lines. There was a warning shout, volleys of shot from the walls behind, but the man was already in the enemy's advanced trench, where he was welcomed with joy, and immediately taken to Mustapha Pasha.

This defection was extremely serious. Aguilar was a highly rated and trusted man. He was well informed. He had often been present at discussions between Marshal de Robles and La Valette: he had heard a great deal of confidential discussion about the plight of the defenders—frank talks about the fortifications, details of the guards' daily routines, weapon supplies, and tactics. All this was now in Mustapha's hands.

La Valette immediately set about preparing the defenses against an attack, aware that Mustapha could target the weakest sectors of wall with precision. Incendiary devices were stockpiled at key points; planks with studded nails positioned; cauldrons of pitch readied. The grand master planned to wait with a mobile relief force in the city's square to confront whatever dangers arose.

During the following night, the Ottomans bombarded Birgu and Senglea with fury and mustered their men for the attack. They had emptied the camp and ships of all their fighting men. Columns of men were ferried around from the harbor and landed to the east of Birgu. Anastagi's cavalry, two miles away, waited with their horses in the dark, listening to the pounding of the guns, and watched the camp.

An hour before dawn, Mustapha and Piyale launched a simultaneous massed attack on the two promontories. Eight thousand men converged on Senglea, four thousand on Birgu. The assault opened with the accustomed procedures: the chanting in the dark, the beating of drums, the terrifying shouts. The blackness was lit by the roar of arquebus fire and the flash of incendiary devices, fire hoops, flamethrowers, and cauldrons of boiling pitch. There was confused shouting, church bells clanging, the crashing of cymbals. In the growing light, the defenders could make out a figure brilliantly dressed in red silk scrambling over the ruined parapets, banner in hand. It was Candelissa the Greek, roundly accused by the Turks of cowardice at the Spur, leading the attack with the vow to plant the first banner on the ramparts. He was too visible to miss. The defenders quickly felled him with an arquebus shot; there followed the usual furious scrap for the body. Despite this setback and a terrible casualty rate, the weight of Ottoman numbers gradually began to tell. The defense became more ragged.

On the adjacent front at Birgu, Piyale's men were battling their way into the post of Castile, whose outer defenses had been reduced to hills of rubble by days of concerted gunfire. The Ottomans established themselves on the ramparts and began to plant flags. Word reached La Valette in the square that the situation had turned critical. Taking his helmet and pike from his pages, he hurried to the scene with the mobile relief force, shouting "This is the day to die." The captains at Castile tried to hold him back; they forcibly restrained him from climbing onto the cavalier, where the enemy was already established. Moving to another position, "pike in hand, as if he were a common soldier," he grabbed an arquebus from a soldier and started firing.

By this time, the Ottomans had succeeded in planting the sultan's own royal standard on the walls; the white horsetail surmounted with a golden ball became the center of a furious contest. "Seeing it," wrote Francisco Balbi, "we hurled hooked lines to try and get hold of it, and at last managed to do so. As a result of our pulling one way, and the Turks pulling the other, the ball on top of the shaft fell off, which enabled them to save the sultan's standard, but not before we had burned many of its silk and golden tassels with incendiaries."

The battle raged on. As each wave of Ottoman soldiers fell back, it was replaced with another. Key people on both sides were taken out of the fight. Munatones, the hero of the tunnels, was wounded in the right hand and died later. Ali Portuch Bey, the governor of Rhodes, was killed. La Valette was hit in the leg and was finally persuaded to withdraw. "The assaults on this day were most daring and well fought on both sides with great bitterness and much bloodshed," wrote Balbi. The scene on the battlefield was ghastly; there were many "without heads, without arms and legs, incinerated or with their limbs torn to bits." Sensing that the battle was reaching its height, Anastagi's cavalry picked their way stealthily across the fields toward the Ottoman camp. As they drew near, they broke into a charge.

NEITHER OF THE PASHAS had any intention of quitting the field without victory. There was intense competition to win the day. If the men faltered from the killing field, they were cudgeled forward again by military police. Within the walls, the defenders were weakening. They had been fighting unrested for nine hours. Though La Valette had ensured supplies of bread and watered wine to fortify the men, and the civilian population, both women and children, joined the fray, the situation was deteriorating. The Ottoman commanders could sense the end was near.

And then quite suddenly, and for no visible reason, the attack faltered. The men in the ditch at Castile suddenly turned tail and fled; those at Senglea joined them. They streamed away from the battle, being shot down from behind. No threats or blows from their officers could prevent this sudden flight. If the men on the ramparts were baffled by this turn of events, Mustapha Pasha was even more so. Mounted on his horse, he struggled to get control of the army and to draw it up again out of rifle shot. The word got around that Don Garcia's relief force had landed on the island and fired the camp. There was a muffled uproar, and smoke could be seen rising from the tents. Panic spread throughout the Ottoman army; every man, woman, and child in the beleaguered citadels climbed onto the ramparts and stared down at the deserted trenches in disbelief. Then they started to shout: "Victory and relief!"

Both sides were wrong. It was not a powerful Spanish army from Sicily. Anastagi's small force of cavalry—perhaps no more than a hundred, a mixed force of knights and Maltese militia—had swept down on the unguarded camp. Only the sick and wounded had been left behind, with a limited band of sentries and supply staff. The horsemen swung into camp, sabres swinging, with the force of vengeance. They rampaged through, massacring the sick, cutting down sentries, burning tents, ruining supplies, spreading a blind panic that infected the whole army. Then they were gone again back to Mdina before Mustapha could react, leaving the Ottoman high command furious and humiliated. Another bitter row broke out between Mustapha and Piyale.

Malta survived on August 7 purely through Anastagi's lucky strike. The island was hanging on by the skin of its teeth. A Te Deum was sung in the church of Saint Lawrence, followed by a procession. There was weeping in the streets. But when the defenders saw the state of the walls, there was deep concern that the end could not be far off. To scotch rumors that the knights would retreat into the fortress of Saint Angelo at the tip of Birgu and leave the civilian population to their fate,

La Valette took decisive action. The flinty old man had all the precious icons of the Order carried to the fortress and the drawbridge raised. The whole population would fight on together at the ruined walls; the icons could make a last stand on their own.

The next day, Mustapha decided to deal with the Mdina cavalry. It was a decision he should have taken at the start of the siege, and failure to do so had cost him dearly. Piyale was tasked with wiping them out. A careful ambush was prepared; a detachment of troops was sent out to raid cattle grazing on the plain outside the city. When the Christian cavalry rode out to see the raiders off, they found their return barred by large formations of Ottoman infantry. It took a fierce fight and the loss of some thirty men and horses for the men to scramble back to the city, some on foot making it back only the next day. Piyale's men then advanced on the city. As they drew near, they were surprised to see a large number of soldiers on the battlements. The Ottomans had believed the place to be weak and poorly defended; instead the walls were crawling with troops who unleashed a torrent of gunfire, beat their drums, and rang the church bells. Piyale's advance may have been opportunist rather than planned—they had brought no heavy cannon with them—but they decided to withdraw. The Ottomans were running out of time; there was little spare energy to attend seriously to Mdina. They marched back to camp. The "army" on the walls breathed a sigh of relief; a large part of it was composed of civilians—peasants and their wives, even children, dressed in spare uniforms and parading on the ramparts.

When the captives from this ambush were marched before Mustapha, he heard some unwelcome news. Don Garcia had dropped Don Salazar, an experienced captain, onto the island the day before to reconnoiter the situation before mounting a full-scale rescue bid. Mustapha played down this morsel of information but realized its significance. Time was running out, and he was under pressure from all sides. On August 12 he received the letter Suleiman had written on July 16. With it came an oral account from a herald, outlining the sultan's mood: he was uttering terrible threats in the case of defeat, which would be "to the affront to the sultan's name and his unconquerable sword." Victory would bring matching rewards. Mustapha was evidently keeping his head down, unwilling to send Suleiman bad news. When the sultan wrote again on August 25, he still had had no direct word from his general.

The tone was more insistent: "The *chaush* Abdi, who had brought some good news about the conquest of certain towers in the harbour of the fortress of Malta, has been sent back to you. But up to now I have had no news from you. I have decreed that you should send me some information on the siege of Malta. Have you got enough provisions and weapons for the soldiers? Is the day of conquest of the Malta fortress near? Have you sighted any enemy navy? You should send me some information on the situation of the enemy navy and our navy. Up to now I have sent you seven ships carrying provisions. Did they arrive? Send me some messages."

Both Suleiman and his general were seriously concerned about Don Garcia's buildup. When Piyale snatched some men from the Sicilian coast on August 17, the pashas realized that a formidable rescue operation was in progress. Day and night Piyale's galleys were patrolling the island, firing shots across the Malta channel to intimidate the Christians. Anastagi had been tracking their movements from the shore and found this guard duty perfunctory; morale was obviously low. "I have often left guards to discover what they are doing. . . . They always leave at one hour in the night. At times we saw a fire ten miles out to sea which we believe belonged to them and that they do it to put their mind at rest; this is all the guarding they do."

Both commanders were struggling for morale. La Valette gave out that relief was on its way, Mustapha that it was small and badly equipped, but the pasha's problems were growing by the day. The men were being thinned out daily by war and disease; supplies of gunpowder and munitions were short; it was becoming harder and harder to force men out of the trenches to run to certain death. Mind games became more ingenious; on the night of August 18, thirty Ottoman galleys sailed out to sea under cover of darkness with a large number of men on board. The next day they reappeared, pretending to be a new relief of crack troops. The men were dressed up as janissaries and sipahis, welcoming cannon were fired, and flags planted on Mount Sciberras to show this huge new force to the defenders. Mustapha knew from the deserter Aguilar that the defense must be close to breaking. He pressed on with the siege.

Throughout August, slogging trench warfare continued around the post of Castile. The Ottomans attempted to snake trenches forward,

This miniature shows Hayrettin Barbarossa in Istanbul,
receiving instructions from Suleiman to rebuild the Ottoman fleet
and wreak havoc on the realms of Charles V.

Charles V, the stern and resolute emperor of war, by Titian.
Charles spent large sums commissioning images of martial and imperial power.

Charles's expedition to Tunis in 1535 to destroy Barbarossa: his galleys
advance in waves to bombard the outer port of La Goletta. Tunis is beyond
the lake, where Barbarossa's fleet is bottled up.

Winter 1543: Barbarossa's lean predatory galleys in Toulon harbor
terrified his nominal allies, the French, almost as much as his enemies.

The Ottoman sultans' triumphs at sea were celebrated in books
of exquisite miniatures. Here Ottoman galleys row into battle,
with bow guns firing and flags flying.

Admirals and enemies: Hayrettin Barbarossa and Andrea Doria as aged men.

The start of the siege of Malta: on May 27, 1565, the Ottoman army
converges on Saint Elmo. White turbans swarm up the Sciberras Peninsula;
to the right, miners and siege engineers lug up materials and tools; to the left,
shrouded corpses are carried off into tents; center foreground, the pashas
discuss tactics, flanked by janissaries with arquebuses.

A reconstruction of the land front of Saint Elmo, seen from
the Ottoman trenches. The cavalier looms over the fort from behind.

RECONSTRUCTION BY DR. STEPHEN SPITERI

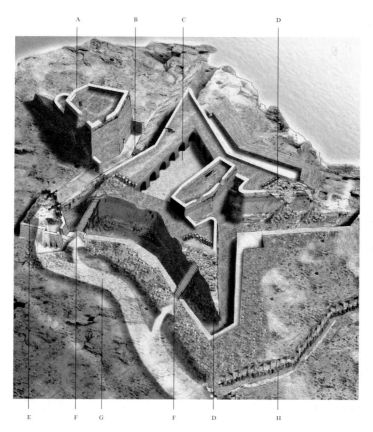

An aerial reconstruction of Saint Elmo under attack: A) the cavalier,
B) drawbridge into the fort, C) central parade ground, D) the points of the stars
pounded into rubble, E) the ravelin, captured on June 3 and furnished with two guns,
F) Ottoman bridges, G) route of the Ottoman assault, H) the forward Ottoman trench.

RECONSTRUCTION BY DR. STEPHEN SPITERI

August 7, 1565: the moment of supreme crisis for Christian Malta.
Ottoman arquebusiers in turbans and white headdresses try to storm the post of
Castile and plant their flags on the wall. They are met by counterfire from the
well-armed knights. La Valette stands, suicidally visible, at center foreground.

A nineteenth-century print of the fall of Famagusta. Bragadin,
tied to an ancient column that stands to this day, is prepared for
a ghastly death. Lala Mustapha Pasha watches from a balcony.

The victorious commanders at Lepanto: from left, the dashing Don Juan of Austria, Marc'Antonio Colonna, and Sebastiano Venier, the gruff Venetian lion.

The tomb of Barbarossa on the shores of the Bosphorus.

A modern reconstruction of the *Real*, Don Juan's flagship, showing the highly decorated stern.

"It's as if men were extracted from their own bodies and transported to another world": Vicentino's great painting of Lepanto summons up the smoke, noise, confusion, and shattering impacts of the battle. Violent death is meted out randomly by guns, arrows, pikes, swords, and the sea itself. The water is matted with corpses. Ali Pasha on the *Sultana*, center, rallies his men to fight to the finish.

prepare mines, mount diversionary attacks, and scale walls. They laid down a blanket of fire for days at a time. The Christians responded with surprise sallies and constant observation. Both sides lodged snipers behind makeshift barricades and hunted their enemy. It was almost a form of sport, "an enjoyable game hunt." On August 12 the Ottomans shot dead Marshal de Robles, one of the iconic heroes of the defense, who had been peering incautiously over a parapet without his bulletproof helmet. The defenders took to smearing their bullets with fat; as the bullets hit their victims, they also set the Turks' robes alight. When the Muslims tried to recover their dead, which they invariably did, they became sitting targets. The unyielding La Valette forbade his men to attempt to do likewise—it was simply too expensive. In the rubble of the walls men sniped at one another; hurled hand grenades, rocks, and incendiaries; hit one another at close range with field guns; jumped into one another's positions with sabres and scimitars. They were so close—sometimes no more than twenty paces apart—that they could call to each other. Renegade Christians now took to shouting encoded messages of support to their coreligionists. At moments, something like a fellow feeling developed among men on opposite sides of a single embankment enduring the same fate.

The days pass in a blur of violence and death, noise and smoke, the clanging of Christian church bells, the sound of the Muslims praying in the dark before each attack. Men die in a hundred ways. They are shot through the head, or burned alive by incendiaries or cut down by a blade or blown into fragments by a cannonball. The positioning of banners becomes an obsession. The Ottomans raise green and yellow flags on the parapet, red ones with horsetails—the defenders try to tear them down. The battle for these markers of territory is as fierce as the struggle to recover the body of a dead commander. Flags raise morale; their loss is a signifier of ill omen. On August 15 the standard of the knights is shot down on the post of Castile; the Muslims in the trenches take it as an omen of impending victory. When they are forced back on August 18, a soldier on the ramparts grabs the red-and-white flag of Saint John and runs the length of the walls "out of sheer joie de vivre," so fast "that an infinite number of arquebuses can't touch him." No one wants to be taken alive; capture inevitably means torture, and both sides despoil the enemy dead, acting out rituals stretching back to the Mediterranean bronze age—Achilles dragging Hector around the walls of Troy.

MUSTAPHA WAS PUSHING HIS MEN as hard as he could for one more major assault. Four days of bombardment from August 16 to 19 were followed by sullen dissent from the janissaries. They refused to leave the trenches unless he led the way. The pasha was no coward. He led the charge—and swelled the numbers of crack troops by dressing up camp servants as janissaries, and promising them promotion if they fought well. The fighting was fierce, but to no avail; Mustapha had his turban knocked from his head and fell to the ground, stunned. Both sides were drawing on their last reserves of strength; Mustapha started to siphon off the fleet's resources of gunpowder. La Valette presented himself at the infirmary and requested a muster of the sick and wounded; those able to walk were judged fit to fight. The same day an arrow was shot over the wall with a one-word message attached: Thursday—warning of yet another attack. It was beaten back.

The siege was grinding slowly to a halt in a murderous stalemate, similar to the impasse at Rhodes forty years earlier. The councils in Mustapha's ornate tent became longer and more heated; the pasha wanted to follow the example of Suleiman at Rhodes, and continue a winter campaign. Piyale flatly refused. The fleet was far from home. It was impossible to repair it over the winter on Malta, and the enemy was close. One or two more attacks and they would have to head back to Istanbul. Mindful of Suleiman's warnings, on August 22 they planned yet more assaults. Huge prizes were offered for bravery and success. On Saturday, August 25, it started to rain.

# CHAPTER 14

# "Malta Yok"

August 25 to September 11, 1565

THE NORTH WIND that the Italians called the tramontana, "the sunset wind," is brewed in the Alps. It sweeps down the length of Italy, bringing heavy rain and squally sailing conditions to the central Mediterranean. In late August 1565 the tramontana hit Malta with torrential downpours—the first indications of winter.

The rain heightened a scene of unrelieved devastation. After three and a half months of fierce fighting, the harbor area had been reduced to an apocalyptic wasteland. The defenses of Birgu and Senglea had been literally pulverized; heaps of rubble were all that separated the two sides. The Ottomans crouched miserably in their waterlogged trenches, the Christians behind makeshift barricades. Each front line was marked by tattered flags and the rotting heads of their enemies. Though the Muslims worked hard to carry away their casualties and bury them in mass graves dug with enormous effort from the solid rock on Mount Sciberras, it was a landscape of death. Snipers, cannon, swords, pikes, incendiaries, malnutrition, waterborne diseases had all taken their toll. By the end of August, perhaps ten thousand men had died in the equatorial summer heat. Bloated corpses bobbed gaseously in the harbor or lay dismembered across the battlefield after each successive attack. The Ottoman camp at Marsa was fetid with sickness; the air stank of rotting flesh and gunpowder. Both sides were hanging by a thread.

Within the Christian compounds, there was a sense that one more concerted attack could finish them off. "Our men are in large part dead," wrote the knight Vincenzo Anastagi, "the walls have fallen; it is easy to see inside, and we live in danger of being overwhelmed by force. But it is not seemly to talk of this. First the Grand Master, then all the Order, have determined not to listen to anything [defeatist] that is whispered outside." It did indeed seem that only the willpower of La

Valette was keeping the defenders alive. When it was suggested on August 25 that Birgu could no longer be defended and that they should retreat to the fort of Saint Angelo at the tip of the peninsula to make a last stand, La Valette had its drawbridge blown up. There would be no retreat. Rounds of church services and thanksgiving prayers for each successful defense fortified the morale of the people.

At the front line it was impossible for the defenders to show their heads over the parapet without being shot. At times only heavy-duty siege armor kept them alive. On August 28 an Italian soldier, Lorenzo Puche, was talking to the grand master when he was hit in the head by an arquebus shot. His plate helmet took the full force of the blast. The man fell to the ground stunned, picked up his dented headgear, and asked permission to carry on with a sortie—under the circumstances it was refused. To lessen the risks from sniper fire, arquebuses were lashed together, hoisted above the parapet on poles, and fired remotely by long strings.

The two sides were in places only feet apart, crouching behind their barricades in the rain. "We were sometimes so close to the enemy," recalled Balbi, "that we could have shaken hands with them." Commanders on both sides noticed—and feared—the sense of common suffering across the front line. At Senglea it was reported that "some of the Turks talked to some of our men and they developed the confidence to discuss the situation together a bit." These were brief moments of mutual recognition, like footballs kicked into no-man's-land. On August 31, a janissary emerged from his trench to present his opposite numbers with "some pomegranates and a cucumber in a handkerchief, and our men gave back in exchange three loaves and a cheese." It was a rare moment of common humanity in a conflict devoid of chivalry. As the two groups of men talked, it transpired that morale in the Ottoman camp was dropping. Food supplies were dwindling, the situation was at stalemate with the defenders repairing the breaches as fast as they were made; the friendly janissaries gave the impression that it was now a common belief in the Ottoman camp "that God did not want Malta to be taken."

The rain probably dented Ottoman morale more; La Valette issued his men with mats of woven grass to protect themselves from the wet, and the change in the weather altered the dynamics of the siege. Mustapha knew that time was running out. The councils in the pasha's ornate tent became heated and recriminatory. All the old arguments were picked over again: Could they overwinter? What would the sultan do if they retired without a victory? How serious were the rumors of a rescue fleet?

Piyale again refused to countenance overwintering, but peremptory orders were sent out to strengthen marine patrols of the island: "Due to the urgent need to guard and watch the regions of the island of Malta, I have ordered that you set up a mission to guard and watch around the island by means of 30 galleys. . . . You are to punish whosoever opposes or contradicts your words, by a fitting punishment." At the same time, the wet weather provided Mustapha with an opportunity. Heavy rain doused the fire of arquebuses and other incendiaries. It provided a chance to tackle the defenses without answering gunfire.

In the last days of August the pashas threw everything into a series of desperate assaults in the driving rain. Miners were set to work planting explosive charges under the walls; siege towers constructed; handsome rewards offered for success. The pashas moved their tents closer to the front line to inspire the men, and Mustapha led attacks in person. He sensed again and again that the ultimate prize was almost within reach; yet it continually eluded him. The defenders were still fighting with spirit, countermining, leading sorties, shooting down Mustapha's wooden siege engines. When it was too wet to use their arquebuses, La Valette issued the men with mechanical crossbows from the armory. The Ottomans were unable to use their conventional bows in the rain, but the crossbow—an anachronistic device from medieval warfare—caused heavy damage. They were so powerful, according to Balbi, "that their bolts could pierce a shield and often the man behind it."

On August 30 it rained all morning and Mustapha led a determined attempt to clear the breaches of fallen stone, then to storm through the opening. Some Maltese ran to La Valette shouting that the enemy had got into the city. La Valette hobbled there in person as fast as he could with all the men he could muster, together with the women and children hurling rocks down on the onrushing men. They were probably saved only by the weather. The rain stopped; the defenders were able to use incendiaries and guns to drive the enemy back. Mustapha was struck in the face but remained resolute; according to the Christian sources, "stick in hand, he began furiously to urge his men on." They fought from noon until nightfall, to no avail. The attack faltered. The following day, the defenders braced themselves for yet another attack, but none came. "They did not move for they were exhausted as we were," Balbi recorded. The whole siege had ground to a halt. By now Mustapha knew that a Christian rescue fleet would soon be on its way from Sicily. He offered lavish rewards for victory: for the men promotion to the salaried rank of janissary, for the slaves freedom. It made little difference.

Mustapha was not the only commander growing anxious to discern, and fulfill, his sovereign's wishes. Malta was a struggle for the Mediterranean fought by proxy—peering over the shoulder of the combatants were the looming figures of Suleiman and Philip II, like dominant figures at either end of a chessboard. In Sicily, Don Garcia waited anxiously for permission from Madrid to mount a rescue bid. By early August he had collected eleven thousand men and eighty ships on Sicily; the men were largely hardened Spanish troops, pikemen and arquebusiers, together with a small band of Knights of Saint John and some gentleman adventurers—freelancers come to fight for the glory of Christendom. Among those who failed to make it in time was Don Juan of Austria, Philip's illegitimate half brother. The military force was to be led by Don Alvare Sande, the commander at Djerba, ransomed back from Istanbul, and a famous condottiere, the one-eyed Ascanio della Corgna, who had been released by the pope from prison, where he was being held for murder, rape, and extortion. Apparently one could be lenient in the cause of Christendom. They were ready to depart, and Don Garcia was being assailed by furious requests to sail. Daily the reports became more desperate. "Four hundred men still alive. . . . Don't lose an hour," wrote the governor of Mdina on August 22. Yet Philip dawdled in an agony of indecision, and when permission finally reached Don Garcia on about August 20 it was hedged about with caveats. A rescue attempt could be mounted "providing it could be done without any real danger of losing the galleys." There must be no clash with the Ottoman fleet. It was an almost impossible injunction. After lengthy deliberations, the decision was taken to pack their force into the sixty best galleys, make a dash for the Malta coast, drop the men, and then retire. To increase their chances of evading detection, they would make an approach from the west, feinting an attack on Tripoli.

The rescue force set sail from Syracuse on the east coast of Sicily on August 25 and immediately found themselves sailing into the teeth of the gales that were striking Malta. August 28 saw the fragile galleys snouting into a breaking sea, dipping and plunging, the rain falling in sheets, so that the men were drenched "from the water both from the sky and the sea"; the fighting spurs were ripped off the ships, oars snapped, masts shattered. With the boats in danger of foundering, the landlubber soldiers, cold and terrified, turned to prayers and the promise of votive offerings. The spectacle of Saint Elmo's fire flaring in blue and white jets from the masts added to their alarm, along with the date: it was the day of the decapitation of John the Baptist, a particularly ill-omened marker in the church calendar. Somehow the whole convoy survived the night and was blown far off course to Trapani on the west coast of Sicily. It was to be the start of a nightmarish week of missed rendezvous and contrary winds that carried the expedition right around Malta, where they were sighted by the Ottoman fleet, and back to Sicily again. The soldiers, green and seasick from the whole experience, would have deserted to a man if Don Garcia had not forcibly prevented them. Finally on September 6 the fleet set out again to make a direct dash across the straits to try to catch the Ottoman fleet off guard. The ships departed in silence to cross the thirty miles of open water. Strict orders had been issued: the cockerels on the boats were to be killed, all instructions were to be given to the crews by voice rather than the usual whistles, and the oarsmen were forbidden to raise their feet—the rattling of chains carried far over a calm sea.

But the element of surprise had already been lost on September 3, when they were sighted by the corsair Uluch Ali, scouting off the west coast of Malta. The Christian relief force was now the subject of intense discussion in the pasha's tent.

IN THE EARLY DAYS OF SEPTEMBER it became apparent to the defenders that although the attacks continued, their tenor was changing. "They continued to bombard Saint Michael's and the Post of Castile with equal fury," wrote Balbi on September 5, "but with all their brave bombardment we saw them daily embarking their goods and withdrawing their guns. This afforded us great satisfaction." The Ottomans were dragging their precious cannon away against the threat of a landing on the island. This was a long and laborious process that caused much trouble. Two giant bombards caused particular difficulty; one had come off its wheels and had to be abandoned. The other fell into the sea. Increasingly encouraging news leaked out to the defenders. They learned that some of the corsairs had taken their ships and sailed away; a boom had been placed over the mouth of the harbor to prevent further defections. At the same time a Maltese captive escaped back to Birgu. In the main square he publicly proclaimed that the Turks were so weakened they were leaving. Later, two more Maltese arrived with news that the enemy would give one more major attack then depart. On the night of September 6, hearing nothing from the enemy lines, a number of men crept into the Ottoman trenches. The trenches were completely deserted; they found just some shovels and a few cloaks. The whole force had been temporarily withdrawn to man the galleys against the possibility of attack.

Yet Mustapha had still not given up hope that victory might be snatched from impending failure. The untrustworthy Christian sources are the only record that we have of the final agonized debates in the pasha's tent on the night of Thursday, September 6. Mustapha apparently reread a letter from Suleiman brought by a eunuch of the palace, of which we have no trace, stating that the fleet must not return from Malta without victory. What followed was an intense discussion about the sultan's likely reaction. Mustapha was of the opinion that the nature of his master was so terrible that their end would be "miserable and horrible" if they returned from Malta without victory. Perhaps he recalled the execution of the cartographer, Piri Reis, killed on the sultan's orders ten years earlier for a failed campaign in the Red Sea, at the age of ninety. Piyale, supported by one of the army commanders, demurred: Suleiman was the wisest and most reasonable of sultans; they had made superhuman efforts to capture the island; the weather had broken; it was most important to save the fleet; risking it now would hasten the destruction of the whole force. Mustapha declared himself ready to die in one more assault the following morning. If this failed, they would withdraw.

Mustapha had already given a specific order that suggested he was preparing himself for the inevitable. The chief eunuch's huge galleon, taken by Romegas before the start of the siege, had been an ostensible cause of the whole campaign. It had rocked gently at anchor in the inner harbor the whole summer; Mustapha had sworn at the outset that it would be sailed back in triumph to Istanbul as proof of victory. Now on September 6 he ordered it to be sunk by gunfire. As the first shots came whistling across the water, La Valette had the galleon strapped to the quay with hawsers. It was holed but remained afloat.

Dawn on Friday, September 7, brought a fine day. Like every other point in the year, the date was a marker in the Christian calendar; it was the eve of the feast of the Virgin Mary. The weather had reverted to intensely stifling equatorial heat. The nights became so unbearable that no one could sleep. The Ottoman troops were again in the trenches waiting for the order to attack. In order to add weight to the attempt, the galley squadron of Uluch Ali had just been ordered down from its lookout station at Saint Paul's Bay. It was Mustapha's final piece of bad luck. Two hours later, Don Garcia's rescue force swept into the adjacent bay at Mellieha, disembarked ten thousand men on the sandy beach in an hour and a half, and put to sea again. They had landed unopposed. It was a complete fluke.

Ten miles away, the defenders on Birgu and Senglea, already sweltering in their plate armor, crouched in the dust of their ruined defenses and braced themselves for another day of fury. As they waited, an unfamiliar noise reached them from the Ottoman trenches: a murmuring of discordant voices like the buzzing of angry bees. It transpired that the janissaries and sipahis were arguing among themselves, each wanting the other to be the first into the breach. From the walls the defenders watched in openmouthed astonishment as the enemy spontaneously abandoned their trenches and withdrew. While they wondered what this might mean, they heard gunfire from Saint Elmo—an evident signal to the Ottoman camp. Around the point came a small boat, rowing hard for the shore. A turbaned figure hurried ashore, "who by his clothing and bearing was evidently a man of authority," jumped onto a waiting horse, and galloped toward Mustapha's tent. So great was his haste that the horse stumbled and fell; in fury the man drew his scimitar and cut off the horse's legs. "And having done that, he continued at a run toward Piyale Pasha's tent. And toward Corradino and the front line at Saint Margaret could be seen three or four other Turks on horseback, with scimitars in hand; who, hurrying there, set the whole camp into uproar and commotion. And as a result, they ordered the army to hurry and embark with all the provisions of the fleet." Word of Don Garcia's landing had stirred the Ottomans into a

*The relief force marches to Mdina*

fury of activity. They regrouped on Mount Sciberras and started to re-embark their provisions and equipment with miraculous speed and effi-ciency; but Mustapha left behind an ambush of arquebusiers to massacre the defenders should they venture forth.

In the event, they did not. La Valette remained wary to the bitter end, refusing to permit anyone to leave the fortifications. Within Birgu there were celebrations in the streets. All the church bells were rung to celebrate the eve of the feast of the Virgin; trumpets, drums, and flags provided a welcome gaiety in the forlorn streets of the ruined city. There were extraordinary displays of mass emotion. People fell to their knees and raised their hands to heaven, thanking God. Others leaped and cried "Relief, relief! Victory! Victory!" running about wildly. And Vespasiano Malaspina, a knight "of the most holy reputation," climbed up onto the ramparts with a palm leaf in his hands and sang the Te Deum. He had just got to the end of the first verse when Ottoman snipers shot him dead. It must have been a grimly satisfying Parthian shot.

Night fell on Birgu and Senglea with an extraordinary, amplified si-lence after months of continuous bombardment; only the distant rum-ble of wheels grinding on the stony ground disturbed the hot night air, as the Ottomans dragged their guns back to the ships.

All day, while the Ottomans had been withdrawing to their ships, the relief force had been slogging across country the seven miles from the landing spot to Mdina. The men were wearing steel helmets and breastplates, carrying weapons and heavy loads of food. The day was oppressively hot and they were exhausted by their weeklong ordeal in the boats. Strung out across the parched landscape, the force was highly vulnerable. Some started to drop their supplies to make the march more bearable, and had to be sent back to collect them. As they struggled uphill to Mdina, Ascanio della Corgna and Anastagi rode down to meet them, and the local population brought pack animals to carry away the supplies. Ascanio, fearful of ambush, urged the men mercilessly on; by the end of the day all ten thousand had been safely garrisoned in and around Mdina.

As the Ottoman expedition anticipated ignominious departure, there came a sudden twist of fate. On Sunday, September 9, a soldier from the relief force defected to the Ottoman camp. He was a Morisco, a Spanish Muslim converted under duress to Christianity, prompted by the Islamic banners still fluttering on the shoreline to return to the faith of his fathers. He put a new slant on the arrival of the relief force: there were not ten thousand men, the true number was nearer six thousand; they were exhausted from the traumatic maritime maneuvers and were so short of food they could scarcely stand on their feet; moreover, their different leaders were jostling for authority. This was one fact that was almost certainly correct: The Spaniard Alvare and the Italian Ascanio did not get on; it was a split command structure replicated in the Ottoman camp.

To Mustapha, still unable to confront the possibility of defeat, this information offered a chance to salvage something from the wreckage. He decided on one last throw of the dice. Before daybreak on Tuesday, September 11, he disembarked ten thousand men from the galleys in the dark, so that his intentions could not be detected, and started to march north in battle formation with the aim of defeating the relief force before it could recover from the voyage. At the same time Piyale's fleet put out from the harbor and sailed north, to stand off Saint Paul's Bay. From Birgu and Senglea the defenders watched the Turks go, then climbed Mount Sciberras and planted the red-and-white flag of the Knights of Saint John on the battered ruins of Saint Elmo. The Ottomans could now be seen on the march, setting fire to the countryside as they went.

In fact, Mustapha's plan had been very quickly leaked back to the Christians by a Sardinian renegade who had switched sides, and Maltese scouts were monitoring the Ottomans' movements closely. La Valette had sent urgent messages up to Mdina to prepare the troops. In the early morning, the ten thousand men of the relief force were drawn up on the high ground beyond Mdina. They had had two days of rest and something more than ship's biscuit to eat: each company had been given a cow or an ox. Many of the men were Spanish veterans from Philip's Italian possessions, pikemen and arquebusiers, accustomed to open field warfare and experienced in fighting in organized formations. The troops were drawn up for battle. The Spanish banners were unfurled, and the kettledrums beat a battering tattoo. The bristling squares of steel-helmeted men waited for the Ottoman charge.

As the Turks approached, the Spanish and Italian commanders found their men increasingly difficult to control: "Not even at the point of the sword could they restrain their men, so great was the desire of all to come to blows with the Turks." Both sides realized the advantage of the high ground and rushed to command a hillock beyond Mdina surmounted by a tower. The Spanish won the race, raised their banners, and started to force the enemy down the hill. The Ottomans tried to stand and fight but were driven back; the fighting was fierce—men were shot down by arquebuses or by arrows—and the sun, now at its zenith, was intensely hot, "so great that I maintain I never knew it so hot in all the siege as on that day," wrote Balbi. "Christians and Turks alike could hardly stand from exhaustion, heat and thirst, and many died." Mustapha's decision to attack was now shown to be a terrible error of judgment. The Christian force was larger than the Morisco had claimed—and they were far fresher than the Muslims, who had been in the field for four months. The Ottomans started to waver. Mustapha's arquebusiers held the line for a short while, but the onward momentum of the Christians proved unstoppable. The impact of the Spanish pikemen led to a rout. Mustapha, brave to the last, tried to halt his men's flight. He killed his horse to demonstrate there would be no retreat and ran forward to place himself in the front line. It was to no avail; his men were fleeing in disorder down to the sea before the rapidly advancing enemy, flags flying, drums beating, the knights in their red-and-white tunics, the Spanish levies stabbing and jabbing with their pikes. Ascanio was wounded; Don Alvare had his horse shot from under him, but the forward momentum of the Christians was now irresistible. The Ottoman officers were unable to control the men at all; they turned in disorderly flight. Mustapha dispatched an urgent order to the fleet to bring their ships in close to the shore, prows forward with their guns ready to cover the retreat. The arid plains leading down to the sea became a scene of slaughter. It was so hot that men from both sides collapsed under the weight of their armor and died; but the Spanish relief force was stronger and fresher. Shouting "Kill them!" they swept forward with the force of vengeance. With the memory of Saint Elmo still vivid, the order was given to take none alive. Some of the Turks fell to the ground and could not, or would not, get up. They were killed where they lay.

The final ghastly moments of the battle for Malta were played out on the shores of Saint Paul's Bay, the site of the legendary shipwreck of Saint Paul and a place of intense Christian significance to the Maltese. For the retreating Muslims it was now just a matter of personal survival. While the scores of galleys stood off from the shore, a throng of smaller rowing boats surged into the bay to take the men away. The retreating soldiers were driven onto the beach and the sandstone ledges that surrounded the bay, then into the sea. The young Maltese and the Spanish troops splashed into the lagoon, slashing and hacking at the floundering Turks. Men tried to scrabble into the boats and overturned them. Bodies floated in the blue water, trailing ribbons of blood. Eventually the last survivors scrambled onto the ships. The galleys then turned their guns on the shore, and Don Alvaro and Ascanio ordered the men to withdraw. They stood in the hot sun, exhausted and drained, watching the fleet go. The beach and the water were littered with turbans, scimitars, shields, and an unknown number of dead. "We could not estimate exactly the number of their dead at that time, but two or three days afterwards the bodies of the drowned floated to the surface," wrote Balbi. "So great was the stench in the bay, that no man could go near it."

After dark, the galleys returned to the shore, took on water, and sailed away—the Barbary corsairs back to North Africa, the imperial fleet to make the long voyage home to face the sultan's displeasure, leaving perhaps half its army, some ten thousand men, dead in the barren landscape. Behind them a shattered island, "arid, ransacked, and ruined" in the words of Giacomo Bosio; of the eight thousand defenders, only six hundred were still fit to carry arms, and two hundred fifty of the five hundred knights were dead. Malta stank of death. The Christian survivors rang their bells and gave thanks to God; there were bonfires in the streets of Rome and prayers of thanksgiving all the way to London. For the first time in forty years, Suleiman had received a major check in the White Sea. In the face of all previous experience, the ravelin of Europe had held, shielding the Christian shore from certain depredation. Malta had survived through a combination of religious zeal, irreducible willpower—and luck. In the process La Valette had fired up all Europe.

THE INEVITABLE NEWS found its way back to Suleiman in Istanbul. Mustapha and Piyale took the precaution of sending word ahead of them, then slipping the fleet into the Golden Horn at night. When word got about the city, there was collective grief. Christians "could not walk in the streets for fear of the stones which were hurled at them by the Turks, who were universally in mourning, one for a brother, another for a son, husband or friend." Yet Suleiman's response was unusually muted. Both commanders kept their heads, though Mustapha lost his post. Piyale would be at sea again the following year raiding the Italian coast, and Suleiman was generous to the janissaries who had survived a tough fight. He ordered that those "who fought during the Siege of Malta should be rewarded by being promoted in rank and should be given some money as a reward." The failure at Malta was swiftly airbrushed from the imperial record; "Malta yok" ran the Turkish saying—Malta doesn't exist. Like Vienna, it was considered a negligible check in the onrush of Ottoman victories.

And for all the victory bells and the bonfires, no one in the central Mediterranean saw Malta as closing a chapter on Ottoman ambitions. A sense of terrible and impending danger continues to sound in the Christian diplomatic exchanges after the enemy fleet had sailed home. Malta was in ruins, its fortifications shattered, its population indebted and impoverished; few of the surviving knights could ever fight again. There was certainty that Suleiman, wounded by the debacle of 1565, was rebuilding his fleet and would strike again. "He has given orders," a report from Istanbul declared in October, "that fifty thousand oarsmen and fifty thousand soldiers be in a state of readiness by mid-March." Europe remained panic-stricken and insecure. There was little time to collect troops and money and rearm the island. Feverish work began on Mount Sciberras to build a new citadel named Valletta in honor of the grand master. People looked nervously east.

But despite an inconsequential raid on Italy, the Ottomans abandoned the sea. Imperial ambitions swung north to Hungary. The following year Suleiman led the troops in person. It was his thirteenth campaign and his first for twelve years. The sultan was seventy-two years old and unwell; unable to ride, he traveled ponderously in a carriage. With him marched the largest army he had ever assembled. It was to be an exercise in imperial power. After Malta, Suleiman wanted to reassert his credentials as leader of the holy war, to demonstrate that the writ and power of the "Sultan of Sultans, Distributor of Crowns to the Rulers of the Surface of the Earth," still ran in the world. The momentum of Islamic conquest was to be inexhaustible.

By mid-September, after the labored annihilation of the fortress of Szigetvár in the marshes, where a tiny Hungarian force fought and died with the spirit of Saint Elmo, Suleiman was on his way home. The imperial carriage jolted and rattled over the long plains. Six pages walked by its wheels reciting verses from the Koran. The sultan sat upright inside, white-faced and hawk-nosed, hidden by curtains. Sometimes half-visible reassuring glimpses of the Shadow of God on Earth were shown to the troops.

EXCEPT THAT THE MAN INSIDE was not Suleiman; he was a body double from the imperial household. The sultan was dead; his disemboweled, embalmed corpse jolted along secretly behind. When Suleiman died, on September 5 or 6, 1566, Szigetvár was still holding out. Impatient and irritated by the fort's resistance, he wrote a few hours before his death, "This chimney is still burning, and the great drumroll of conquest has yet to be heard." The words fall like a coda on the life of the great sultan, whose career had started so brilliantly nearby at the capture of Belgrade. They suggest disappointment, bitterness, a sense of failure. No matter how many islands were captured, how many citadels stormed, the dream of the world empire of Islam had slipped through his fingers, like grains of sand. He was thirty-seven miles from Mohacs, where he had shattered the Hungarians in 1526. The Christian skulls were still whitening on the long plains.

And within the Mediterranean basin, everyone knew that the propulsive thrust of Ottoman conquest would go on. Malta was unfinished business that lacked a conclusion. Southern Europe had escaped by the skin of its teeth.

# Part Three

## ENDGAME: HURTLING TO LEPANTO

# CHAPTER 15

# The Pope's Dream

I T HAD TAKEN CHRISTIAN EUROPE perhaps one hundred fifty years to understand the true nature of Ottoman succession. To scotch the possibility of civil war, the news of a sultan's death was always stage-managed; when word reached the West, it was invariably greeted with a collective sigh of relief. Pious hopes would be expressed that the new sultan would prove more amenable, less aggressive than his predecessor, as if the propensity for war derived from personal choice; even Mehmet, the conqueror of Constantinople who campaigned continuously for thirty years, had been considered at first too callow to threaten. By the time Selim ascended the throne in September 1566, Europe had been largely disabused of such notions: a change of ruler required fresh wars.

The new sultan had survived the murderous selection process through the death or execution of his more talented siblings. No one had a high opinion of Selim. He was physically unprepossessing; he was lazy and unpopular with the army—the janissaries referred to him as the Ox; he was said to be a drunkard. The ambassadors filed back unfavorable reports: "by nature irascible and bloodthirsty, he is given to all kinds of carnal pleasures, and above all he is a great wine lover." But by the middle of the sixteenth century Europe understood that personal qualities were almost irrelevant. The idea of conquest was central to the sultanate, intricately interwoven with its holder's position as leader of the Muslim world. Conquest was expressed repeatedly in the visible trappings of power; the high-sounding titles proclaimed dominion over the earth. The elaborate campaign tents and banners, the jeweled swords and ceremonial helmets decorated with the victory suras from the Koran, emphasized his role as an Islamic warrior. Only spectacular conquests could legitimize a sultan. War was not dependent on personal volition; it was an unceasing imperial project, authorized by

Islam. The whole machinery of the Ottoman state required it; if conquest momentarily faltered, as at Malta, it was a temporary check, soon to be overcome. "Turkish expansion is like the sea," a Serbian had observed a hundred years earlier, "it never has peace but always rolls." Once, the sultan had led every campaign. Now he could be there just through the presence of his horsetail banners and splendidly decorated flagship, while proxy commanders conducted the fighting. Distance from the battlefield lent Selim a certain disregard for the odds; the Venetians, inquisitive judges of Ottoman sultans, thought him to have "too high an estimation of himself, contempt for all the other potentates of the world; he considers himself capable of putting into the field infinite armies, refuses to listen to all who oppose him."

The internal necessity for war was immediately impressed on Selim. On the day he made his triumphal entry into Istanbul through the Edirne Gate—the gate of conquest—the janissary corps mutinied. They barred the palace gates to the new sultan and demanded their customary gifts. Piyale Pasha, still admiral of the fleet, was knocked from his horse. It took the hurried distribution of gold coins to resolve the matter, but the lesson was not wasted on Selim. The standing army was a tiger every successive sultan had to learn to ride; harnessing it

*Sultan Selim*

required victories and the accompanying rewards of booty and land. Selim, fearful of coups, was the first sultan never personally to go away on campaign—in this respect his reign marked a watershed—but the conquests would proceed anyway. And the Mediterranean remained a project in which he was keenly interested.

The man who orchestrated Selim's succession with consummate skill was the Bosnian-born chief vizier, Sokollu Mehmet Pasha. It was Sokollu who concealed Suleiman's death with the cooperation of his doctor and quelled the janissary revolt back in Istanbul. Tall, thin, inscrutable, susceptible to bribes but utterly loyal to each successive sultan—and he served three before he fell—Sokollu was a man of exceptional talents. He had proved his abilities to Suleiman as general, judge, provincial governor, even admiral of the fleet after Barbarossa's death, before his appointment as grand vizier in 1565 and marriage to Selim's daughter. Sokollu was wary of Mediterranean ventures after the failure on Malta; he would have preferred a land campaign in Hungary, but he had other contenders for the sultan's loyalty. The Venetians carefully appraised Sokollu's strengths and weaknesses: "He is extremely skillful and has a deep understanding of diplomatic negotiations. . . . The sultan leaves all the care of government to him. . . . Despite this, [Sokollu] Mehmet is not sufficiently confident of keeping the sultan's favor to dare speaking to him without fear. . . . He sometimes says that despite the important power that he enjoys from the sultan, he does not risk, in cases when he is ordered to arm two thousand galleys, to tell him that His Majesty's empire is not in a fit state to do so. This timidity arises in part from the sultan's nature . . . partly from the fact that [Sokollu] is the constant object of jealousy on the part of the other pashas." Sokollu's principal aim was to cling to the pinnacle of power, but from the start of Selim's reign, he was confronted by ambitious rivals, foremost of whom were Selim's childhood tutor, Lala Mustapha Pasha, and Piyale Pasha. The swirling factions that surrounded the stay-at-home sultan were to have potent effects on Ottoman decision-making in the White Sea. All the candidates for imperial favor were also keenly mindful of the blood-spattered walls that marked the downfall of Ibrahim Pasha; it did not encourage failure in the sultan's service.

SELIM'S SULTANATE COINCIDED with another significant succession. In the complex matrix of European power politics, no institution provided such consistent opposition to the sultan as the papacy. Rome and Istanbul stood at the centers of two worlds, implacable and unwavering opponents. On December 9, 1565, Pius IV, who had shepherded Christendom through the terrors of the Malta siege, died in his apartment in the Borgia Tower. During the short days of midwinter, the cardinals of the Catholic Church withdrew into whispering seclusion to horse-trade for a successor.

With the white smoke from the Vatican chimneys on January 8 came a name that almost none had foreseen. Michele Ghisleri was a different type of prelate from his predecessor. Pius IV, as coolheaded and tolerant as was possible in the eye of the gathering Protestant storm, had been a man of the world—scion of a wealthy family, political, urbane—a pope of the Renaissance. Ghisleri was a son of the poor, who had begun life as a shepherd boy in the hills of Piedmont and owed everything to the church. He had served it with a startling zeal; latterly as grand inquisitor. The new pope took the name of Pius V. It was a somewhat inappropriate choice under the circumstances, as his predecessor had disliked him intensely. Ghisleri was not a prelate to sit down at table with the nobility of Rome or Florence. With his bald head and flowing white beard, Pius V was intransigent, ascetic, and uncompromising, more an Old Testament prophet than a Borgia pope. He had no political subtleties, lived frugally, worshipped zealously, never rested. The man who owned only two coarse woollen shirts—one to wash and one to wear—crackled with pious energy. He was filled with a fervent zeal to defend and enhance the Catholic Church in the face of its enemies, Protestants and Muslims, a zeal that harked back to the spirit of the medieval Crusades. It was Pius V who excommunicated Elizabeth of England as "a slave of wickedness." There was a whiff of brimstone about his presence, a sense of violent and intolerant energy that divided opinion. Philip II's agent at the Vatican reported him to be "a good man ... of great religious zeal. ... He is the cardinal we need as pope in the present times." More worldly observers were less enthusiastic. "We should like it even better if the present Holy Father were no longer with us, however great, inexpressible, unparalleled and extraordinary his holiness might be," wrote back an imperial councillor dryly within the year.

The project that caught the old man's glittering eye was the revival of the crusading dream. It was more by luck than judgment that Eu-

*Pius V*

rope had survived at Malta. There had been no unity of purpose before
the siege; recriminations over the relief left a sour taste in the mouth
afterward. Christendom was still in terrible peril, from the frontiers of
Hungary to the shores of Spain. Only by unified action could it successfully oppose the Ottoman Empire: "No one alone can resist it," the
pope insisted. Pius set his heart on succeeding where his predecessors
had failed: to wake the Christian powers from their dangerous slumber
and to align their disparate interests in the formation of a durable Holy
League to confront the infidel. He brought the inquisitor's zeal to the
task. Four days after his succession he renewed the papal subsidy to
Philip II for galleys to protect the Christian seas. It was a small first
step, but in the turbulent years of the late 1560s, Pius was to emerge as
the champion of Christendom, a force of nature propelling the crusade
against Islam.

The enormity of his task in 1566 was self-evident. Europe was a ferment of violent passions, torn apart by different interests, imperial dreams, and religious tensions. Philip's attention was divided among a score of conflicting priorities: the New World colonies, the security of his outposts on the North African shore, the internal crusade against Spain's remnant Muslim population, the threat from the Turks, the mutual suspicion with rival France, and the smoldering Protestant rebellion in the Netherlands. These all successively commanded the Catholic King's attention at his gloomy palace high above Madrid. His dispersed empire was riven with fault lines and difficulties; only the steady argosy of galleons laden with South American silver could keep the Spanish imperial venture afloat—and still there was insufficient money for the need. Philip had no strategy for the Mediterranean, only piecemeal responses to a thousand problems. When sullen dissent in the Low Countries burst out into open revolt in 1566, Philip was compelled to march his best troops across a tense and suspicious Europe; within the Mediterranean he was largely powerless to act. The French offered no better prospect to the pope. They still had treaties with the Ottomans and a religious war—in 1566 the Protestant revolt burned brightly across Southern France—while no one trusted the self-serving Venetians at all. In order to mount a unified response against the Turks, Pius needed at least to triangulate the resources of the papacy with those of Venice and Spain. It would take five years and the trigger of particular events for him to succeed.

In the years immediately after Malta, Philip resisted the pope's pleas for a Holy League while continuing to take his crusading subsidies; he was distracted by the Netherlands and had no wish to provoke new wars. The king could be surprisingly pragmatic; he even toyed secretly with a formal truce with Selim. At the same time Philip had not forgotten the lessons of Djerba; with quiet calculation he continued building galleys in Barcelona; by 1567 he had one hundred—not enough to take on the Ottomans alone, but sufficient to deter a long-distance strike.

BUT THE OTTOMANS CONTINUED to be largely absent from the sea. In 1566 Piyale had caused further tremors in the Christian world by appearing in the Adriatic with one hundred thirty galleys. All the defenses of Sicily, Malta, and La Goletta were readied, then stood down again after the Turks conducted a halfhearted raid on the Italian coast. This pattern of expectation and anticlimax continued in successive years. The Turks were quiet, their behavior inexplicable. The Mediterranean once again became a sea of rumors, a shadowy world of unattributed intelligence reports. Throughout the northern ports, spies profited, picking up scraps of gossip and passing them on, among whom was Venice's man in Dubrovnik, paid by the word for his intelligence. Both sides spread false reports, which rival intelligence services patiently unpicked. There were whispers, suggestions, threats: the Turks were preparing strikes against one of a dozen places—La Goletta or Malta, Cyprus or Sicily—or nowhere. There was shadowboxing—the Ottomans would put out a cruising fleet, then withdraw it again—a war of nerves; each side scanned the horizons for sails that did not materialize. Caught between the two, the Venetians became alarmed and edgy; they began to fear for Crete and Cyprus. The Ottomans meanwhile seemed almost to be disarming; they concluded a new agreement with the jumpy Venetians in 1567, sealed a peace in Hungary the following year. The deceptive quiet at least bought time: Malta was rebuilt; Spain worked to clear its waters of corsairs.

In Madrid, Venice, Genoa, and Rome a hundred theories were circulating about Ottoman intentions. It was said that the sultan had no appetite for war: "The Turk is only interested in amusing himself, having a good time and eating and drinking; he placed all affairs of state in the hands of his chief minister," came back a Spanish report. Others claimed that the Ottomans were busy in the East or were just biding their time.

The true sources of Ottoman policy were hidden from foreign powers, no matter how hard agents in Istanbul pressed their ears to the wall; nor did anyone possess a panoptic vision of the sea. There were larger rhythms at work in the Mediterranean in the years 1566–68 that interfered with human plans: harvest failures and grain shortages in cities with swelling populations, outbreaks of plague and famine. People were dying of hunger in Egypt and Syria in 1566; in 1567, Spanish agents reported a terrible shortage of bread in Istanbul; plague carried off many people there. The narrow margins of human survival quieted war talk.

At the same time the energetic Sokollu Mehmet was occupied with trouble farther east. The Ottomans learned early the difficulty of managing Arab lands; there were revolts in the marshes north of Basra, more serious trouble in the Yemen. Simultaneously Sokollu conceived visionary projects to overcome the barriers to new conquests; he ordered the construction of a Suez canal that would give Ottoman ships direct access to the Indies, and he developed a matching plan for a second canal linking the Black and the Caspian seas to enable an attack on the Persian foe by water. Neither project came to fruition and these failures were significant. There would be no New World for Ottoman navigators. Hemmed in, they necessarily had to push forward again into the Old.

The checks and balances of motive and initiative in the late 1560s were the play of new globalizing forces in the world. The Mediterranean was the center of a vast arena of turmoil whose interconnections could be grasped only from space. Events in the Yemen, in the Netherlands, in Hungary and North Africa, were intertwined. The Protestant revolution in northern Europe was facilitated by the Mediterranean pressure the Turks applied to Philip. And for the first time, the New World was exerting an influence on Europe. France and Spain bristled with particular hostility after the Spanish massacre of French settlers at Fort Caroline in Florida in 1564. More dramatically the silver mines of Potosi in Peru were making and wrecking the economies of the Old World. From the 1540s, bullion fleets across the Atlantic were supplying the Spanish crown with the means to fight. The king could build ships, pay for professional armies, wage wars, on an unprecedented scale. But with this inflow of wealth came an inflationary pressure the Hapsburgs failed to understand. Warfare had always been costly; in the sixteenth century it rocketed. The price of ship's biscuit—a critical expense in sea warfare—quadrupled in sixty years; the commensurate total cost of operating Spanish war galleys tripled; price increases rippled across Europe and lapped at the shores of the Ottoman world too. War had become an expensive game. "To carry out war, three things are necessary," remarked the Milanese general Marshal Trivulzio presciently in 1499, "money, money and yet more money."

Only two superpowers—the Ottomans and the Hapsburgs—had the resources now to wage war on a significant scale, and they were evenly matched. In the age of empire both could extract resources, tax, and aggregate matériel on a hitherto unimaginable scale. By midcentury, power was being concentrated in Madrid and Istanbul; formidable bureaucracies managed the logistics of war in distant provinces with impressive skill. In the Mediterranean the exponential weight of numbers was driving smaller players to the wall. Venice had been the great naval power of the fifteenth century; by the time of Preveza in 1538, though her fleet was five times larger, it was still dwarfed by the Ottomans'. The impact of fleet sizes was shrinking space; where wars within the Mediterranean had once been local, they could now encompass the whole sea. Spain and the Ottomans had been sniping blindly for thirty years, since Barbarossa and Doria. They had fought each other to a standstill at Malta. A decisive clash for control of the center of the world still awaited.

No one moved more warily in the shadow of power than the Venetians. They struggled to live on the shrinking frontier between Istanbul and Madrid. Venice was continually torn between trade and war. Her position kept her ambiguous, a liminal place between two worlds, of neither the land nor the sea, the East nor the West, interpreting each to the other—and treated by both as a double agent. Nobody invested so much energy in watching and understanding "the Grand Turk," or in conniving with him. Deep in the maze of passages beneath the doge's palace, a busy secretariat monitored Ottoman intentions in scrupulous detail; thousands of pages of memoranda, reports, international briefings poured from the tips of Venetian pens. At the same time, the republic's diplomats worked tirelessly to appease her voracious neighbor—cosseting and cajoling, toadying to Ottoman sultans, bribing ministers, supplying information and rich gifts—and spying. A ceaseless flurry of encoded messages from the republic's residents in Istanbul made it back to the doge's palace on trading galleys and swift brigantines, interpreting palace politics, fleet movements, and rumors of war. The Venetians briefed shamelessly on both sides according to the set of tested maxims: "It is better to treat all enemy rulers as friends," one seasoned politician advised, "and all friends as potential enemies." Venice followed this to the letter. To the pope they presented themselves as the front line of Christendom, to the sultan as a trading partner and friend. When Philip appointed his half brother Don Juan of Austria to command his resurgent fleet in 1568, Venice sent honeyed messages of congratulation but kept Istanbul fully informed of his movements.

Venice played her cards with extreme care, but after Malta this delicate balancing act became increasingly fraught. Despite the new peace treaty with Selim in 1567 and the quiet waters of 1568, the Venetians were edgy and disquieted. Why were the Turks so amenable? Were they concealing something? Was the new treaty designed to lull? There were worrying signs. Intelligence reports suggested new works in the Istanbul arsenal; and Selim was quietly constructing a fort on the mainland opposite Cyprus. Seasoned sea watchers feared for the safety of the Most Serene Republic's overseas colonies. La Valette, who evidently knew a thing or two, sold all his Order's landholdings in Cyprus in 1567 shortly before he died. The Venetian senate took tentative steps—modestly increasing troop numbers and building cannon foundries on Crete and Cyprus—but war was expensive and the hard-nosed Venetians were reluctant to lay out speculative cash. They continued to guard their hand.

The difficulties for the papacy of corralling Venice and Spain into a Holy League against the Turks seemed as great in 1568 as they had ever been. Philip was still busy in the Low Countries. He had no sharp motivation for aggressive war; nor was there any reason to help the self-serving Venetians if they were attacked on Cyprus or Crete. Had they helped at Djerba? Had they not openly rejoiced at the fall of Saint Elmo? And the Venetians, for their part, were quite happy trading with Islam until a blow fell—then they would appeal to all Christendom. But not until.

And yet, for those who could see, the underlying conditions were there: Selim's need for a confirming victory, the incendiary blasts of Pius V, the aggregation of resources among the two superpowers, the shrinking sea—it was only a matter of time before something triggered a headlong rush to war. In the dying days of 1567, events in Spain started to quicken the pace.

THE CLIMATE OF RELIGIOUS fervor in Spain had been sharpened by Protestant rebellion in the Netherlands. The Catholic Church felt itself under attack on all sides, nowhere more so than in the land of the Catholic King himself. The infidel was never far away; he was just across the straits of Gibraltar, a short sail away; he surrounded Spain; closer even, he was within its very heartlands. The Moriscos, the remnant Muslim population of southern Spain, forcibly converted to Christianity by imperial decree, remained unfinished business; they were somehow inassimilable. As the shadow of the Turk lengthened over the whole sea, fear grew that the Moriscos were still crypto-Muslims, a fifth column of Ottoman holy war in the homelands. Christian Spain became increasingly wary of its home population. Year after year, tightening decrees attempted to determine the zeal of the suspect new Christians. On January 1, 1567, Philip issued an edict to erase the last cultural traces of Islam in Spain: Arabic could no longer be spoken, the veil was prohibited, and so were public baths. It was the last straw for a goaded people, backed into a corner by intolerance and religious dogma. On Christmas night 1567, Morisco mountaineers from the Alpujarras scaled the walls of the Alhambra Palace in Granada and called for uprising in the name of Allah.

The southern mountains of Spain crackled with revolt. Catholic Spain found itself suddenly embroiled in internal holy war with Islam, and its best troops were hundreds of miles away in the Netherlands. The uprising projected all the fears about the Turks onto a huge screen. The Moriscos had been appealing for aid from Istanbul for seventy years. In the late 1560s they sent out cries for help, dispatching representatives to the sultan. Selim ordered men and arms from Algiers in early 1570; arquebuses were shipped across the straits; there were soon four thousand Turkish and Barbary troops in the mountains of southern Spain. There was live fear that the Turks were planning a long-distance invasion of Spain; it was claimed they would sail in 1570 "to give heart and help to the Moors of Granada." Sokollu Mehmet openly asked the French king for use of Toulon as a base. And in the confusion the corsair Uluch Ali dethroned a Spanish puppet regime and recaptured Tunis. At a stroke, Charles's proudest achievement had been undone. Suddenly distance was telescoped: Istanbul was no longer a thousand miles to the east. The spectre of the Turk was very close indeed.

The Morisco revolt served to concentrate Philip's mind firmly on the Mediterranean; troops were recalled from Italy; more were levied in Calabria. Don Juan of Austria was given the task of crushing the rebels. It was a dirty fight, driven by the long-repressed resentment of the Moriscos and the matching fear of the Christians. Fought with visceral hatred across the fault lines of culture and faith, it prefigured the horror of Goya's firing squads, the pitiless mutilations of the Spanish civil war. The Moriscos were buoyed up by the encouragement of

Turkish intervention; they fought desperately and horribly in the snow-blocked passes of the Alpujarras. But the Spanish operated with slamming brutality. On October 19, 1569, Philip gave the army the right to take booty from the Moriscos. The war of fire and blood dragged on through 1570. On November 1 of that year Philip made the drastic decision to order the expulsion of the whole civilian Morisco population from the lowlands for tacitly abetting the revolt. Don Juan approved its logic but found it heartrending. "It was the saddest sight in the world," he wrote on November 5, "for at the moment of departure there was so much rain, wind and snow that the poor people clung together lamenting. One cannot deny that the spectacle of the depopulation of a kingdom is the most pitiful anyone can imagine." The rebellion collapsed. The promised Turkish armada never came; it was probably never intended to come: it seems likely that Sokollu used the Moriscos to distract attention from deeper intentions. The cornerstone of Sokollu's thinking was to ensure the development of Ottoman plans without provoking unified Christian action.

On this occasion the strategy confounded its own purposes; Sokollu had probably intended to tie Philip up with the problems of his internal revolt. The revolt had quite the opposite effect. It enabled Philip to grasp a strategic truth: until the Turk was defeated in the central Mediterranean, Spain would always be under threat. The Morisco revolt rendered Philip susceptible to the pope's call for unified Christian warfare.

What the true Ottoman purposes might have been was suggested by a small incident at the other end of the sea. In early September 1568, a fleet of sixty-four Ottoman galleys appeared off the southeast coast of Cyprus, under the vizier Ali Pasha. At Famagusta the Venetian rulers of the island tensed themselves, then dispatched one of their ships, "with a fine present of a thousand piastres in a silver bowl," to exchange courtesies. The vizier declared that there was no cause for alarm; he was on his way to load timber on the Anatolian coast and simply wanted to hire a pilot. Furthermore the Venetians should discount rumors of a military buildup in Istanbul. A fleet was being prepared to aid the Moriscos in Spain, and the army would march on Persia. The Venetians had every reason to be wary of such "visits"; friendly landfall on the Genoese island of Chios in 1566 by Piyale had resulted in its capture. Nevertheless a contingent of Turkish officers was treated to a courtesy tour of the fortifications of Famagusta; Ali Pasha himself came ashore the following day in disguise. With him he brought an Italian engineer in the sultan's service, Josefi Attanto, with a request that he should be allowed to tour the island to find four classical columns suitable for a building he was constructing for Selim. Attanto dutifully scoured the island; despite the extensively colonnaded ruins at Salamis just a few miles north of Famagusta, he was mysteriously unable to find anything suitable. He did however give close attention to the fortifications of both Famagusta and Nicosia.

Ali's fleet departed. A few days later Cyprus learned that it had never gone for timber but returned directly to Istanbul, snatching a boatload of Venetian soldiers from Famagusta as it sailed off.

# CHAPTER 16

# A Head in a Dish

### 1570

$M$AYBE THE VENETIANS HAD SEEN this coming for a long time. Maybe after thirty years of peace they hid from themselves the truth about Ottoman power. After the fall of Rhodes, Cyprus was an anomaly, Christianity's forward position in a Muslim sea, isolated, fertile, hundreds of sea miles from Venice, both a provocation and a temptation to the sultans in Istanbul—"an island thrust into the mouth of the wolf," one Venetian called it.

Like Malta, Cyprus had always lived in the shadow of empires and holy wars. From the air it looks like some primitive marine dinosaur, with a swordfish beak and crude flippers pushing hard into the corner of the sea. Beirut is a mere sixty miles to the southeast; the snow-capped mountains of Anatolia are visible to the north. Too big, too fertile, too close to ignore, everyone had made a claim on the place and left their mark. The Assyrians, the Persians, the Phoenicians had been and gone. The island's root population of Greek speakers had been converted to Orthodox Christianity by the long rule of Byzantium. The Arabs held it for three centuries, and Islam never forgot the claim. When Crusaders came from the West, they turned Cyprus into the mart and marshaling yard of Christian war. They built Gothic cathedrals among the palm trees and transformed its inland capital, Nicosia, into a polyglot meeting place of diverse worlds, and the port of Famagusta briefly into the wealthiest city on earth. By the time the Venetians acquired it by sleight of hand in 1489, the current of holy war had reversed again, and the Ottomans were already halfway masters of the Eastern Mediterranean.

Almost from the start of Venetian rule, Cyprus had been on the checklist of Ottoman conquests. The Venetians paid tribute to the sultan and bribes to his viziers to preserve their neutrality; theirs was an undignified policy of appeasement, slipping ducats into complacent hands year after year. It was, on the whole, cost-effective and cheaper than maintaining war fleets, now let to rot in the backwaters, but this policy permitted no fallback position. It encouraged belief in Istanbul that the republic had grown soft with peace and would never fight.

In the short run, appeasement had been worth it. Cyprus supplied the mother city with a stream of wealth: grain from the great central plain, salt from the southern shore, strong wine, sugar, and cotton—"the plant of gold"—produced by serfs under conditions of plantation slavery. Venice held the island strictly for its commercial utility and treated it as badly as Crete. In the imagery of Venetian artists, Neptune poured the riches of these marine colonies from an inexhaustible conch into the city's lap; their wealth went to construct everything that rose like a mirage from the malarial lagoon—the stone churches, the paintings of Titian and the music of Saint Mark's, the palazzos, the Grand Canal by moonlight—all this had been brought or paid for by the merchant galleys beating their way home from the eastern seas.

It was a one-way trade. Venice gave nothing back. The downtrodden Greek Cypriot peasantry were ruled corruptly and taxed viciously. They were poor beyond belief. "All the inhabitants of Cyprus are slaves to the Venetians," wrote the visitor Martin von Baumgarten in 1508, "obliged to pay to the state a third of all their increase or income . . . and which is more, there is yearly some tax or other imposed on them, with which the poor common people are so flayed and pillaged that they hardly have the wherewithal to keep soul and body together." When in 1516 the administration of Cyprus proposed to generate extra cash by selling some of their twenty-six thousand serfs out of bondage, only one man could raise the fifty ducats. Nor was the tone of the island improved by its employment as a Botany Bay for the republic's undesirables. Murderers and political dissidents were exiled to Famagusta to swell the population. It was, all in all, a recipe for nervous occupation: the Cypriots would not reliably fight for their overlords as the Maltese had done. They slipped across the straits and made appeals to the sultan. Two Cypriots appeared in Istanbul in the 1560s with letters to Suleiman that the serfs would welcome Ottoman rule on the island; the Venetian agent in the city bribed Sokollu to hand over the men; they conveniently disappeared, but the incident did not increase Venetian confidence. The 1560s brought growing civil disturbances and ill omens: a proposed peasants' revolt in 1562; violent storms, famine, plague, earthquakes, and bread riots—all interpreted as signs from God; and the repeated, dull mutter of invasion scares, despite the renewal of treaties in 1567.

Selim had always been attracted by Cyprus. As early as 1550, the Venetian senate had been warned that if Selim came to the throne, there would be war. By the late 1560s there were pressing dynastic and strategic reasons for eliminating the Venetian colony so close to the Ottoman shore. Selim needed full legitimacy for his regime—and only a brilliant victory could bind the army to their less than charismatic sultan. The great Ottoman architect Sinan was preparing plans for a new mosque complex at Edirne, but according to custom and tradition a sultan's mosque had to be constructed with funds provided by the infidel; these could come only from conquest. Selim's early forays in expanding the empire farther east had come to nothing; there was a turning back to the Mediterranean again. At the same time, the Venetian island was a legitimate strategic problem. It sat across the crucial hajj routes to Mecca and trade routes to Egypt, through which the wealth of the East flowed into Istanbul, and the Venetian authorities had been less than effective in clearing out Christian corsairs from the area; the Knights of Saint John continued to be a particular menace. Cyprus lay uncomfortably within the Ottoman center of influence, and when pirates captured the ship carrying the treasurer of Egypt in 1569, Selim's mind was finally made up. The island must be taken.

Behind this decision lay a power struggle at the heart of the Ottoman court. Selim's favorites included Lala Mustapha Pasha, his boyhood tutor, and Piyale Pasha, both keen to regain military glory after personal setbacks—and to steal an advance on the chief vizier. Sokollu Mehmet himself was wary of an initiative that might unite Christian Europe, and unwilling to see his rivals triumph, but the sultan was not to be gainsaid. Sokollu's personal strategy was now to attempt to wheedle Cyprus from the Venetians by diplomacy.

As Venice was at peace with the empire, a religious opinion was sought from the chief mufti as to the legitimacy of breaking a treaty with the infidel; the mufti duly found precedent in the Arab occupation of the island: it was Selim's duty to recover these places for Islam. It was the only treaty the Ottomans would break in the sixteenth century. From the outset the Cyprus campaign carried particular overtones of holy war.

MAHOMET SOKOLLI.

*Sokollu Mehmet, the chief vizier*

When the sultan's emissary, Kubat, delivered his message to the Venetian authorities on March 28, 1570, the broad contents were already known and a response framed; even before Kubat was heard, the red banner of war had been carried in the doge's procession. The Venetians listened in silence to the familiar, peremptory crash of Ottoman rhetoric and reported it thus:

> Selim, Ottoman Sultan, Emperor of the Turks, Lord of
> Lords, King of Kings, Shadow of God, Lord of the Earthly Paradise and of Jerusalem, to the Signory of Venice: We demand of
> you Cyprus, which you shall give Us willingly or perforce; and
> do you not irritate our horrible sword, for We shall wage most
> cruel war against you everywhere; nor let you trust in your
> treasure, for We shall cause it suddenly to run away from you
> like a torrent; beware to irritate Us.

It was the measure of how intimately the Ottomans—or Sokollu— understood Venice that their direst threat was on cost grounds, but the senate was resolute and voted for war by the unprecedented margin of

195 to 5. Kubat had to be slipped out of a back door to avoid the attentions of the mob.

DESPITE THIS THUNDERCLAP, the Ottoman plan was not a sudden whim; the visit of 1568 indicated that it was years deep, part of a clear intention for final Ottoman control of the Eastern Mediterranean. Reconnaissance had been accompanied by planning that conformed to all the verities of Ottoman diplomacy and turned on careful calculations. Whatever Sokollu felt, he was instrumental in preparing the ground. He had made peace in Hungary and the Yemen, then thrown dust in the eyes of Christian Europe: the promised support for the Morisco revolt was intended to distract Philip in faraway Madrid; in France, Charles IX was receiving from the Turks offers of new treaties, to keep Christendom in diplomatic turmoil. As for the Venetians, they had been encouraged to use their bribes on Sokollu as "the friend of Venice" who could pour oil on the troubled waters of Ottoman aggression and who would then offer, at the last moment, to take the island peacefully off their hands. Sokollu reasoned that Venice was too far from Cyprus to mount an adequate defense—if it fought at all—and, crucially, that Europe was too disunited to mount a joint response. Fear of crusade always dominated Ottoman thinking, but two hundred years' experience of disorganized pan-Christian actions had reasonably led Sokollu to hope that Venice could be teased into peaceful surrender. It was a reasonable bet that proved wrong. No one in early 1570 could have predicted that the Cyprus war and the Morisco revolt—events at the far ends of the sea—would trigger a chain reaction that would surprise everyone. Nor had anyone made adequate allowance for the messianic personality of Pope Pius V, or the daring of Don Juan of Austria, or the velocity that events in Famagusta would impart to a united sense of Christian purpose.

EVEN BEFORE KUBAT'S dramatic ultimatum, the Venetians had started to make overtures to Christian Europe and, against their better judgment, to raise the question of Holy League again. On March 10, the doge was writing to his ambassador at Philip's court in Madrid with oily disingenuousness that "the forces of his Catholic Majesty should be united with ours in order to oppose the fury and power of the Turks, to which we have readily assented because of our desire for the universal good, and because we hope that the Lord God has turned His compassionate eyes toward Christendom, and that He is willing at this time to repress the audacity of the infidels." The problem was that no one believed in Venice's sincerity; people wondered, even as Venice made this offer, if the republic was still negotiating with Sokollu—which indeed they were. If the Ottomans withdrew their threat, the merchants on the Rialto would cheerfully forget the greater good of Christendom and go back to trading with the infidel. Philip could doubtless still recall Venetians cheering at the fall of Saint Elmo and had no intrinsic interest in helping Venice; indeed the Ottoman concentration on Cyprus seemed an ideal moment to retake Tunis and consolidate the Western Mediterranean.

Everyone, however, had reckoned without the pope. The Cyprus crisis was just the opportunity to reanimate the Holy League for which Pius had been waiting. He threw himself headlong into the project with a frightening passion; he immediately committed the papacy to supplying galleys for the venture and loosed the papal purse strings with a promptness that left the recipients slightly openmouthed after the tightfistedness of his predecessor. "His Holiness has demonstrated the truth of one of our Castilian proverbs," quipped the Spanish cardinal Espinosa, "that the constipated die from diarrhea."

Pius dispatched the Spanish churchman Luis de Torres to Philip with cogent arguments for combined action. "It is clear that one of the principal reasons why the Turk has quarreled with the Venetians is that he thought he would find them unaided, without any hope of uniting with Your Majesty, who is so occupied with the Moors of Granada." That had indeed been Sokollu's calculation; it was a reasonable one, but it had unintended consequences.

Philip was suspicious of the whole idea of Holy Leagues, and it was not in his nature to act spontaneously. God's bureaucrat, who dressed soberly in black, read everything, ruled absolutely, thought suspiciously, and acted cautiously, was not one to make up his mind quickly— nor to reveal his intentions prematurely. "He is one of the greatest dissimulators in the world," complained the French ambassador. "He knows how to pretend and conceal his intentions better than any king . . . up to the time and the hour at which it suits him to let them be known." Where Selim delegated the affairs of state, Philip wanted to weigh every detail and manage every operation personally. His decision-making was a byword for sloth. "If we have to wait for death," joked his officials, "let us hope that it comes from Spain, for then it would never arrive."

Yet Torres arrived at a critical moment and initially appeared to achieve unexpected results. The Morisco war was at its height and Philip was at Cordoba, overseeing the campaign. Spain crackled with religious fervor; the fear that the Turks might be aiding the revolt loomed large in Philip's mind. In an atmosphere of heightened emotions, distances telescoped and it seemed to Philip that nothing less than a direct challenge to Ottoman power could now solve his internal problems and resolve the whole issue of Mediterranean security. And Torres had brought with him the promise of substantial papal subsidies, for money always concentrated Christian minds. Torres had his answer within two days. The Catholic King agreed in principle to involvement in a Holy League, the terms for which must be scrupulously worked out, Philip's natural caution quickly reasserting itself on this point. In the interim, prompted by the prospect of cash up front, he committed himself to providing "immediate" aid to "please the Pope and provide always for Christendom's need." He would send his naval commander Gian'Andrea Doria—the inglorious survivor of Djerba—with a galley fleet to the south of Italy. For the first time in many years, the Mediterranean witnessed a unified Christian attempt to turn back the Ottoman tide.

It was to be a tripartite force. Venice, the Papacy, and Spain, oiled by church money and indulgences for the sins of those who participated, were to combine their fleets in a concerted attempt to save Cyprus. Each force appointed its own commander. The Venetians gave the baton of command to Gerolamo Zane, in a typically elaborate service in Saint Mark's. He departed the lagoon with an advanced galley fleet on March 30, 1570. Doria, the most experienced seaman in the whole operation, was captain general of the Spanish galleys, while to the pope fell the choice of overall commander. He made what was effectively a political compromise. Marc'Antonio Colonna was an Italian but also a vassal of the Spanish king; it was felt he could appeal to both parties and draw Philip into the league. The problem was that he was a diplomat and a general, not an experienced naval man. Off the record there were snorts of derision in the Spanish camp—Cardinal Espinosa declared that his sister knew as much about ships—and Philip initially dragged his heels over accepting the appointment, annoyed that

Colonna had accepted without consultation, reminding his man that there was as yet no such thing as a league. But Pius was unmovable in his choice. On July 15, Philip wrote to the commander expressing pleasure at his appointment.

BENEATH SUCH FELICITOUS WORDS lay oceans of mutual suspicion and unstated but divergent objectives. The expedition of 1570, under-taken under no agreed terms, was an exercise in bad faith, held together by the willpower and subsidies of the pope. Philip had no intrinsic inter-est in saving Cyprus for the Venetians, but welcomed the papal subsidy and would have liked to divert the expedition to North Africa; natural caution—and the catastrophe at Djerba—governed his secret instruc-tions to Doria. The loss of his carefully reconstructed fleet would lay Spain open to North African corsairs again; he had no intention of risk-ing it for the treacherous Venetians, who were quite capable of cutting a late deal with the sultan. The Venetians, for their part, had a profound distrust of the Genoese in general and the Doria clan in particular after the Preveza debacle of 1538. And neither party had any faith in the pope's choice of Colonna as a naval commander. They quietly ordered their admirals to obey him only in so far as it accorded with their expe-rience. The small print of Philip's directive to Doria hedged these instructions in particularly ambiguous terms: "You shall obey Marc'An-tonio Colonna as General of the Galleys ... and with the practical ex-perience you possess, you should at all times draw the attention of [Colonna] to what you judge the correct course of action in all things." Behind this lay a larger command: "You should look carefully where you put our galleys because of the great harm that any misfortune would bring upon Christendom." Philip was actually giving Doria the selfsame command he had given Don Garcia de Toledo at Malta: not to engage the enemy fleet at all. Doria's brother was said to have offered a wager "that there would be no combat with the enemy's armada, because Gian'Andrea had orders from his Majesty not to engage in such for this year." This chimed exactly with Doria's own peculiar relationship to the endeavor: he was present both as commander of the king's fleet and as a private contractor. Twelve of the galleys were personal property rented out to Philip: he had no intention of risking them in a fight.

It was against this background that the allies launched their fleets. The enterprise was ramshackle, ill-conceived—and late. The Venetians

*Gian'Andrea Doria*

had been at peace for thirty years and were playing catch-up. They built and recommissioned ships with extraordinary speed; in June the arsenal turned out 127 light and 11 heavy galleys, but the search for reliable manpower was, as ever, a problem. The sea, and the conditions on board, quickly thinned out Zane's force still further. He was at Zara on the Dalmatian coast, waiting for Colonna and Doria, when typhus took hold of the rowing benches. The men started to sicken and die. He sat there under orders for two months, then moved to Corfu, where things failed to improve. Inaction demoralized the fleet; when more rowers were recruited from the Greek islands, they died too. Exasperated at the nonappearance of their allies, the Venetian senate ordered Zane to push on to Crete with his depleted ships in late July.

Doria, meanwhile, was making the usual laborious preparations, collecting troops in Southern Italy and awaiting Philip's exacting but conflicting instructions. Reverting to type, the king had not as yet actually pledged to join his fleet with the Venetians', merely to send it to Italy. It took further clarifications to get Philip to instruct Doria accordingly, but in such ambiguous terms that Doria complained to his father-in-law that "the king commands and wishes that I serve him and guess [his intentions]. Yet the more I read his letter, the less I understand it. ... Thus, I have no other choice but to go, but slowly." He acted accordingly, dawdling around the south coast of Italy to a meeting with the papal galleys of Colonna at Otranto. Colonna had been waiting fifteen days, then had to endure Doria playing games with naval protocol. Doria failed to make the customary visit to his superior officer; eventually Colonna went aboard the Genoese flagship, where Doria informed him of his overriding "obligation of preserving intact the fleet of Your Majesty" and that he would stay with the combined fleet no later than the end of September.

Eventually Colonna and Doria set sail for a rendezvous with the Venetians on Crete on August 22, "and all this was done," Colonna reported ruefully afterward, "despite Gian'Andrea who, for fear of being discovered, went so far out to sea that he could hardly make the landing in Crete."

IT WAS ALL HAPPENING too late. The Ottomans had planned their operation carefully and sailed early. Piyale left Istanbul in late April with eighty galleys; the army commander, Lala Mustapha, departed twenty days later; the cavalry and janissaries marched across Anatolia to the collection point at Finike on the southern coast, one hundred fifty miles from Cyprus. By July 20, the Ottomans had landed somewhere between sixty thousand and eighty thousand men on the island.

The expedition was the echo of Malta, though on a far larger scale. There were two competing objectives. Nicosia, the inland capital in the center of the island, and Famagusta, "the eye of the island," its heavily fortified port on the eastern coast. Venice's most competent commander, Astorre Baglione, guessed the Ottomans would go for Famagusta, and Piyale again argued for capturing the safe harbor. But somewhere in the back of Lala Mustapha's brain lurked the lesson of Mdina, which had been his namesake's nemesis on Malta. He was anxious not to leave Nicosia unguarded in the rear.

Lala Mustapha was part of the sultan's inner circle. His honorific forename—Lala, "guardian"—denoted his care of Selim as a child; he was a passionate opponent of Sokollu Mehmet, who tacitly disapproved of the whole venture. Success was now critical for Mustapha, who shared two attributes with his namesake General Mustapha on

Malta—an explosive temper in the face of stubborn opposition and a matching propensity for acts of exemplary cruelty. It was a character trait that would not serve the Ottoman cause well.

UNLIKE THE KNIGHTS AT BIRGU, the Venetians had at least given some foresight to defending their Cypriot strongholds. Nicosia lies at the center of the island's great plain—a dusty thirty-mile-long expanse, flat as a billiard table, that shimmers in the summer heat. The open terrain had allowed the unsentimental Venetians to rip the heart out of one of Europe's most beguiling and cosmopolitan cities. During the 1560s they blew up palaces and churches, evicted thousands of people, and demolished the island's most precious building—the monastery of Saint Domenico with its royal tombs—in the name of defensive engineering. In its place they constructed a perfectly symmetrical star fortress, three miles in circumference, taken straight from the pages of an Italian siege manual. It had a few shortcomings—some of the bastions were faced with turf, rather than stone—but it was considered by visiting experts to be of "the finest and most scientific construction." In the summer of 1570 it had provisions for a two-year siege. In the right hands it might have held out for a long time.

The problem was that Nicosia required twenty thousand men to defend its whole perimeter; the city's total population was put at fifty-six thousand, of which only twelve thousand were fit for military service, and many of these were untrained Greek levies. The priest Angelo Calepio, who later wrote a startling eyewitness account of what transpired at Nicosia, commented coolly about these men: the government "had neither muskets nor swords to give them, no arquebuses, no defensive armour. . . . Many of the soldiers were brave enough, but many had so little training that they could not fire their muskets without burning their beards." Effective defense also required a competent commander, and in this respect Venice had been unlucky. Death had stripped the island of its most experienced generals; the best remaining soldier on the island, Astorre Baglione, was in Famagusta. By default, control of Nicosia passed to the utterly disastrous Nicolas Dandolo. "Would to God we had lost him too!" wrote Calepio bitterly. Dandolo was cautious, uncharismatic, scornful of the opinions of others, and remarkably unintelligent. Throughout the whole siege he managed to frustrate the best efforts of his skilled Venetian officers and local Greek cavalry.

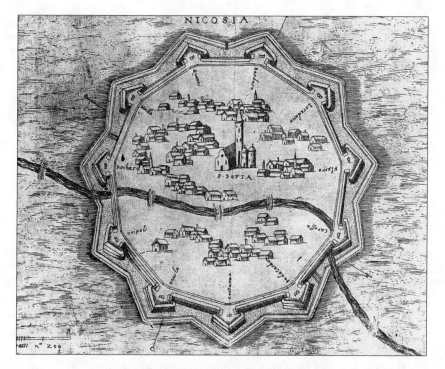

*Nicosia: "the finest and most scientific construction"*

He botched almost everything. Lala Mustapha was surprised to be able to land unopposed. Dandolo had forbidden the cavalry from repulsing the invaders. The Venetian senate had sent the island permission to free their Greek serfs, in a last-minute attempt to win their goodwill; the release was never implemented. From the start the Ottomans treated the local population with great clemency. "No liberty did they get," Calepio recorded, "except such as Mustapha gave them." It was all too easy to detach the Greek Cypriots from their Italian masters. When the unfortified village of Lefkara submitted to the Turks, a force from Nicosia sallied forth and massacred the local population. Unsurprisingly, later appeals to the outlying villages for help went unanswered.

Lala Mustapha marched on Nicosia unopposed and was quick to erect the gun platforms and snake his trenches forward. Dandolo seemed frozen into immobility, forbidding sorties, hoarding gunpowder, snuffing out initiative. Calepio, subsequently bitter from personal loss and imprisonment, could not restrain himself:

We were anxious to harass [the enemy] with our cavalry to stop their horses from bringing up faggots, but were not allowed to do so: even when some of the most daring of them came close up to our ditch to cut away the bridges and fronts of the bastions, and to bore into the walls, the Lieutenant [Dandolo] would not allow our men to fire on them if they were one or two, but only when they were ten or more, saying that he could not justify it to St Mark. So that the enemy had all the convenience for damaging our walls and bastions which they themselves could desire, whilst I and very many others have heard with our own ears the haughty commands and threats addressed to our gunners and their chief about wasting powder, which was doled out with the utmost niggardliness, as though to avoid injuring men who with such furious and incessant firing were trying to take our lives. Even what they had the Lieutenant wanted to hoard, so that very many people began to think he was a traitor. More than once Signor Pisani asked [him] why he did not let our men do what was necessary for the defence, and they almost came to blows when [Dandolo] was told, "Illustrious Sir, we ought to clear the ditch, and drive out the enemy, so that they may not with spades and picks undermine our ramparts, and lay them low." Signor Dandolo answered that our bastions were so many mountains.

There were fault lines within the city between Greek Orthodox and Venetian Catholics, and between rich and poor, that Dandolo—no La Valette—was unable to mend. "I saw but little charity where I ought to have found it," lamented Calepio, who delivered two mule loads of food and wine to the soldiers on the front line "to stir the hearts of the rich and great . . . but I found few to imitate me." The aristocratic leaders took to abandoning the defenses at nightfall and returning to their houses, which led to murmuring among the men.

The decisive moment came on August 15. The inspirational bishop of Paphos at last persuaded Dandolo to permit a sortie to spike the Ottoman guns. It went badly awry. Some of the undisciplined Greeks took to looting the enemy camp, then Dandolo forbade the cavalry to ride out in support of the operation. The core of professional Venetian soldiers was cut to bits.

Lala Mustapha tried repeatedly with a mixture of promises and threats to persuade Nicosia to surrender. By August 30, he was confident that the rescue fleet would not come. He made one more attempt, but the Venetians, fueled by a deep patriotism, refused to concede. "Everyone shall know again at this crisis," ringingly declared the Venetian aristocrat Count Giacomo, "by our brilliant deeds, by our very blood, how loyal we are; how we would rather die by the edge of the sword than change our masters." The vassal Greeks were probably less excited by these sentiments, but the example of Malta was firmly in everyone's mind. When signal fires were lit on the distant hills, men, women, and children ran to the walls and jeered at the Ottomans, reminding them of their failure before the walls of Birgu five years earlier. The authorities in outlying areas had ordered the fires to raise the morale inside the city, though they knew no relief was in sight. Dandolo took to protecting himself with an armed bodyguard against the ill will of the people.

While the siege of Nicosia was entering its last desperate phase, three hundred fifty miles away on Crete the allied fleet was acting out its own pitiful tragedy of bickering and deceit. The Spanish and papal fleet finally rendezvoused with Zane at Souda Bay on northern Crete on August 30. The Venetian commander had lost perhaps twenty thousand men to disease and had been scrabbling for replacements around the islands. The Christians now had a sizeable fleet—205 sails as against 150 of their opponents'—but there was no consensus of how to proceed and no agreed chain of command. On September 1, Colonna called a council of war on his flagship. The commanders talked for thirteen days. Doria was unimpressed by the condition of the Venetian fleet and accused Zane of concealing its true state; during the fleet review Zane had drawn up all his ships in the harbor and shifted his men from ship to ship as each was inspected, to disguise the truth about his depleted force. Doria argued it was too late now to attack Cyprus and roundly declared that he had no intention of letting Venice "acquire honour with my goods." He demanded that the Venetians should promise security of two hundred thousand ducats for his private galleys, should they be lost in the venture. The Venetians refused and insisted on a relief of Cyprus: Nicosia was still holding out, and Zane had orders to make for Cyprus and destroy the Ottoman fleet; it was imperative that they make the attempt. Doria continued to object. Zane wrote back to Venice describing Doria's obstructive attitude: "Though he pretends he is willing to fight the enemy, he does not wish to do so at all, and never ceases to make difficulties." Further intelligence was dispatched to determine the situation on Cyprus. As time and willpower dribbled away, Colonna became increasingly desperate to achieve something, anything. Finally on the night of September 17 the whole fleet weighed anchor with a view to unsettling the Turks by a strike on the island of Rhodes in their rear.

MEANWHILE PIYALE HAD DISPATCHED scouts to determine the intentions of the Christian fleet. Helpful Cretans informed him that the Christians were hopelessly bogged down and unlikely to achieve anything. Piyale duly detached sixteen thousand men from the galleys to join Lala Mustapha's final assault. At dawn on September 9 they closed in for the kill, spurred on by the pasha's promise of lavish rewards for the first men into the city.

The Ottomans concentrated their attack at four points. The inexperienced Greek levies were terrified by the pandemonium of the first assault and ran away almost at once. It was left largely to the Venetians to hold back the tide. Bells clanged throughout the city summoning men to the walls. Calepio came upon the bishop of Paphos, "who had on a breastplate ... [and] made me put on him arm pieces and a helmet, and went to join his men." For two hours they held back the Ottomans but "our men were cut in pieces, and the little fosses of the shelter were choked with corpses." Calepio saw the men being shot down one by one: "The Coadjutor fell killed by a musket ball; Messer Bernardo Bollani fell, and lay awhile under the corpses, but was picked up and went down to the gate. Nicolo Sinclitico withdrew at last with a wound on the face, likewise his brother Geronimo. Thomas Visconti, their brother, died; Colonel Palazzo died on the spot; the Governor Roncome died in his house; and (to be brief) after two hours' continuous fighting nearly all were left dead." Among the defenders still holding their ground, there was confusion and fury. The chief gunner at one of the bastions, now short of powder, rounded violently on his field commanders: "You dogs, enemies of God, of yourselves and the realm, do you not see that the enemy is gaining ground? Why have we no powder that we may drive them out? As long as I had powder to batter their flanks, they made no way. The devil take you. Have we eaten the powder? Have we swallowed the balls? Your saving for St Mark will, I can see, lose us the day." But by this time Dandolo was nowhere to be seen. He had abandoned his post and fallen back on the palace.

There was confused fighting in the streets "but with no kind of order" as the Ottomans poured in. A large number of Greek priests were killed outside their church. Calepio and another priest tried to rally the fleeing Greek levies: "we took a great cross and exhorted them as earnestly as possible ... but though we spent two hours haranguing them, it did little good." Some tried to slip through the embrasures of the walls; others opened the gates in an attempt to escape. "Many were killed by the Turkish cavalry, others were made prisoners, and a few escaped."

Around the palace in the central square, the defenders grouped for a last stand. By this time there were Venetians more intent on killing Dandolo than the Turks. The nobleman Andrea Pesaro sought out Dandolo and tried to cut him down. Crying "here I say, we have the traitor," he raised his word but was felled by the commander's bodyguard. Dandolo wanted to arrange an organized surrender but it was futile. Those who laid down their arms were just slain in the onrush. Fighting yard by yard, the last survivors held out for a while in the upper rooms of the palace, hurling Turks out of the windows, until they themselves were reduced to a mound of corpses. Dandolo dressed himself in his crimson velvet robe in the hope of being spared as an important person. He was beheaded anyway. "Then," according to Calepio, "a drunken Greek hoisted over the palace the Turkish standard, pulling down that of St Mark."

Finally the guns stopped firing and the din subsided, "but the change was a sad and mournful one." All that could be heard was the wailing of the women and children separated from their families and driven off into slavery. Calepio recorded terrible snapshots of collective and personal grief: "The victors kept cutting off the heads of old women; many of them as they marched along, to prove their swords, split open the heads of old women who had already surrendered. ... Among the slain were Lodovico Podochatoro and Lucretia Calepia, my mother, whose head they cut off on her serving maid's lap." The day after the capture of the city, the prisoners and plunder were put up for sale. It was said that no such quantity of loot had been taken from a city since the fall of Constantinople.

LALA MUSTAPHA SENT TO KYRENIA on the north coast a Venetian captain in chains with two severed heads attached to his saddlebow. To the commander at Famagusta, Marc'Antonio Bragadin, he dispatched Dandolo's head in a dish.

On the evening of September 21 the Christian fleet was sheltering from a storm off the Ottoman coast when scout ships returned with the news they had been dreading: Nicosia had fallen. The following day, on the poop deck of Colonna's flagship, the Christian relief effort played out its last act. The majority of the commanders were for turning back; Zane at last and reluctantly conceded. The bedraggled fleet sailed home, not without the bickering continuing on and off. Doria wished to wash his hands of the fleet and hurry back alone, mindful of the lateness of the season and his trumping instruction to keep his ships safe at all costs. In this at least he showed good judgment. In early October the fleet was hit by gales. Thirteen galleys foundered off Crete, though Doria, probably a better seaman, lost none. Typhus hit the galleys again; Colonna's vessel was damaged by lightning, and more ships went down. By the end of the year both Colonna and Doria would be publicizing their own partisan accounts of the fiasco. If the pope was dispirited, the Venetian senate was appalled; Zane would end his days in prison, a broken man, while Philip, who was as responsible as anyone for the humiliating failure, promoted Doria to the rank of general.

On Cyprus, the Venetian fortress at Kyrenia promptly surrendered when the captured officer rode clanking into the courtyard with the heads attached to his saddle. But at Famagusta, Marc'Antonio Bragadin buried Dandolo's head with honor and sent Lala Mustapha a ringing reply: "I have seen your letter. I have also received the head of the lord lieutenant of Nicosia, and I tell you herewith that even if you have easily taken the city of Nicosia, with your own blood you will have to purchase this city, which with God's help will give you so much to do you will always regret having encamped here."

The Ottoman army marched on to surround Famagusta. With it, Lala Mustapha sent booty and the pick of the young men and women taken from Nicosia. These captives were loaded onto a galleon belonging to Sokollu and two other vessels as presents for Selim. On October 3, off Famagusta, an explosion in the galleon's magazine ripped all three ships apart and rocked the defender's walls. Legend had it that it was an act of deliberate destruction by the daughter of an Italian noblewoman, determined not to be taken alive.

# CHAPTER 17

# Famagusta

RAIN FELL BLEAKLY on the Venetian lagoon during the winter of 1570–1571. The weather was wretched, the price of grain high, the fleet in tatters. There was still typhus in the galleys, and the ships' priests, fearful of contagion, were leaving the men to die unconfessed. The war was hurting Venice badly. Money was short, but the republic dared not stand down her fleet for fear the men would simply melt away.

Within the city, blame for the debacle of 1570 was hurled back and forth. An anonymous pamphlet, *The Notable Errors Committed by the Venetian Signoria in Their Resolution and Administration of the War Against the Turk*, excoriated the authorities for naïveté, bad judgment, poor appointments. The author held them responsible for "the loss of Nicosia, the death or imprisonment of 56,000 persons, as well as the loss of more than 300 pieces of artillery and of almost the entire island except for the walled enclosure of Famagusta." The ignominious fall of Nicosia seemed to mark another chapter in the unhalted decline of the republic's fortunes. Now the fate of Famagusta hung finely in the balance. "God knows whether Famagusta will be strong enough to hold out for so long a time against the forces of the Turk," wrote the French cardinal de Rambouillet to Charles IX. It was a view widely shared in Venice. Five hundred miles east, Selim was in Edirne, already preparing for the new campaigning season; after the rich pickings at Nicosia, volunteers thronged to the cause.

The pope was distraught. He personally blamed the expeditionary failure on Doria's refusal "to render the Venetians more satisfactory service." In Rome, the new year opened badly with one of those natural occurrences that unsteadied people. On January 3, during a violent storm, a bolt of lightning struck the campanile of Saint Peter's and caused extensive damage. More seriously, negotiations for the formal constitution of a Holy League seemed bogged down in the winter mud.

Talks had started brightly enough in July 1570 with Philip's representatives and those of Venice meeting in Rome under the auspices of the pope. There was initial jousting about terms of reference and costs—the Spanish wanted the league to be directed generally against all heretics and infidels; the Venetians, who had no intention of fighting Protestants in the Low Countries, countered that the term "the Turk" would be sufficient. The papal negotiators proposed using the league of 1537 as a template for the arrangement, and it appeared by September that all the major issues had been discussed; talks then had to be suspended while the Spanish negotiators trundled back to Madrid. By October, Philip, despite reservations, was ready to sign—at which point the Venetians started to quibble; they changed their team and demanded to negotiate everything again from scratch, point by point. There followed months of stop-start negotiations, wrangling, and distortion. For Pius, driven by Christian zeal, it was like herding geese into a pen.

The process was a clear reflection of the forces that destroyed the parallel naval expedition: bad faith, hidden agendas, mutual lack of confidence, conflicting objectives. Philip, the Catholic King, wanted the kudos of heading the league as temporal leader of the Christian world; his strategic interests extended no farther east than Sicily. In fact the fall of Cyprus had some advantages in that it reduced the power of Venice. Philip wanted to direct the league to a defense of the Western Mediterranean and the recapture of Tunis; he was also keenly interested in money. The dangled papal subsidies were crucial to Spanish participation. The Venetians demanded an offensive operation to secure Cyprus and gave not a thought for Tunis, while both parties were secretly appalled by Pius's vision that the league's ultimate objective must be the recapture of the Holy Land.

The Venetians remembered the league of 1537 with distaste and played a complex double game. Whilst strenuously denying it, they conducted on-off negotiations with Sokollu during the hammering out of the deal—and even after it was signed—for an ending of the war. Their representative in Istanbul, Marc'Antonio Barbaro, while ostensibly under house arrest for the duration of the war, was in constant contact with the chief vizier. The republic used the threat of a deal with the sultan as a pressure for better terms from the league, and vice versa. "I have no doubt," wrote an observant cardinal at the negotiations, "that if [the sultan] should offer these lords some sort of accord, and the league is not quickly settled, they will accept it, even though it means simply surrendering Cyprus to him." In fact the Venetians were bargaining hard with Sokollu for the retention of Famagusta, even as the Turks prepared to capture it. And the chief vizier had his own ruthless game of power politics to play; he had not wanted the Cyprus war, but now that it was under way, he was determined that his bitter rivals in the divan—Lala Mustapha and Piyale—should not gain military glory at his expense. If he could wheedle Famagusta from the Venetians by diplomacy, he could still spike their guns.

FAMAGUSTA, "THE CITY SUNK IN THE SAND" the Greeks called it, was the easternmost outpost of the Venetian sea empire. The lion of Saint Mark, carved in stone on the sea gate, glared unblinkingly into the brilliant sunlight; his flag rustled in the salt wind, above the palm trees and the Crusader chapels and the church of Saint Nicholas, a gothic fantasy modeled on the cathedral at Rheims, somehow beached on a tropical shore.

The Venetians had fortified the place heavily in the years before Lala Mustapha came. The two-mile perimeter, shaped like a rhombus, presented a formidable obstacle for the pasha. "A very fair stronghold, and the strongest and greatest on the island," an English visitor called it in 1553—five gates, fifteen bastions, a deeply excavated dry ditch, walls fifty feet high and fifteen feet thick—and the terrain was low-lying and malarial, not a place for an army to linger. The pasha was keen for a quick result.

As soon as he arrived in late September, Lala Mustapha tried to persuade the Venetians to give up without a fight. He paraded heads and live captives in front of the walls, and forged letters to the Venetian ambassador in Istanbul, requesting Bragadin's permission to surrender. From the start he received a flinty response. Bragadin, like the hapless Dandolo, was a scion of one of the great families of Venice, but a stouter patriot. Matters at Famagusta were put on a very different footing from those at Nicosia. There was strong internal discipline; the soldiers were paid; food distribution was systematic and fair; accordingly to the patriotic Venetian accounts, "as long as there was a drachm of food, Bragadin distributed it; and where there was none, there remained his goodwill." Despite a huge discrepancy of forces—eighty thousand to eight thousand—morale was high. The Greek population and their priests participated wholeheartedly in the defense, and Bragadin was wise enough to leave practical military command to the inspirational Astorre Baglione, who was adored by his men.

Winter passed in desultory fashion. The Ottoman fleet had returned to safe harbors on the mainland, and Lala Mustapha was left awaiting the spring. In the interim there were sorties and skirmishes and Homeric bouts of single combat to relieve the tedium, in which Baglione himself took part. The whole population watched from the walls and accused the Turks of cheating by wounding horses and running away when beaten, rather than yielding to the victor. Baglione offered prize money to up the sporting interest—just two ducats for killing an opponent, five for unseating him from his horse.

In the midst of this low-level engagement, Venice delivered a small, sharp military blow to their enemy that was to have unforeseen consequences. In January, the republic appointed the energetic Marco Querini as commander of the galleys in Crete. The new man discovered that the Ottomans had withdrawn their fleet from the winter seas; there was just a token force left to support the army at Famagusta. He decided on an audacious, high-risk, and unseasonal strike, timed to coincide with the start of Ramadan. On January 16 he set sail with a dozen galleys and four high-sided sailing ships laden with seventeen hundred soldiers assigned to reinforce the town. Running east on the winter seas, he reached Famagusta in ten days; as the four ships made for the harbor, they were sighted by the Ottoman galleys, but Querini had laid a careful trap. His own galleys, lurking out of sight, caught the Ottomans totally by surprise and shot three of their vessels to bits before towing Querini's sailing ships into the harbor, to the great joy of the defenders. For three weeks Querini rampaged around the coast, destroying fortifications and harbor installations, capturing merchant ships and putting new heart into Bragadin's men.

On the night of Querini's departure, Bragadin and Baglione prepared an ambush. They ordered that no one was to appear on the walls the next morning, then loaded their cannon with grape and chain shot, their arquebuses with bullets, and readied their cavalry behind the gate.

At dawn, the Ottomans looked up at silent ramparts. Nothing moved; the ships had gone. They scrambled out of the trenches. Still no sign of life. They began to think the Venetians had sailed away with Querini. When this was reported to Mustapha, the whole army moved forward. As the Turks came within range, a signal shot was fired, followed by a furious volley of fire from the walls that mowed down swaths of men. It was then followed by a devastating cavalry charge.

Querini had departed with promises of substantial relief; he also apparently left Bragadin with a boatload of captured hajj pilgrims to employ as hostages—though the details of this would be later disputed. These unfortunates were destined to play a pivotal role in what ensued.

QUERINI'S "VISIT" ALSO SERVED as a vivid reminder of what Venice was still capable of; it shocked the Ottoman high command and triggered a series of reactive measures that would aggregate large consequences. Selim was outraged and disturbed at this jolt to his pride; for protector of the faithful, keeping the hajj routes open was critical. He executed the bey of Chios, nominally responsible, by way of example. Piyale kept his head, but was dismissed from his post—a useful blow for Sokollu to inflict on one of his rivals. Command of the navy passed to the fifth vizier, Muezzinzade Ali—Ali Pasha—a far less experienced commander and another potential rival. Some have detected Sokollu's malign hand in this appointment, a deliberate attempt to sabotage a military operation whose success might weaken his position. Whatever the motive, the appointment would prove crucial. At the same time, fear of another relief effort forced the Ottomans into unfamiliar procedures. To guard Cyprus, they sailed much earlier than usual.

In mid-February, twenty galleys were sent to watch Crete; on March 21, Ali Pasha also departed from Istanbul. By sailing early, the fleet was inevitably committed to a long campaigning season. And in his pocket, as he sailed out of Istanbul, the new admiral carried a set of unprecedented instructions. In principle, the Ottomans had little interest in open-sea warfare. They used their ships to transport troops and to support amphibious operations against enemy ports and islands; the sieges of Malta and Rhodes were typical uses of Ottoman sea power. In this respect Ali Pasha's orders were extraordinary. They instructed him "to find and immediately attack the Infidel's fleet in order to save the honour of our religion and state." It is impossible to know if these were issued by Sokollu, or by the incautious sultan himself. It was to prove a fateful prescription.

BACK IN ROME the talks went on. In March the Spanish tried to divert the principal objective of the league to Tunis, but Pius was obdurate—the expedition would go east—and kept a tight fist on the purse strings. When all parties were finally invited to sign, the Venetians suspended the talks without explanation and went back to talking to Sokollu; as the noose tightened on Famagusta, the peace faction in Venice grew clamorous. The pope was reduced to tears; it seemed as if all his efforts were bound to fail; but by this time Sokollu's terms had grown more demanding—and Colonna was dispatched by Pius to persuade the Venetians back to the table. Eventually in May 1571, after ten months of wrangling and distortion, the final terms were agreed.

On May 25, 1571, the three parties signed the historic document in the Sala del Concistoro in the Vatican. It was followed a week later by huge public celebrations in the streets of Rome; specially minted coins were thrown to the crowd "as a sign of joy and gladness." On June 7, the league document was formally published in Venice in front of a huge crowd; a mass was sung in Saint Mark's and the doge walked in solemn procession. There was a thrill of expectation throughout Italy, mirrored in the stirring words of Pius himself, conscious that he had made history. He spoke, according to one observer, "with lively and loving words, thanking the Divine Majesty that in the time of his pontificate He had conceded the grace to Christendom that the Catholic princes had united and drawn together against the common enemy."

The terms of the league gave something to everyone. It was conceived not as a temporary alliance but, in the lofty words of its formulation, as an alliance in perpetuity—a permanent crusade that harked directly back to the causes of the Middle Ages. It was to be both offensive and defensive in nature, a war waged not just against the Turk, but against his vassal states in Algiers, Tunis, and Tripoli, this clause being of crucial importance to Philip. The league's financial arrangements were spelled out: Spain would pay a half, Venice a third, the papacy a sixth of the costs. And the short-term objectives were defined. The league was to prepare an immediate expedition of two hundred galleys and attendant forces for the recovery of Cyprus and the Holy Land—

the latter objective being one that both Venice and Spain prayed would be honored more in the breach than in the observing.

It was an extraordinary diplomatic coup by Pius; he appeared to have succeeded where fifteen of his predecessors had failed. To forge a united front to push back the infidel had long been one of the most ardent papal objectives. Pius, by sheer willpower, persistence, and money had achieved what many had believed was impossible, but despite the fine words in which the agreement was couched, many seasoned observers remained skeptical. In January, Philip had predicted that "as the League is now, I do not believe it will do or achieve any good at all." As if to justify these remarks, the ink was hardly dry before Spain tried to renege on the terms. Pius had to whip the Spanish back into line by threatening to withdraw the crusading subsidies again. Many others remained equally unconvinced. "It will look very fine on paper ... but we shall never see any results from it," wrote the French cardinal de Rambouillet during the negotiations. He saw nothing later to change his mind, and in Istanbul they were hopeful too, after the failed expedition of 1570, that the whole thing would collapse of its own accord.

The fact that the league held together for any time at all was largely the conjunction of two remarkable circumstances. The first was the choice of leader of the joint Christian battle force, Don Juan of Austria, Philip's half brother, the illegitimate son of Philip's father, Charles V. The second was the violent and extraordinary denouement to the siege of Famagusta that was unfolding as the delegates signed and the crowds cheered.

THE SPRING SAILING had brought Lala Mustapha fresh men; Cyprus was so close to the Ottoman coast that no matter how many men died, replenishment was an easy matter. Word of the rich pickings at Nicosia had got about, and the pasha proclaimed, perhaps unwisely, that the booty at Famagusta would be better still. Adventurers and irregulars flocked to the cause. By April, Lala Mustapha had a vast army, somewhere in the region of one hundred thousand men. The Ottomans boasted that the sultan had sent so many to the siege that if each one threw a shoe into the ditch, they would fill it up. Crucially, a large number of these were miners, armed only with picks and shovels. Within the walls, there were four thousand Venetian infantry and the same number of Greeks.

By mid-April, Lala Mustapha was ready to press forward in earnest. Bragadin counted his finite food stocks and decided that there was no alternative but to expel the noncombatants. Five thousand old men, women, and children were given food for one day and marched out of a sally port. Any ruthless besieging general might now be expected to take advantage. Julius Caesar let the women and children die of starvation, hemmed in between the Roman legionnaires and Vercingetorix's fort in 52 B.C.; Barbarossa forced them back to the walls of Corfu in 1537. The mercurial Lala Mustapha did neither. He let them return to their villages. It was both compassionate and astute, a guarantee of goodwill toward the Greek population.

Bragadin was determined to emulate the defense of Malta, but there were crucial differences—not only was Famagusta fourteen hundred miles from any help, but the geology was different too. Birgu and Senglea had been built on solid rock; tunneling had required superhuman effort. Famagusta was constructed on sand—easy to mine, even if it required constant propping. In late April, Lala Mustapha's huge labor force started to shovel their way toward the city. The Christians jeered at the Turks for waging war like peasants, with picks and shovels, but the strategy was terribly effective. A vast network of trenches zigzagged toward the moat, so deep that mounted men could ride along them with only the tips of their lances showing, so extensive that the

*Famagusta under siege*

observers declared the whole army could be accommodated within them. Earth parapets were thrown up that concealed all but the tops of the Ottoman tents, and earth forts constructed fifty feet wide and bulwarked with oak beams and sacks of cotton. If these were destroyed by gunfire, they were quickly rebuilt. When the platforms overtopped the walls, they were mounted with heavy cannon.

The defenders fought with the confidence of the Knights of Saint John for the honor of their little republic. Baglione conducted sorties and ambushes, picked off miners, threw gunpowder into their trenches, hid planks in the sand studded with poisoned nails, knocked out gun emplacements, and killed alarming numbers of men. The fortitude of the defense astonished and worried the Ottoman high command. Men wrote home to Istanbul that Famagusta was defended by giants. When Lala Mustapha sent a message to Bragadin on May 25 with yet another request for surrender, he was met with shouts of "Long live St Mark." One of these parleys was rebuffed with a hotter response. The Venetians lived in eager hope of relief, and Bragadin invited the messenger to tell his master that when the Venetian fleet came, "I shall make you walk before my horse and clear away on your back the earth you have filled our ditch with." These were not wise words.

Eventually the weight of numbers started to tell. In early May, as the Holy League prepared to append their signatures in Rome, the Ottoman cannon started a heavy bombardment. Day after day they poured shot into the houses to break the citizens' morale, and against the walls to batter them down. Despite heroic repair work, Lala Mustapha's men inexorably degraded the fortifications; tunneling allowed them to plant mines and blast the front off the ravelins and bastions. On June 21 the Ottomans opened a definitive breach and delivered the first of six furious assaults that gradually whittled away the defense. Supplies of food and gunpowder began to dwindle. "The wine is finished," wrote the Venetian engineer Nestor Martinengo, "and neither fresh nor salted meat nor cheese could be found, except at a price beyond all limits. We ate horses, asses, cats, for there was nothing else to eat but bread and beans, nothing to drink but vinegar with water and this gave out." On July 19, the bishop of Lemessos, a talismanic figure for the people, was killed at his table by an arquebus. The Greek citizens had supported their Venetian masters faithfully; now they had had enough. Mindful of the end of Nicosia, they petitioned

Bragadin for surrender. After an emotional mass in the cathedral, Bragadin begged them for fifteen more days. They assented, but the Ottomans too knew the end was near. On July 23, Lala Mustapha, increasingly frustrated by what he regarded as pointless resistance, shot a blunt message over the wall to Baglione, yet again repeating Suleiman's formula at Rhodes:

> I, Mustapha Pasha, want you milord general, Astorre, to understand that you must yield to me for your own good, because I know that you have no means of survival, neither gunpowder nor even the men to carry on your defence. If you surrender the city with good grace, you will all be spared with your possessions, and we shall send you into the land of the Christians. Otherwise we shall seize the city with our great sword, and we shall not leave a single one of you alive! Mark you well.

# CHAPTER 18

# Christ's General

WHILE LALA MUSTAPHA WAS CLOSING in on Famagusta, the Holy League's naval preparations lumbered into action. In all the ports of Spain and Italy—Barcelona, Genoa, Naples, Messina—men, materials, and ships were being laboriously gathered. The Western Mediterranean was a hubbub of disorganized activity: badly coordinated, unprepared—and late. The Venetian ambassador in Spain watched the proceedings in impotent fury. "I see that, where naval warfare is concerned, every tiny detail takes up the longest time and prevents voyages, because not having oars or sails ready, or having sufficient quantities of ovens to bake biscuits, or the lack of fourteen trees for masts, on many occasions hold up on end the progress of the fleet." It all contrasted so badly with the central coordination of the Ottoman military machine: its plans were laid far in advance, their execution ensured by unbreakable imperial edict. The governor of Karaman had lost his post for being ten days late in collecting men for the Cyprus campaign the previous year. The Ottomans had a battle plan to meet the Christian threat, and they followed it rigorously in the spring of 1571. The admiral, Ali Pasha, had sailed to Cyprus in March; another fleet under the second vizier, Pertev Pasha, left Istanbul in early May; the third vizier, Ahmet Pasha, marched the land army west in late April to threaten Venice's Adriatic coast; Uluch Ali sailed east from Tripoli. The campaign was to be much more extensive than the conquest of Cyprus. It was intended to carry the fight into the heart of the Adriatic, even to capture Venice or beyond: "The domination of the Turks must extend as far as Rome," Sokollu rhetorically informed the Venetians. By late May, Ali and Pertev, judging the siege of Famagusta to be nearly over, combined their fleets and started to ravage Venetian Crete.

The Venetians were desperate for something to happen. Their galley fleet was at Corfu by late April, under the new commander Sebastiano Venier. After the shameful display of the previous year under Zane, the Venetians had now entrusted their enterprise to a formidable man. Venier, already seventy-five years old, with the looks of a bad-tempered lion from some Venetian plinth, was a redoubtable patriot; though no sailor, he was a resolute man of action—impetuous, decisive, and possessed of an explosive temper. He received news of the plight of Cyprus with growing impatience and tried unsuccessfully to persuade his officers that they should strike out for Famagusta on their own, without waiting for the prevaricating Spaniards. It was judged to be too risky; the fleet was still understrength. There was nothing to do but wait. Slowly the allies started to converge on Messina, on the north coast of Sicily, the agreed rendezvous for the operation. Marc-'Antonio Colonna was again appointed to command the papal galleys at the insistence of Pius V, despite the previous year's debacle. By June, Colonna was at Naples. Now all they could do was await the arrival of the Spanish and the leader of the whole expedition.

It fell to Philip to choose this commander; his first nominee had been the ever cautious Gian'Andrea Doria. This was immediately ruled out by the pope—he personally blamed Doria for the failure of 1570, and the Venetians detested him. Philip's second suggestion was his young half brother, Don Juan of Austria. It was to prove an extraordinary choice.

Don Juan, twenty-two years old, good-looking, dashing, intelligent, chivalrous, and daring, driven by an unquenchable appetite for glory, was the antithesis of his half brother, the prudent Philip. He had already proved himself as a military commander during the Morisco revolt, but not without taking what Philip considered unacceptable risks. When Don Juan had placed himself in the front line and been hit on the helmet by an arquebus bullet, Philip was outraged. "You must keep yourself, and I must keep you, for greater things," he wrote reprovingly. For Philip, Juan represented the only possible dynastic successor in 1571; he was determined not to risk him in battle. To keep him in check, and to ensure astute maritime advice—for Don Juan had no sea experience—he closely shackled his authority with a team of seasoned advisers that included Gian'Andrea Doria, Luis de Requesens, and the marquis of Santa Cruz, Álvaro de Bazán, an experienced seaman. Though Bazán was by nature more likely to favor aggressive action, Philip felt that any likelihood of actual battle had been removed by his

*Don Juan*

insistence that no engagement with the enemy should be undertaken without the unanimous agreement of these three men. He thought that he could count on Doria to deliver a veto.

These restraints irked the young prince. His appetite for glory had been stoked by the circumstances of his birth. His illegitimacy made his position within the royal household anomalous, and Philip went out of his way to deliver casual slights to the over-popular young man. He refused Don Juan the title of Highness; he was merely to be called Excellency. In an age of touchy protocol these niceties mattered. He might be Philip's default successor, but in the interim the king was not going to confirm his royal status. Worse still, Philip undercut Don Juan's position as commander by communicating the order to seek the consent of his advisers to Don Juan's own subordinates. There is a tone of deep hurt wrapped around Don Juan's elaborate written replies to his half brother: "With due humility and respect, I would venture to say that it would be to me an infinite favour and boon if Your Majesty would be pleased to communicate with me directly with your own mouth . . . [rather than] reducing me to an equality with many others of your servants, a thing certainly in my conscience not deserved." Don Juan longed for glory, confirmation, ultimately a crown of his own. Shadowed by graybeards who had been tasked with preventing him from achieving anything at all, he was a man with something to prove. As he prepared to depart from Madrid in early June, the papal delegate in Spain understood, with approval, that Don Juan was eager to throw off these shackles. "He is a prince so desirous of glory that if the opportunity arises he will not be restrained by the council that is to advise him and will not look so much to save galleys as to gather glory and honour."

TWELVE HUNDRED MILES AWAY, the man who would oppose him as admiral of the Ottoman fleet was preparing to raid Crete. At first glance Muezzinzade Ali Pasha—Ali, "the son of the muezzin"—seemed a creature from a different world. Where Don Juan was born half into the royalty of Europe, Ali was the son of the poor; his father called people to prayers in the old Ottoman capital at Edirne, one hundred forty miles west of Istanbul. Through the meritocratic system of Ottoman preferment, Ali had risen to the position of fourth vizier, and now to the exalted position of *kapudan pasha*—admiral of the sultan's fleet—the post once held by the great Hayrettin Barbarossa. Ali was a man of whom people spoke well: "brave and generous, of natural nobility, a lover of knowledge and the arts; he spoke well, he was a religious and clean living man." Yet like Don Juan, he was also something of an outsider. It had become the custom for the sultan's ruling elite to be drawn from the ranks of converted Christians, usually captured as children—men who owed everything to the sultan and were brought up in his court. Sokollu was a Bosnian; Piyale had been taken as a child from the battlefields of Hungary. Ali was unusual in being an ethnic Turk; "coming from and growing up in the provinces, he was considered an outsider in the eyes of the important people of the sultan's palace, and this was considered a fault." He was not part of the ruling elite. Like Don Juan, he was a man with something to prove; he was ambitious for success in his sovereign's eyes. He too was brave to the point of recklessness, and he was driven by a matching code of honor: to draw back would be cowardly.

Crucially, neither man possessed much experience of sea warfare. It was not coincidental that the contest for the Mediterranean had been marked by a singular absence of large-scale sea battles; even Preveza had been little more than a glancing blow. The men who had maneuvered their fragile galley fleets so skillfully—Hayrettin Barbarossa, Turgut, Uluch Ali, Andrea Doria and his great-nephew Gian'Andrea, Piyale, and Don Garcia—had been deeply cautious. It was with good reason. They understood the conditions of the sea and its fickleness; a sudden stopping of the wind or its increase, an unwise maneuver close to shore, a minuscule loss of tactical advantage, could cause havoc. Long experience had taught that the margin between victory and catastrophic defeat was paper-thin; these men weighed the risks accordingly. The two admirals now assembling the largest galley fleets ever seen had none of this experience—they were eager to seek out the enemy directly and fight. Ali carried explicit orders to this effect. It was a combustible set of circumstances.

MANY OF THE SEASONED OBSERVERS on the Christian side doubted that the whole laborious gathering of ships, men, and materials could amount to anything, especially if led by the Spanish. Don Juan's progress toward Italy was tortuous. He left Madrid on June 6. It took him twelve days to reach Barcelona, then he waited a month for everything to be readied. "The original sin of our court is never to get a thing done with dispatch and on time," wrote Luis de Requesens to his brother from Barcelona, watching and sighing. Eventually, on July 20, Don Juan stepped aboard his sumptuously ornate galley, the *Real*, and departed to cheering crowds and gunfire. Every step of the way he was slowed down by rapturous receptions, huge crowds, illuminations, fireworks, festivities, monastery visits, and church services. Everyone wanted to catch a glimpse of the charismatic young prince, to detain and honor him. It was less a march to battle, more a royal progress, touched by explosive expressions of religious and crusading zeal, as if the ports along the route—Nice, Genoa, Civitavecchia, Naples, and Messina—were stations of the cross.

At Genoa, the Dorias entertained Don Juan as they had entertained his father, Charles V, with masked balls. "Everybody was surprised and delighted by the spirit and grace of the dancing of Don Juan," it was reported, like a court circular. Not to be outdone, Naples laid on a brilliant reception for the young man. News of his progress swelled across Southern Europe, each landfall amplifying the sense of expectation and crusading zeal. A breathless communiqué to Rome captured the spectacular arrival of Christ's general there on August 9: "Today at 23 hours Don Juan of Austria made his entrance to the enormous delight of the people. Cardinal Granvelle went to receive him at the harbour mole, and gave him his right hand. The said lord is fair-skinned with blond hair, a sparse beard, good-looking and of medium height. He was mounted on a very fine grey horse in handsome battle dress and he had

*Don Juan receives the banner of the League*

a very good number of pages and footmen dressed in yellow velvet with deep blue fringes." The next day he drove through cheering crowds from the port to the palace in the cardinal's coach in a spectacular outfit of gold and crimson, followed by a long procession of nobles. At each harbor, the ships boarded detachments of Spanish and Italian troops, all King Philip's men.

The pope had sent Cardinal Granvelle to Naples to consecrate the young commander in magnificent style. Granvelle was something of an ironic choice; as one of Philip's representatives at the league negotiations, no one had shown more ill will to the proceedings with his interminable quibbling and foot-dragging. At one point the exasperated Pius had forcibly driven him from the room. Now, at an elaborate service in the church of Saint Clara on August 14, Granvelle conferred on Don Juan the badges of office as leader of the Holy League. Kneeling before the high altar, Don Juan received his general's staff, and an enormous twenty-foot-high blue banner—the color of heaven—a gift of the pope, bearing the elaborately wrought image of the crucified Christ and the linked arms of the league participants. "Take, fortunate prince," intoned Granvelle in a sonorous voice, "take these symbols of the true faith, and may they give thee a glorious victory over our impious enemy, and by thy hand may his pride be laid low." The banner was carried high through the streets of Naples by Spanish soldiers and hung ceremoniously from the mainmast of the *Real*.

FOUR MONTHS EARLIER, a matching ceremony had taken place in Istanbul. Selim had conferred on Ali Pasha a similar swallow-tailed banner, but even larger. This one was vivid green—the color of paradise—and seamlessly embroidered with the ninety-nine names and attributes of God, repeated 28,900 times. Now it was dazzling splendidly in the autumn sun from the masthead of the *Sultana* in the Adriatic. The two banners were markers of matching aspirations and the assumption of God-given victory.

The consecrated Christian banner was given to mark the league's first objective—the relief of Famagusta—but by now the war had drawn closer. During July and early August, Ali Pasha's fleet had been blazing a trail of destruction across the Venetian sea empire. Working their way west along Crete and around the coast of Greece, the Ottomans made themselves lords of the Adriatic. Along the coast of modern Albania, they seized a string of fortified posts—Dulcigno, Antivari, and Budva—while the army moved overland in a coordinated pincer movement. Venier was forced to abandon his base on Corfu to avoid being bottled up, and moved the Venetian fleet west to Messina, to await the Spanish fleet. Venice was now totally without protection; the news worsened daily. In late July, the experienced corsairs Uluch Ali and Kara Hodja—"the black priest," a defrocked Italian friar—carried their raids to the city's very doorstep. Their ships came in sight of the city itself; an Ottoman squadron under Kara Hodja sustained a brief blockade of the basin of Saint Mark. Panic-stricken defensive measures were put in place; fortifications and cannon were mounted on the islands around the city. The Ottoman crescent moon was very close indeed.

FAR AWAY AT FAMAGUSTA, the siege was entering its final act. Lala Mustapha's offer of negotiated surrender was fiercely resisted. Bragadin was in personal agony: "You must know that by the commission which I hold, I am forbidden on pain of death to surrender the city. Forgive me," he cried, "I cannot do it." It took Baglione and two more punishing assaults to talk him around. By July 31, the city was on its knees. The last cat had been eaten; only nine hundred Italians were left alive, of whom four hundred were wounded. The survivors were exhausted, shell-shocked, and hungry. Many of the city's beautiful buildings were in ruins. The Famagustans had paid the highest price for their loyalty. There were no ships on the horizon. Baglione reassured Bragadin that "having discharged our debt in defence [of the city], we have not failed in any way. . . . I tell you, on my word as a gentleman, that the city has fallen. At the next assault we shall not be able to meet them, not only because of our few troops, now so depleted, but because of the gunpowder, which has been reduced to five and a half barrels." Famagusta had been pummeled for sixty-eight days, absorbed 150,000 rounds of cannon fire, and used up, through warfare or disease, perhaps sixty thousand Ottoman troops. Bragadin gave way. On August 1, in the network of interconnecting tunnels under the walls, Venetian miners handed their counterparts a letter for the pasha. The white flag was raised on the ramparts.

The generous terms were a measure of the toll on Lala Mustapha's army. All the Italians would be allowed to leave the island with colors flying; safe passage on Ottoman ships would be afforded them to Crete; the Greek inhabitants could go if they wished or stay and enjoy personal liberty and property. The Italians wanted to take all their cannon, but Mustapha refused to allow more than five. At this point there is a small but significant difference in the sources. All the Venetians agree that these, give or take a few minor details, were the terms on which Mustapha sealed the document and granted the safe conduct. Mustapha Pasha subsequently narrated his own version to the chronicler Ali Efendi, who took part in the siege. In this there is a further clause: the Venetians were still holding fifty hajj pilgrims captured by Querini in January, and it was agreed by both parties that these pilgrims had to be surrendered. In the space between these two accounts, something terrible arose.

On August 5, the Venetians started to embark on the Turkish ships. "Up to that hour the Turks' relations with all the rest of us had been friendly and without suspicion, for they had shown much courtesy toward us in both word and deed," wrote Nestor Martinengo, although by this stage, against the terms of the agreement, Ottoman soldiers were already entering the city and engaging in opportunistic looting. It may have been difficult to restrain men who had been promised lavish booty by the pasha.

At the hour of vespers, with the ships almost loaded, Bragadin set out to take the city keys to Lala Mustapha. The proud Venetian aristocrat departed from Famagusta in a show of pomp—some suggested less the defeated general than the victor. He walked in state, preceded by trumpeters and wearing crimson robes. A crimson parasol was carried above his head as the symbol of his office. With him went Baglione and the other commanders and a personal bodyguard—about three hundred men in all. They walked with their heads held high between the jeering ranks of the Ottoman army, but were safely conducted with due ceremony to Mustapha's tent. The commanders left their swords at the threshold and entered. Mustapha rose from his seat and gestured them to stools covered with crimson velvet; they duly kissed the pasha's hand, and Bragadin began his formal declaration of surrender: "Since the Divine Majesty has determined that this kingdom should belong to the most illustrious Grand Signore, herewith I have brought the keys to the city, and herewith I give the city up to you in accordance with the pact which we have made with each other." And then, at the moment of greatest vulnerability for the Venetians, it all started to go horribly wrong.

Negotiated surrender hangs on a thread of mutual trust. Whether it was the Bragadin's visible pride, or his earlier taunt to Mustapha, or the pasha's exasperation at the sheer pointlessness of a siege that had cost at least sixty thousand men, or a need to justify the lack of booty to his men, or a justifiable grievance about the prisoners, whether it was spontaneous or premeditated, none of this is clear, but when Bragadin inquired if they were now free to depart, the thread snapped.

According to the Ottoman accounts, it started with a tetchy exchange about guarantees of safekeeping for the return of the ships from Venetian Crete. Mustapha wanted a hostage from among the nobles. Bragadin cursed him angrily: "You shan't have a noble, you shan't even have a dog!" Angry now, Mustapha asked where the hajj prisoners were. According to Ali Efendi's account, Bragadin admitted that they had been tortured and killed after the peace treaty had been signed: "Those Muslim captives were not under my personal control. The Venetians and native Beys killed them on the day of surrender and I killed those who were with me."

"Then," said the pasha, "you have broken the treaty."

There were other matters too to add fuel to Mustapha's fire: the destruction of a large quantity of cotton and ammunition—booty might well have been a subtext to the pasha's displeasure—and there were something haughty in Bragadin's words and manner that riled the conqueror unbearably.

The Venetians told the story differently. In one, Querini had taken most of the Muslim prisoners away with him in January; in another, it was claimed that only six were left, and they had escaped; in a third, that Bragadin was ignorant of the fate of these men. "Do I not know," came the angry reply, "that you have murdered them all?" Then getting into his stride, all Mustapha's grievances came tumbling out. "Tell me, you hound, why did you hold the fortress when you had not the wherewithal to do so? Why did you not surrender a month ago, and not make me lose 80,000 of the best men in my army?" He wanted a hostage against the safe return of his ships from Crete. Bragadin replied this was not in the terms. "Tie them all up!" shouted the pasha.

In a flash they were hustled outside and prepared for death. The executioners strode forward and Bragadin was made to stretch out his neck two or three times. Then Lala Mustapha thought again; he decided to reserve him for later and ordered his ears and nose to be cut off—the punishment for common criminals. Baglione protested that the pasha had broken his faith; he was executed in front of the tent along with the other commanders. In the Venetian account, Mustapha then showed Baglione's head to the army: "Behold the head of the great champion of Famagusta, of him who has destroyed half my army and given me so much trouble." Three hundred fifty heads were piled in front of the ornate tent.

Bragadin's end was lingering and dreadful. He was kept alive until August 17, a Friday. The wounds on his head were festering; he was crazed with pain. After prayers, he was processed through the city to the sound of drums and trumpets, accompanied by his faithful servant Andrea, who had accepted conversion to Islam in order to serve him to the last. Because of his earlier words to the pasha, he was made to carry sackfuls of earth along the city walls and to kiss the ground each time he passed the pasha. He was taunted to convert to Islam. The Venetian hagiographers record a saintly response: "I am a Christian and thus I want to live and die. I hope my soul will be saved. My body is yours. Torture it as you will." They probably heightened the horror for a receptive audience, but the stark facts are beyond doubt. These were ritual acts of humiliation. More dead than alive, he was tied in a chair and hoisted to the top of a galley's mast, ducked in the sea, and shown to the fleet with jeers and taunts: "Look if you can see your fleet; look, great Christian, if you can see succour coming to Famagusta." Then he was hustled into the square beside the church of Saint

Nicholas, now converted into a mosque, and stripped naked. The butcher ordered to commit the final act—and this would not be forgiven in Venice—was a Jew. Tied to an ancient column from Salamis still standing to this day, Bragadin was skinned alive. He was dead before the butcher reached the waist.

The skin was stuffed with straw. Dressed in the commander's crimson robes and shaded by the red parasol, it was mounted on a cow and paraded through the streets. Later the hideous dummy was exhibited along the coast of the Levant, then sent to Selim in Istanbul.

This theatrical act of cruelty was not universally applauded within the Ottoman domain. Sokollu was said to have been appalled. Maybe he understood, as with the massacre at Saint Elmo, that such acts only stiffened resolve; or he read a deeper motive. With the butcher's knife Lala Mustapha had wrecked his rival's attempt to broker surrender by peaceful means; Sokollu's diplomacy turned on the need to keep the republic from alliance with Spain. All this was probably now in ruins. Bragadin had given the Venetians a martyr and a cause. He had not died in vain: the time spent on Famagusta and the losses incurred had seriously impeded the Ottoman war with Venice. His stuffed skin, now dangling from the yardarm of a Turkish galley, still had its part to play.

# CHAPTER 19

# Snakes to a charm

August 22 to October 7, 1571

THE FATE OF FAMAGUSTA was still hidden from the Christian fleet when Don Juan reached Messina on Sicily on August 22. He was again treated to extraordinary displays of ceremonial pomp. Don Juan stepped ashore beneath a triumphal arch emblazoned with heraldic devices, to be presented with a charger with silver trappings—a gift from the city—to the roar of cannon, and buildings festooned with banners, inscriptions, and images of Christ triumphant. At night the city was brilliantly illuminated. All the congregated strength of the Christian Mediterranean seemed to be assembled in one place. Two hundred ships rocked at anchor in the harbor; thousands of Spanish and Italian fighting men crowded the narrow streets; thousands of chained galley slaves rested on the rowing benches. It was Pius's personal triumph to have gathered the great commanders of the age to fight in the name of Christ: Romegas and the Knights of Saint John were there, and Gian'Andrea Doria, Colonna with the papal galleys, the experienced Spanish admiral Bazán, the one-eyed Ascanio who had relieved Malta, the combustible Venetian Sebastiano Venier, Marco Querini whose daring raid on Cyprus had caused the Ottomans so much trouble early in the year, detachments from Crete and the Adriatic. It was an Olympic gathering, a test of Christendom's resolve. "Thank God that we are all here," wrote Colonna, "and that it will be seen what each of us is worth."

Beneath the surface, this magnificent pan-Christian operation was a brawling, bad-tempered, quarrelsome assortment of conflicting egos and objectives. There had been trouble all the way around the coast between the Italian and Spanish soldiers; fighting in the streets of Naples, fighting again at Messina; the men had killed each other. The officers had been forced to hang a few scapegoats to restore order. The commanders eyed one another with jealousy and suspicion. The Venetians hated Doria, whom they described sneeringly as looking like a corsair; their irascible commander, Venier, was fuming with impatience at the endless delays. He suspected the Spanish of something less than enthusiasm for battle and was hardly willing to take orders from Don Juan. Everyone regarded the Venetians as unreliable. They had brought a large quantity of ships but were woefully short of men. The Knights of Saint John were virtually the sworn enemies of Venice, a feeling enhanced by the recent execution by the city of one of their number for counterfeiting the republic's coinage. Meanwhile many of the men were simmering with discontent at the lack of pay. In short, the expedition of 1571 was riven with all the divisions that had surfaced at Preveza, during the relief of Malta and the ill-fated attempt to relieve Cyprus the previous year. It was a fair calculation, in the Ottoman camp, that the Christian enterprise would fail, as it had so often in the past. Yet if the Ottomans were wrong, the stakes could be high; and the possibility certainly caused anxiety in Istanbul.

Behind all the trumpet calls and celebrations, the critical issue by late August was simply whether to risk battle or not. The season was late, the enemy rampant. Opinions were sharply divided. There were men with something to prove, such as Colonna smarting from the failed expedition the previous year; Venier and the Venetians, desperate for battle; and the aggressive Spanish admiral Bazán. Then there was the prince himself carrying the weight of papal expectation. Among all the gifts and celebrations he received, one outweighed all the others. Pius dispatched the bishop of Penna to Messina as his special envoy with the promise that victory would be rewarded with an independent crown. On the other side there was the majority Spanish opinion— Doria with the mandate not to risk the Spanish fleet; Requesens with orders to shackle Don Juan; and the cautious spirit of Philip, who had paid the majority share of the expedition, hovering in the background.

Don Juan was being lobbied with advice from all sides, some of it extremely helpful. The duke of Alba had written from faraway Flanders to urge him to manage the men well: "Your Excellency should always try to present a cheerful face to all the soldiers, for it's commonly known that they set great store on this and on Your Excellency bestowing a few favorable words on one national contingent one day and on another the next. And it's most advisable that they understand that Your Excellency takes great care over their pay and gives it to them whenever possible, and when not that you order that care should be taken that they are given their due rations at sea and that their provisions are of good quality, and that they understand when this is done that it's by your order and diligence, and when it's not, that you regret it and order punishment." Don Juan followed this to the letter and grew in the process. On August 3 he had quelled a pay mutiny at La Spezia by personally promising that the men would be paid. The Spanish meanwhile were working hard to rein in the enthusiasm of their young commander. Even Don Garcia de Toledo, dismissed from Philip's service after Malta, had advice to give.

The old man was two hundred miles away, taking a cure for his gout at the hot springs near Pisa. He was a repository of knowledge about the Mediterranean wars. He had been at Charles's triumph at Tunis in 1535, seen the destruction of his fleet at Algiers eight years later, and relieved Malta. Above all he remembered the lessons of Preveza in 1538, the nearest thing to a major sea battle in thirty years, when Barbarossa got the better of Andrea Doria. He had cautious words for the young man, which he unfolded in a series of letters. He understood the risks, the problems with naval alliances, and the physical and psychological superiority that the Ottomans now had at sea: "If I were in charge, I would be reluctant [to fight] with your majesty's fleet lacking eight or nine thousand experienced soldiers from Flanders, because were defeat to happen—God forbid—it would do far more harm than the benefits of any victory could bring. Bear in mind also that our fleet belongs to different owners, and sometimes what suits some of them doesn't suit others, whereas our enemy's fleet has just one owner, and is of one mind, will, and loyalty, and those who fought at Preveza know the value of this. The Turks have gained the psychological advantage over the Venetians, and I believe that even against us they haven't much lost it."

Behind the Spanish position lay fifty years of maritime defeat. Preveza and Djerba hovered behind all their thinking; be cautious, he repeated, be cautious. "For the love of God," Don Garcia wrote again to Requesens, "consider well what a great affair this is, and the damage that may be caused by a mistake," before going on to emphasize the convoluted secrecy of the Spanish position. "But as it will be better for various good reasons that the Venetians should not know how much or why it is in His Majesty's interest that there should be no battle, I pray you after having read this letter to Don Juan to destroy it." There was a determined aim to ensure that the expedition should fail, while saving the face of the Catholic King.

But Don Juan's personal inclination was already clear from the sets of questions he was now firing back to Don Garcia. If he were to fight, how should he organize his fleet? How should he use his artillery? When should he give the order to fire? Don Garcia's advice, some of which failed to reach him in time, was very specific, drawn from the accumulated knowledge of half a century of sea warfare. Full frontal sea battles had been extremely rare—and none on the scale that was now being planned—but those fought had been illuminating. He advised Don Juan to learn the lessons of the past: "You should be warned not to order all the fleet into one squadron because such a large number of ships will certainly lead to confusion and some ships obstructing other ships—as happened at Preveza. You must put the ships into three squadrons, and put at the outer extremity of the wings those galleys in which you have greatest confidence, giving the tips of the wings to exceptional captains, and ensure that enough sea remains between the squadrons so that they can turn and maneuver without impeding one another—this was the arrangement employed by Barbarossa at Preveza."

These words were to prove highly influential. As to when to fire, his advice was horribly specific, a vivid reminder of the realities of sea battles. There were no second chances; the shots had to count: "In reality it's not possible to fire twice without causing the greatest possible confusion. In my opinion the best thing is to do what the cavalry say, and to fire the arquebuses so close to the enemy that their blood spurts over you. . . . I've always heard captains who know what they're talking about say that the noise of the bow spurs breaking and the report of the artillery should be simultaneous or very close together." He was advocating point-blank range.

As the ships continued to gather in early September, Don Juan decided to hold a final meeting to agree on the plan of action. Wisdom dictated that all the senior officers should be present; given the prickly sensibilities of the various factions, Don Juan was determined to act openly. On September 10 seventy senior officers gathered on board the *Real* for the fateful conference. Don Juan put forward two options: to seek out the enemy or, in line with Don Garcia's advice, not to seek battle "but rather have the enemy to come to us, seeking every occasion to force them to do so." The opinions divided predictably: the papal fleet and the Venetians for immediate attack, Doria and a Spanish contingent for caution. But when Don Juan roundly declared his intention to attack and win, the vote was carried unanimously. Under silent peer pressure, Doria and Requesens caved in. "Not everyone willingly agrees to fight, but nonetheless [is] forced and pressured by shame to do so," wrote one commander.

In hindsight, despite Philip's attempts to shackle the fleet, this outcome was inevitable. Against all expectations, the Christians had assembled an enormous fleet. To turn back now would involve massive loss of face—and Don Juan had let it be known that if the Spanish would not participate, he would proceed with the papal and Venetian fleets alone. The failure of the previous year, the huge weight of religious expectation imparted by the pope, the crowds, the banners and the celebrations, the dashing pronouncements of Don Juan—the expedition was being impelled forward, "like snakes drawn by the power of a charm," as one observer put it.

Doria, mindful of Philip's orders, was still hopeful that battle might be avoided. It was resolved that the final objective would be decided at Corfu. There might yet be time to halt the impetus to war, but every sea mile east of Messina would make the decision harder to overturn.

Crowds cheered; officers and men thronged churches to receive the sacrament; the papal ambassador pronounced his blessing. Early on the morning of September 16, Don Juan scribbled a final letter to Don Garcia that would soon have the old man shuddering in his steam bath. He was sailing in pursuit of the enemy. "Although their fleet is superior in size to that of the league according to the information we have," he wrote, "it isn't better in terms of quality of either ships or men, and trusting in God our Father, whose cause this is, I have decided to go and seek it out. And so I leave tonight—may it please God—on the voyage to Corfu and from there I will go wherever I learn that their fleet is. I have 208 galleys, 26,000 soldiers, six galleasses, and twenty-four ships. I trust in our Lord that, if we meet the enemy, He will give us victory." The papal nuncio stood on the mole at Messina in his red robes, and blessed the vast contingent of ships, decked with their flags and pennants, as they rowed past the breakwater and out into the open sea.

—

AS THE ARMADA SWUNG OUT along the Italian coast, questions about the Ottoman fleet became more pressing. Where exactly was the enemy, and what condition were they in? How many ships did they have? What was their intention? The need for reliable intelligence was crucial. Don Juan had sent the Maltese knight Gil de Andrada forward with four fast galleys to hunt for clues. Three days later, Andrada returned with worrying news. The Turks had attacked Corfu, then retired to Preveza. There was a fear that the Ottoman fleet was now dispersing for the winter. That night, scanning the sky and the dark sea, the whole fleet witnessed a celestial phenomenon that raised their spirits. A meteor of unusual brilliance coursed across the sky and burst into three trails of streaking fire. It was taken as a good omen. Then the weather turned dirty; for several days the fleet toiled through rainy squalls that blotted out the horizon and held them back.

Andrada's intelligence had been partially correct. The Ottomans were withdrawing from the Adriatic after a highly successful campaign. They had captured key fortresses and taken a large quantity of booty. They raided Corfu for eleven days but withdrew as the Holy League left Messina, and then sailed south to seek the safety of their base at Lepanto, tucked into the mouth of the Gulf of Corinth, to watch and wait for orders from Istanbul.

It had been an exceptionally long season. Ali Pasha's ships had been at sea since March; the hulls of the galleys were now fouled with weed and needed cleaning; the men were tired. The Adriatic raids, despite their dramatic success, had exhausted the fleet. There was a general feeling that it was too late in the year for large-scale naval maneuvers; soldiers who had been in the ships for months asked to be released, or defected to the land army of Ahmet Pasha. Additionally there was a strong belief from past experience that the Christian fleet would collapse in disunity of its own accord or draw in its horns for the winter.

The Ottomans had also been carrying out their own information-gathering and, unknown to the Christians, had scored an extraordinary intelligence coup. One night in early September the Christian fleet had been lying at anchor in Messina harbor; all Marc'Antonio Colonna's papal ships were decked in black mourning for the death of his daughter. Unnoticed, a black galley rowed quietly through the lanes between the anchored vessels, up and down. It was the ship of the Italian-born corsair Kara Hodja, counting the enemy's strength. He also took back with him Don Juan's battle plan, either from spies or perhaps even from printed news sheets, so widely circulated were its details. He knew exactly how they intended to organize their fleet and the intention to push on to Corfu—though their purpose after that remained obscure.

The problem was that Kara Hodja had miscounted. He had missed a complete Venetian squadron of sixty galleys in the inner harbor. He put the tally at no more than one hundred forty. Don Juan had 208. Ali was puzzled by the aggressive intentions of an enemy with inferior numbers but reported this news back to Istanbul by swift frigate. At the same time, Don Juan, sighting the mountains of Corfu through the drizzle, was given equally unsafe intelligence. Some Venetians, returned from the enemy fleet in a prisoner exchange, reported that the Ottomans had one hundred sixty galleys and lacked fighting men, that Uluch Ali had departed the fleet. In fact they had about three hundred galleys, and Uluch Ali had gone to unload booty at Modon and return. A few days later, Gil de Andrada, scouting ahead, quizzed some Greek fishermen who seemed to confirm the weakened state of the enemy; they assured him that the Christians might offer battle with every certainty of victory. The same Greeks had just given identical messages of hope to Ali Pasha's scouts. The two sides had underestimated each other. Intelligence failures were about to aggregate serious consequences.

By September 27, the Christian fleet was anchored in Corfu harbor. It was the final moment of decision: to seek out the enemy or to pause. The mood of the Venetians, particularly, had been further darkened by the state of their island. Irritated by their inability to reduce the fortress, and bad-tempered by the length of the campaign, elements of the Ottoman army had indulged in wanton atrocities and ritual desecrations of holy shrines that fired up the crusading zeal of the Italians. Doria and sections of the Spanish contingent again pressed on Don Juan the risk and the lateness of the season; they suggested a face-saving raid on the Albanian coast before withdrawing for the winter, but Don Juan and the Venetians were not to be turned. They would seek out the enemy fleet.

The next day, in faraway Madrid, Philip wrote a letter ordering Don Juan to winter in Sicily and start again the following year. In

Rome the pope was urging exactly the opposite course of action through the power of prayer; "he fasts three times a week and spends many hours every day at prayer," wrote the Spanish cardinal Zuniga. On September 29, Andrada's scouts reported that the whole Ottoman fleet was at Lepanto. And somewhere off the southwestern tip of Greece, a fast frigate from the Venetian governor of Crete was hurrying north with news of Famagusta.

As September rolled into October, the Holy League was at Gomenizza on the Greek coast. Don Juan held a final review of the fleet. The galleys were stripped for action and put through precise maneuvers. Every captain was made fully aware of the battle plan. Don Juan passed through the fleet, observing the condition of the ships minutely. He was greeted by arquebus salutes as he passed—a not inconsiderable risk: twenty men had been accidentally shot dead since leaving Messina.

MEANWHILE, ALI PASHA had been receiving a string of orders from Istanbul. There was a fifteen- to twenty-day time lag between the commanders at the front and the imperial center, yet it is clear from the Ottoman documents that Selim—or Sokollu—was attempting to impose considerable central control over the running of the campaign. A steady stream of directives instructed Ali about fleet maneuvers, food supplies, and troop collection. Sokollu and Selim were evidently aware that the fleet was exhausted and manpower a problem, yet the orders dispatched on August 19 were emphatic: "If the [enemy] fleet appears, Uluch Ali and yourself, acting in full accord, must confront the enemy and use all your courage and intelligence to overcome it." Another directive, not dispatched until after the battle, was even more emphatic: "Now I order that after getting reliable news about the enemy, you attack the fleet of the infidels fully trusting in Allah and his Prophet." It is impossible to determine the division of responsibility between Sokollu and his master for these remarkable orders. They seemed to leave the commander on the ground no freedom of maneuver. Even Suleiman's thunderous commandments to Mustapha on Malta did not contain detailed instructions on how to proceed. Maybe the sultan and his vizier refused to believe that the Christians would actually risk battle, or believe that the Christians' morale would collapse, or maybe the sultan, buoyed up by the final conquest of Cyprus and a zeal for holy war, was overconfident, but they committed Ali Pasha to fight.

—

BY LATE SEPTEMBER, Ali was at Lepanto, the fortified port the Turks called Inebahti, a bare fifty miles south of Preveza and in a similar position to that occupied by Barbarossa against Doria. Like Barbarossa's at Preveza, Ali Pasha's position was virtually unassailable. Lepanto was a well-fortified, tightly walled port tucked into the mouth of the Gulf of Corinth; the entrance of the gulf was protected on both sides by gun emplacements, so that, as the Ottoman navigator Piri Reis had put it, not even a bird could fly through it. In any case, the prevailing winds would make any direct assault on the fleet extremely difficult. Ali could sit tight and wait for the enemy to exhaust themselves offshore, then strike at will, or refuse battle altogether. He had compelling reasons not to fight. The ships needed repairs; believing the campaigning season to be over, many of the cavalrymen had returned home. It seemed hard to believe that the enemy would risk an attack in early October. Furthermore, all the captured prisoners told the same story—that there were serious differences of opinion in the Christian ranks. Ali waited to see what would happen next.

At four in the afternoon on October 2 all the bottled-up tensions in the Christian armada suddenly exploded. The fleet was at Gomenizza on the mainland opposite Corfu when the long-running feud between the Venetians and the Spanish boiled over. Because the Venetian galleys were short of men, the commander Venier had been persuaded with great reluctance to board Spanish-paid soldiers on his vessels. There had been trouble from the start. "In the embarkation of these men and their biscuit, I had many difficulties to contend with, and much insolence from the soldiers to put up with," Venier wrote in his self-defense afterward. On the morning of October 2, as part of the review of battle readiness, Doria was sent to inspect the Venetian galleys. The tempestuous Venier flatly refused the hated Genoese the right to criticize his ships; tempers were already flaring when a brawl broke out on one of his Cretan galleys, the *Armed Man of Rethimno*, between the Venetian crew and its Spanish and Italian soldiers. It started when a crewman disturbed a soldier's sleep, and quickly degenerated into a full-scale fight that littered the deck with dead and wounded on both sides. The captain dispatched a message to Venier's flagship to the effect that the Spaniards on the *Armed Man* were killing the crew.

*The position of Lepanto in the Gulf of Corinth*

Venier was still fuming from his encounter with Doria and ordered four men and his provost marshal to board the ship and arrest the mutineers. The leader of the revolt, Captain Muzio Alticozzi, met them with arquebus fire. The provost marshal was shot through the chest; two of the men were thrown into the sea. Venier, now beside himself with fury, ordered the galley to be boarded, then stood by to blast it out of the water. When a Spanish ship offered to intervene, he erupted in fury. "By the Blood of Christ," the old man roared, "take no action, unless you wish me to sink your galley and all your soldiers. I will bring these dogs to heel without your assistance."

He ordered a party of arquebusiers aboard the *Armed Man* to seize the ringleaders and deliver them to his ship. He then had Alticozzi and three others hanged from the mast. By this time, the captain of the Spanish ship had reported the situation to Don Juan, who could now see four bodies dangling from the mast of Venier's ship. Don Juan himself was equally incandescent at these unauthorized executions of Spanish-paid men. He threatened to hang Venier on the spot. For Doria it was another chance to suggest returning to Messina and leaving the Venetians to it. The Venetian and the Spanish galleys primed their cannon with powder and held lit tapers at the ready. There was a tense standoff, the two galley fleets squaring up to each other for several hours. Eventually tempers cooled sufficiently for reason to prevail. Don Juan declared that he would no longer deal with Venier; henceforward all communications with the Venetians were to be by way of Venier's second-in-command, Agostino Barbarigo. The incident had brought the whole expedition to the brink of ruin, and word quickly reached the

Ottoman high command. When captives reported to Ali and Pertev that the Venetians and Spanish had come close to blowing each other out of the water, it doubled the belief that the outnumbered and divided Christian fleet would not fight. More likely they would carry out a token raid on the Albanian coast and retire.

It was at this moment that the ghost of Bragadin reentered the fray. With tempers soothed, the Holy League fleet sailed on south down the Greek coast. At Cape Bianco, Don Juan ordered a rehearsal of his battle formation; the squadrons were arranged across a five-mile front, each one distinguished by a different-colored flag. On October 4 they had reached the island of Kefalonia, when they spied a lone frigate tacking up from the south. It was the vessel from Crete carrying word of Famagusta. The appalling news had a sudden and electrifying effect on the fleet. It focused the Venetian desire for vengeance and instantly soothed divisions. Rationally it also knocked the bottom out of the whole expedition. If Famagusta could no longer be saved, the expedition's ostensible purpose had gone. When Don Juan held another council of war on the *Real*, there were more Spanish pleas to divert a pointless mission, but by now it was too late. The Venetian commanders thundered for revenge. Forward momentum had become unstoppable. The fleet pushed on in squally weather. By the evening of October 6 the Christians were heading toward the Curzolaris islands at the entrance to the Gulf of Patras, with the intention of luring the Ottomans out to fight.

FORTY MILES AWAY, in the castle at Lepanto, the Ottomans were holding a final council of war. All the key commanders were there: Ali Pasha and Pertev Pasha; the experienced corsairs Uluch Ali and Kara Hodja; two of Barbarossa's sons, Mehmet and Hasan; and the governor of Alexandria, Shuluch Mehmet. It was the mirror image of the debates at Messina and Corfu—to fight or not to fight?—with the same mixture of caution and adventure. Kara Hodja, back from another scouting mission, declared that the Christians numbered one hundred fifty galleys at most, but there were compelling reasons not to risk battle. The season was late; the men were tired and many had deserted from the campaign; their position at Lepanto was unassailable.

There are many different versions of what was said, but the party of prudence seems to have been represented by Pertev Pasha, "a man pessimistic by nature," who pointed out that some of the Ottoman ships were short of men, and almost certainly by Uluch Ali. The weather-beaten corsair, badly scarred on the hand from a mutiny of his galley slaves, was by far the most experienced seaman in the room. He was fifty-two years old and had learned his trade at the side of Turgut. He was intensely feared by the Christians for his courage and cruelty; the previous year he had inflicted a rare humiliation on the galleys of the Maltese knights, and like all the corsairs who had mastered the art of survival, he weighed the odds carefully. It is highly unlikely that Uluch voted for battle. Their argument was clear: "The shortage of men is a reality. From this point of view, it's best to remain in Lepanto harbor and fight only if the unbelievers come to us." Others, such as Hasan Pasha, spoke for battle—the Christians were divided among themselves and were numerically inferior.

Ali Pasha's final verdict was delivered in tones of high bravado. "What does it matter if in every ship there are five or ten men rowers short?" he roundly declared. "If God on high wants it, no harm can

*Uluch Ali*

come to us." But behind this display of disregard, there were the orders from Istanbul. According to the chronicler Pechevi, Ali went on, " 'I continually receive threatening orders from Istanbul, I fear for my position and my life.' Having said this, the other commanders could not oppose him. In the end the decision was taken to go out and meet the enemy." They went and readied their ships.

Toward the end of the day on October 6 the weather shifted. It was a flawless evening. "God showed us a sky and a sea as not to be seen in the finest day of spring," the Christians recalled. By two the following morning, Sunday, October 7, their fleet was working its way toward the Gulf of Patras. In Lepanto harbor the rattle of anchor chains; one by one the Ottoman ships started to row out through the mouth of the gulf, leaving the protective security of their shore-based guns.

# CHAPTER 20

# "Let's Fight"

Dawn to noon, October 7, 1571

*Dawn. The wind from the east. A fine autumn day.*

THE CHRISTIAN FLEET WAS IN THE LEE of a small group of islands, the Curzolaris, that guard the Gulf of Patras and the straits to Lepanto from the north. Don Juan put scouts ashore to climb the hills and spy the sea ahead at first light. Simultaneously, lookouts from the lead ship's crow's nest sighted sails on the eastern horizon. First two, then four, then six. In a short time they could descry a huge fleet "like a forest," scrolling up over the sea's rim. As yet it was impossible to determine the number. Don Juan hoisted the battle signals; a green flag was run up and a gun fired. Cheering rang across the fleet as the ships rowed one by one between the small islands and debouched into the gulf.

Ali Pasha was fifteen miles away as the dawn broke and the enemy ships were spotted threading through the islands. He had the wind and the sun at his back; the crews were moving easily. At first he could see so few ships that it seemed to confirm Kara Hodja's report about the inferior size of the Holy League's fleet. They appeared to be heading west. Ali immediately assumed that they were trying to escape to open sea. He altered the fleet's course, tilting southwest to stop the outnumbered enemy from slipping away. There was a feeling of anticipation in the galleys as they surged forward to the timekeeper's drum. "We felt great joy and delight," one of the Ottoman sailors later recalled, "because you were certainly going to succumb to our force."

And yet there were twinges of unease among the men; a large flock of crows, black with ill omen, had tumbled and croaked across the sky as the fleet left Lepanto, and Ali knew that his boats were not confidently manned. Not all the men were happy at the prospect of a sea battle; in places, the number had been made up by compulsion from the area around Lepanto. As each half hour passed, the distant fleet seemed to grow. Far from escaping, they were fanning out. His first impression had been inaccurate; there were more ships than he had thought. Kara Hodja's count had been wrong. He cursed, and adjusted his course again.

Ali's initial shift of the tiller had sparked a parallel reaction in the Christian fleet—that the enemy was getting away—then a matching correction at the realization of the true size and intent of the enemy fleet. As the hours passed and the two armadas spread across the water, the full extent of the unfolding collision became apparent. Along a four-mile-wide front, two enormous battle fleets were drawing together in a closed arena of sea. The scale of the thing dwarfed all pre-conceptions. There were some 140,000 men, soldiers, oarsmen, and crew, in some 600 ships—something in excess of 70 percent of all the oared galleys in the Mediterranean. Unease turned to doubt. There were men on each side secretly appalled by what they saw.

Pertev Pasha, general of the Ottoman troops, tried to persuade Ali to feign a retreat into the narrowing funnel of the gulf, under the shelter of Lepanto's guns. It was a course of action the admiral's orders and his sense of honor could not permit; he replied that he would never allow the sultan's ships even to appear to be taking flight.

There was equal concern in the Christian camp; it was becoming increasingly clear with every successive sighting from the crows' nests that the Ottomans had more ships. Even Venier, the grizzled old Venetian, suddenly fell quiet. Don Juan felt compelled to hold yet one more conference on the *Real*. He asked Romegas for his opinion; the knight was unequivocal. Gesturing at the huge Christian fleet around the *Real*, he said: "Sir, I say that if the emperor your father had once seen such a fleet as this, he wouldn't have stopped until he was emperor of Constantinople—and he would have done it without difficulty."

"You mean we must fight, then, Monsieur Romegas?" Don Juan checked again.

"Yes, sir."

"Very well, let's fight!"

There was still an attempted rearguard action by those who remembered Philip's cautious instructions, but it was now too late. Don Juan's mind was set. "Gentlemen," he said, turning to the men assembled in his sea cabin, "this is not the time to discuss, but to fight."

BOTH FLEETS BEGAN to fan out into line of battle. Don Juan's plans had been laid in early September and carefully practiced. They drew on the advice in one of Don Garcia's letters: to divide the fleet into three squadrons. The center, commanded by Don Juan in the *Real* and closely supported by Venier and Colonna, consisted of sixty-two galleys. On the left wing, the Venetian Agostino Barbarigo with fifty-seven galleys, on the right, Doria with fifty-three. Backing up this battle fleet was a fourth squadron, the reserve, lead by the experienced Spanish seaman Álvaro Bazán, with thirty galleys; his brief was to hurry to the aid of any part of the line that crumbled.

It had been Don Juan's policy to mix up the contingents to limit the possibility of defection by any one national group and to bind them together; the experience of Preveza lay behind this plan. Nevertheless, the mix had been weighted in various places to fulfill different roles. Forty-one of the fifty-seven galleys on the left wing were lighter, more maneuverable Venetian galleys, whose function was to operate hard up against the shore, following advice from Don Garcia that "if this happens in enemy country, it should take place as close to land as possible, to make it easy for their soldiers to flee from their galleys." The heavier Spanish galleys occupied the center and the right, where the fight might be more bludgeoning.

The wind was blowing briskly against the Christian ships as they struggled to get themselves into line; Doria's galleys on the right had to travel farthest to take up their positions. It was a difficult exercise, conducted in slow motion. "One could never get the lighter galleys properly lined up," Venier recalled, "and it caused me a lot of problems." It took three hours for the Christians to sort themselves out.

Ali Pasha's task was made easier by the following wind but his arrangement was broadly similar. The admiral took the center of the battle fleet in his flagship, the *Sultana*, diametrically opposite the *Real*; his right wing was commanded by the bey of Alexandria, Shuluch Mehmet, and his left by Uluch Ali, opposite Doria. As the fleets wheeled and turned, it slowly became clear to the Genoese admiral that he was badly outnumbered. Uluch Ali had sixty-seven galleys and twenty-seven smaller galliots, drawn up in a double line. Doria had just fifty-three. The discrepancy had the potential for serious trouble.

Where Don Juan was trying to hold a straight line, the Ottomans favored the crescent. It had both a symbolic function as the crescent moon of Islam and a tactical one. Both sides had a clear understanding of the realities of galley warfare. All the offensive capabilities of the galley lay in its bows; the three or five forward-facing guns were effective only within a narrow arc of fire, and the bows were the only place where fighting men could gather in any number. The conventional tactics were to sweep the opponent's deck with cannon fire, arquebus shot, and arrows, then to ram it with the beaked boarding bridge and pour on board. Galley hulls are fragile shells, horribly vulnerable to impact or shot. To be caught sideways or from behind by another galley was to be left literally dead in the water. Ali's crescent was designed to outflank and encircle the less numerous enemy, then to break up his ranks in a mêlée where the more maneuverable Muslim vessels might catch the ships sideways and pick them off.

FOR BOTH SIDES THE INTEGRITY of the line abreast was crucial. However, for Don Juan, whose galleys were weightier and more ponderous, the principle of mutual support was a matter of life and death. Each galley needed to be a hundred paces apart—sufficiently distant to prevent a clash of oars but close enough to prevent an enemy from inserting himself into the ranks. For the same reason, it was critical that they remained in line. Too far ahead, a galley could be isolated and picked off; lagging too far back, the enemy could again insert himself into the line and cause havoc. Once holes were picked in the fabric of the battle formation, it became a dangerous game of chance, but to maintain this matrix of order across a four-mile front required extraordinary skill. Seen from the perspective of a bird circling lazily in the higher air, the effects were quite clear. The Christian fleet continually expanded and contracted in and out like an accordion while its line abreast rippled back and forward in sinuous curves as the ships kept trying to adjust their relative positions outward from the *Real* at the center.

Ali Pasha had the same problem. The outer horns of his crescent threatened to get too far ahead, an arrangement that could lead to disaster: unsupported, they would be quickly picked off. It was the sheer size of the fleets and the rippling effect of lag times as each ship kept adjusting its position that made these formations so difficult to maintain. Finding the crescent too hard to orchestrate, Ali switched his deployment to a flat line in three divisions that mirrored his opponent's formation, with the *Sultana* as the front marker; no ship's commander was to pull ahead, under pain of death. The two fleets closed at a walking pace as they struggled to keep their shape.

What the Christians lacked in maneuverability they made up in firepower. The Spanish Western-style galleys were weightier than their opponents' and packed a heavier punch. The Christian ships, on average, possessed twice the number of artillery pieces; used judiciously, they could inflict grievous blows. As the slow miles shrank, Ali's lookouts could see that the Christian center was packed with these heavier Spanish galleys. If not disrupted and outflanked by the Ottoman wings, these could bludgeon his center. This started to cause Ali concern.

And the Christians had been innovating. At Doria's suggestion Don Juan had ordered his commanders to shear off the rams from the front of their ships. These structures were more ornamental than practical; their removal permitted the guns to be trained lower and to hit the enemy at close range. Galleys could close the last hundred yards faster than gunners could reload, so there would be only one shot. Don Juan was determined to follow Don Garcia's advice: to keep his nerve and his fire until the last minute, when the enemy was bearing down. He did not want his shots whistling harmlessly overhead. At the same time he ordered nets to be strung along the sides of the ships to entangle and impede would-be boarders.

But it was the Venetians who brought the most radical innovation to the fleet that was now lumbering forward. They had stored for future use the performance of their heavily armed galleon at Preveza in 1538; it had inflicted considerable damage on Barbarossa's galleys and held them off all day. When the Venetians cranked the arsenal shipyard up for war, they dusted off the hulls of six of their merchant great galleys, cumbersome heavyweight oared ships once used for the now-defunct trade with the Eastern Mediterranean. These galleasses, as they called them, had been reconditioned, heavily gunned, and bulwarked with defensive superstructures. On the morning of October 7 galleys were laboriously towing these floating gun platforms up ahead of the line. The Venetians had a definite purpose in mind.

IT WAS A SUNDAY MORNING. Far away in Rome, Pius was conducting a fervent mass for Christian victory. In Madrid, Philip went on signing documents and dispatching memoranda to all parts of his far-

*Venetian galleass*

flung empire in between church services. Selim was departing from Istanbul for his capital at Edirne with the usual pomp of a sultan's progress: a splendid cavalcade of jingling cavalry and plumed janissaries, pages, scribes, civil servants, dog handlers, cooks, and harem favorites. The departure was marked by ill omens: Selim's turban slipped off twice, and his horse fell; a man hurrying to help him had to be hanged for touching the sultan's person.

In the Gulf of Patras, sometime around midmorning, the wind that had been blowing strongly from the east since dawn, faltered and died. The sea glassed, just a light breeze from the west at Don Juan's back. The Ottoman fleet promptly dropped its sails; conditions eased for the oarsmen in the Christian fleet. It was taken as a good sign—a wind from God.

Pius had invested the Holy League venture with enormous Christian hope. The banners, the church services, the papal blessings as the ships left port had imparted to the expedition all the religious fervor of a crusade. The pope had asked Don Juan to ensure his men "lived in virtuous and Christian fashion in the galleys, not playing [gambling] or swearing." Requesen's private response had been muted. "We will do what we can," he murmured, casting his eye over the hard-boiled Spanish infantry and the subspecies of Christian humanity chained to the rowing benches. Don Juan had thought it useful to hang a few blasphemers in front of the papal legate at Messina to encourage virtuous behavior. Moral purpose was critical to the success of the whole endeavor. There were priests on every ship; thousands of rosaries were handed to the men; services were held daily. Now, as everyone could see their fate drawing toward them over the calm sea, sober religious dread seized the Christian fleet. Mass was said on every ship with the reminder that there would be no heaven for cowards. The men were confessed of their sins. Immediately afterward, drums and trumpets sounded with cries of "Victory and long live Jesus Christ!"

WITH THE SHIPS SPREADING OUT, Don Juan stepped down from the elaborately carved poop of the *Real*. He was wearing brilliant armor that glittered in the autumn sun, and carried a crucifix in his hand as he transferred into a light racing frigate and ran along the line of ships, putting heart into the men. As he passed under the stern of Sebastian Venier's ship, the old hothead saluted him. With their minds fixed on ultimate things, all grievances were forgotten.

To each national contingent Don Juan offered words of encouragement. He urged the Venetians to avenge the death of Bragadin. To the Spanish he called for religious duty: "My children, we are here to conquer or to die as heaven may determine. Do not let our impious foe ask of us 'Where is your God?' Fight in his holy name, and in death or victory you will win immortality." He visited two of the lumbering galleasses passing through the fleet line and urged them to hurry to their station. He promised liberation for all the Christian galley slaves if they fought well, and ordered their shackles to be removed. It was in fact a promise that he could not guarantee, as only the oarsmen on his own ships were within his gift. The Muslims were now handcuffed as well as chained, for fear of uprisings during the fight. For them there would be no escape if the ship went down.

Everywhere there were final preparations. Armorers moved among the Christian rowers, striking off shackles and handing out swords; weapons, wine, and bread were stockpiled in the gangways; priests offered words of comfort; the arquebusiers checked their powder and their slow-burning fuses; Spanish veterans of the Morisco wars sharpened their pikes and donned their steel casques. Commanders strapped on breastplates and helmets, flipping their visors up to catch the sea wind and the stink of the ships. Surgeons spread out their instruments and fingered the bite of their saws. Thousands of nameless galley slaves strained at the oars to the crack of the overseers' whips and the steady pounding of drums. With their backs to the enemy, they rowed forward at a steady pace.

A few individual names stand out among the anonymous thousands on the Christian ships: Aurelio Scetti, Florentine musician, had been twelve years in the galleys for murdering his wife. On the *Marquesa*, the Spaniard Miguel de Cervantes, twenty-four years old, bookish and desperately poor, was a volunteer; on the morning of the battle he was ill from fever but tottered from his bed to command a detachment of soldiers at the boat station. Another sick man, sergeant Martin Muñoz, aboard the *San Giovanni* from Sicily, also lay below with fever. Sir Thomas Stukeley, English pirate and mercenary, possibly the illegitimate son of Henry VIII, commanded three Spanish ships. Romegas, detached from the Malta galleys, was with Colonna on his flagship, an appointment that would save his life. Antonio and Ambrogio Bragadin, kinsmen of the martyr of Famagusta, commanding two galleasses, waited in the front line, itching for revenge. And on Don Juan's flagship was one particularly fresh-faced Spanish arquebusier. Her name was Maria la Bailadora (the flamenco dancer); she had disguised herself to accompany her soldier lover to the wars.

Five miles distant, the Muslims were making their own preparations. Ali's fleet was also a mixture of elements: imperial squadrons from Istanbul and Gallipoli, the Algerians and more informal corsair bands in small galliots. All the great commanders were present: the beys of the maritime provinces of Rhodes, Syria, Naplion, and Tripoli; the sons of Barbarossa, Hasan and Mehmet; the commander of the Istanbul arsenal, Kara Hodja the Italian corsair; and Uluch Ali out on the left wing. There was evidently some small chafing between the different factions, between the "deep" Muslims and the opportunist renegades "with pork flesh still stuck between their teeth," as well as between the skillful corsair captains and the sultan's imperial placeholders. Ali Pasha's plan was to run his galleys on the right wing under Shuluch Mehmet hard against the Greek shore; with their shallow draft and the commander's knowledge of the coastal waters, Ali was confident they could outsmart and outflank the opposing Venetians. He ordered cavalry to stand to on the shore if the Venetians tried to beach their ships and run. Uluch Ali was desperately worried by this tactic. The plan turned on a calculated gamble. If it failed, the reverse might happen: the Muslims could be tempted to escape by land. Uluch Ali would have preferred an open-sea engagement, where an outflanking movement would be more clear-cut.

The Muslim fleet carried fewer cannon and arquebusiers than the enemy but many archers, whose vastly superior speed of fire could impale a Spanish hand gunner thirty times over while he was still reloading. They fought without armor, and their ships were not reinforced with wooden parapets that could protect the men against sustained gunfire. The aim was to be quick and agile.

To the calling of the imams, the men performed ritual ablutions and prostrated themselves in prayer. They tensioned their bows and dipped their arrows in poison; the decking was smeared with oil and butter, making it slippery for the heavily shod Europeans to keep their footing in a boarding raid, while the Muslims generally fought barefoot. The Christian galley slaves were forbidden on pain of death to look over their shoulder at the approaching foe, for fear of breaking stroke; when the ships tangled, the slaves were to hide under the benches. But Ali was a generous commander with a strong sense of honor. While Don Juan was double-shackling his Muslim oarsmen, the pasha made his Christian slaves a promise. Speaking to them in Spanish, he said: "Friends, I expect you today to do your duty by me, in return for what I have done for you. If I win the battle, I promise you your liberty; if the day is yours, God has given it to you." It was a promise certainly within his power to fulfill. Ali had his two sons of seventeen and thirteen on board with him. As they were being transferred to another ship, he called them to him and reminded them of their duty. "Blessed be the bread and the salt you have given us," they gravely replied. It was a touching moment of filial piety. Then they were gone.

Ali could now make out the Venetian galleasses becalmed on the water in front of the Christian fleet. They puzzled and worried him. In the Ottoman ranks, there was some general apprehension of heavily gunned round ships. The Turks had been warned of these vessels by captives, but the word was that the ships were armed with only three artillery pieces at bow and stern. It was impossible to understand what the Venetians were up to.

Four miles off, the red-hulled *Sultana* fired a blank shot; it was a personal address to the *Real*, an invitation to fight. Don Juan replied with purpose: his shot contained a live round. Ali ordered his helmsman, Mehmet, to make for the *Real*. The great green banner of Islam, precious above all the emblems of Islamic war, with the names of God intertwined twenty-nine thousand times, was hoisted aloft—the green and the gold thread glittered in the sun that was now catching the Muslims in the eye.

IN THE CHRISTIAN FLEET, Don Juan arranged a matching piece of religious theatre. At a signal, crucifixes were raised aloft on every ship; the pope's mighty sky-blue banner decorated with the image of the crucified Christ was hoisted on the *Real*. Don Juan knelt at the prow in his dazzling armor, imploring the Christian God for victory. Thousands of armed men fell to their knees. Friars in brown or black robes held up crosses to the sun and sprinkled holy water on the men and murmured absolution. Then they stood up and roared the names of their protectors and saints in Spanish and Italian. "San Marco! San Stefano! San Giovanni! Santiago y cierra España! Victoria! Victoria!" Trumpets rang brightly; the low-frequency thudding of the timekeepers' drums beat an insistent tattoo; on the Muslim ships, the blare of zornas and cymbals, the men calling out the names of God, chanting verses from the Koran, and shouting to the Christians to advance and be massacred "like drowned hens." And in a fit of exuberance beyond rational thought, Don Juan, whose dancing had been so noted at Genoa, "inspired with youthful ardor, danced a galliard in the gun-platform to the music of fifes."

THERE WAS STILL TIME, in the words of Girolamo Diedo, a Venetian official at Corfu, for both sides to take in the frightening beauty of the spectacle. "Hurtling towards each other, the two fleets were a quite terrifying sight; our men in shining helmets and breastplates, metal shields like mirrors and their other weapons glittering in the rays of the sun, the polished blades of the drawn swords dazzling men full in the face even from a distance. . . . And the enemy were no less threatening, they struck just as much fear in the hearts of our side, as well as amazement and wonder at the golden lanterns and shimmering banners remarkable for the sheer variety of their thousands of extraordinary colours."

A third of a mile in front of the Christian fleet, four of the galleasses were now in position, spaced out at intervals; two on the right wing lagged and were only just up with the front line. The Venetian gunners crouched with lighted tapers, eyeing the two hundred eighty Muslim galleys closing fast. Arquebusiers fingered their rosaries and murmured prayers. Heartbeats raced. They braced themselves against the wall of noise. At one hundred fifty yards, an order: matches were set to the touchholes. It was just before noon.

THERE WAS A SERIES OF BRIGHT FLASHES, a thunderous roar, then the smoke that would obscure everything. At this distance it was impossible to miss. Iron balls ripped into the advancing ships. Galleys just burst asunder under the impact. "It was so terrible that three galleys were sunk just like that," recorded Diedo. Confusion checked the Ottoman advance; ships crashed into one another or tried to halt. The *Sultana* had a stern lantern shot away. The oared galleasses turned through ninety degrees to deliver a second round. Ali ordered up the stroke rate to shoot past the mouth of the guns as fast as possible. The line tacked and opened to avoid the floating gun towers. Broadside on, the Ottoman line was now raked by arquebus fire. When a helmsman was shot down, the vessel staggered and veered; then a row of turbaned soldiers caught in profile would be felled by a volley of bullets. The galleasses made another quarter turn. "God allow us to get out of here in one piece," shouted Ali, watching the wreckage being inflicted on his battle line, now jagged, holed, and in disarray. Sweeping beyond the guns, the Ottoman galleys opened fire at the main Christian line, but they aimed too high. Don Juan waited for the Ottomans to close; with their rams cut away, the cannon could fire close and low. As Ali's ships pressed forward, the Christian guns erupted, each commander choosing his moment. Black smoke blew favorably on the west wind, obscuring the Muslim aim. Even before the collision of the two lines, a third of Ali's ships had been crippled or sunk, "and already the sea was wholly covered with men, yardarms, oars, casks, barrels, and various kinds of armaments—an incredible thing that only six galleasses should have caused such destruction."

# CHAPTER 21

# Sea of Fire

Noon to nightfall, October 7, 1571

B Y THIS TIME FURIOUS FIGHTING had already broken out close
to the shore. The Ottoman right wing, under Shuluch Mehmet, had
sheered away to avoid the withering fire of the galleasses. Now they
looked to outflank the Venetian-led left under the command of Agostino
Barbarigo. Shuluch aimed to exploit the narrow corridor of the coastal
shallows, into which he knew the weightier Venetians dared not venture. "Shuluch and Kara Ali, outpacing all the other Ottoman galleys,
drove furiously towards our line," wrote Diedo. "As they neared the
shore, they slid between the shallows with the foremost ships of their
squadron. These waterways were familiar to them; they knew exactly
the depth of the sea above the shoals. Followed by four or five galleys,
they planned to take our left wing in the rear."

Before the Venetians knew what was happening, these galleys had
slipped around the end of Barbarigo's line and were assaulting the exposed vessels on the outer tip from both sides. If many more outflanked
Barbarigo's wing, the situation would be critical; the Christians would
be suddenly taken from behind. Barbarigo interposed his own ship to
block the way and was instantly engulfed in a firestorm. So many arrows whipped through the air that his stern lantern was bristling with
shafts; the lead galleys were furiously assaulted, their decks swept by arquebus fire, their commanders and senior officers shot down one by one
as the Ottomans attempted to crush the outer flank. For an hour Barbarigo's ship struggled valiantly, its deck fiercely contested by boarding
parties. Behind his visor, the commander's muffled instructions were
being lost in the din of battle. Incautiously he flipped the visor up,
shouting that it was better to risk being hit than not to be heard. Min-
utes later an arrow struck him in the eye; he was carried below to die.
The battle for the flagship intensified; Barbarigo's nephew Giovanni
Contarini brought his own galley up to help and was, in turn, shot dead.

Shuluch looked close to success, but the Venetians had come for revenge; many of their ships were from Crete, the Dalmatian coast, and the islands, all ravaged by Ali Pasha's summer raids. They fought desperately and without regard. Slowly the tide started to turn: Galleys from the reserve swung up to help; troops were fed onto the stricken ships from the rear. Panic erupted on an Ottoman galley when the Christian slaves broke free and launched a furious assault on their masters, raining smashing blows with their whirling chains. One of the galleasses crept toward the shore and began to pulverize the Ottoman ships. Shuluch's flagship was rammed and had its rudder sheared off; then it was holed and started to sink; it just sat waterlogged in the shallows. Shuluch, identified by his brilliant robes, was fished out of the sea more dead than alive. So severe were his wounds that the Venetians decapitated him on the spot as an act of mercy. Following Shuluch's ship, the whole squadron had drifted toward the shore and was now pinned there. "In this vast confusion," wrote Diedo, "many of our galleys, especially those nearest the centre of the fleet ... made a general turning movement toward the left in good order and came to envelop the Turkish ships, which were still putting up a desperate resistance to ours. By this adroit manoeuvre they held them enclosed, as in a harbour." The Ottoman right wing was trapped.

It was now that Uluch's worst fear was realized. Seeing the temptation of the shore, the Muslims gave up the fight. There was a confused flight for the beach. Ships crashed into one another; men hurled themselves overboard, scrabbling and drowning in the depths and the shallows. Those behind used the trampled bodies of their compatriots as a bridge to land. The Venetians were in no mood for prisoners. They put out longboats and pursued them ashore with shouts of "Famagusta! Famagusta!" One enraged man, finding no other weapon, grabbed a stick and used it to pin a fallen opponent to the beach through the mouth. "It was an appalling massacre," wrote Diedo. In the confusion, a band of Christian galley slaves on the Venetian ships who had been unshackled on Don Juan's orders took stock of their options and decided that instant freedom was better than a general's promise. Leaping ashore with the weapons they had been given, they ran off to take their chances as bandits in the Greek hills.

SHORTLY AFTER MIDDAY the heavyweight centers of the two fleets also collided. The fancifully named galleys of the Venetians and the

Spanish—the *Merman*, the *Fortune on a Dolphin*, the *Pyramid*, the *Wheel and Serpent*, the *Tree Trunk*, the *Judith*, and innumerable saints—shattered into the squadrons from Istanbul, Rhodes, the Black Sea, Gallipoli, and Negroponte, commanded by their captains: Bektashi Mustapha, Deli Chelebi, Haji Aga, Kos Ali, Piyale Osman, Kara Reis, and dozens more. One hundred fifty fully armed galleys plowed into one another.

THE CHRISTIANS HAD ROWED slowly toward this collision, intent on holding their line. The Ottomans were ragged and disarranged by the blizzard of shot from the galleasses but moved forward with eager velocity, skimming the calm sea, their lateen sails raked back, their guns blazing. The principal players on each side clustered at the nerve center of the battle: On the Ottoman side, Ali Pasha in the *Sultana*, with Pertev Pasha, the army commander, on his right shoulder; Mehmet Bey, governor of Negroponte with Ali's two sons on his left; Hasan Pasha, Barbarossa's son; and a group of other experienced commanders. Don Juan steadied himself on the poop of the *Real* with Marc-'Antonio Colonna and Romegas in the papal flagship on one side, Venier on the other. Philip would have been appalled by Don Juan's sense of risk. He was horribly visible standing before the banner of crucified Christ in his bright armor, sword in hand, refusing pleas to retreat into his cabin. Ali stood on his poop in equally brilliant robes, armed with a bow. Both men were playing for high stakes, oblivious of the wise words Don Garcia once addressed to La Valette: "In war the death of the leader often leads to disaster and defeat."

As the ships closed, the *Sultana* loosed off shots from its forward guns. One ball smashed through Don Juan's forward platform and mowed down the first oarsmen. Two more whistled wide. The *Real*, with its forward spur cut off, could shoot lower, and waited until the enemy was at point-blank range, "and all our shots caused great damage to the enemy," wrote Onorato Caetani, captain-general of the pope's troops, aboard the *Griffin*. The *Sultana* seemed to be making for the Venetian flagship, then dipped its helm at the last moment and slammed into the *Real*, bow to bow; its beaked prow rode up over the front rowing benches like the snout of a rearing sea monster, crushing men in its path. The vessels recoiled in shock, but remained interlocked in the entangled mess of rigging and spars.

*Sea of fire*

There were similar shattering collisions all along the line. The papal flagship, directed by Colonna in support of the *Real*, was hit by Pertev Pasha's ship, spun around, and slammed into the side of the *Sultana*, just as another Ottoman galley careered into Colonna's stern. On the other side, Venier also moved up but found himself immediately engulfed in a separate mêlée. The Christian line had already been breached, and the sea was a tangled mass of thrashing ships.

WHAT THE SURVIVORS WOULD REMEMBER—as far as they remembered anything from the flash-lit moments of battle—was the noise. "So great was the roaring of the cannon at the start," wrote Caetani, "that it's not possible to imagine or describe." Behind the volcanic detonation of the guns came other sounds: the sharp snapping of oars like successive pistol shots, the crash and splinter of colliding ships, the rattle of arquebuses, the sinister whip of arrows, cries of pain, wild shouting, the splash of bodies falling backward into the sea. The smoke obscured everything; ships lit by sudden shafts of sunshine would lurch through the murk as if from nowhere and tear at one another's sides.

Everywhere confusion and noise: "a mortal storm of arquebus shots and arrows, and it seemed that the sea was aflame from the flashes and continuous fires lit by fire trumpets, fire pots and other weapons. Three galleys would be pitted against four, four against six, and six against one, enemy or Christian alike, everyone fighting in the cruellest manner to take each other's lives. And already many Turks and Christians had boarded their opponents' galleys fighting at close quarters with short weapons, few being left alive. And death came endlessly from the two-handed swords, scimitars, iron maces, daggers, axes, swords, arrows, arquebuses, and fire weapons. And beside those killed in various ways, others escaping from the weapons would drown by throwing themselves into the sea, thick and red with blood."

AFTER THE FIRST SPLINTERING COLLISION between the two flagships, men on both sides attempted to board. There were four hundred Sardinian arquebusiers on the *Real*, eight hundred fighting men in all, jam-packed shoulder to shoulder so that each had no more than two feet of space. Ali had two hundred arquebusiers and one hundred bowmen. At the first moment, "a great number of them, very bravely, leaped aboard the *Real*; at the same moment many men from the *Real* leaped aboard their ship." According to legend, Maria the dancer was one of the first across, sword in hand. The battle became cut and thrust at close range, the chained rowers trying to duck under the narrow benches, while armed men clattered down the central deck. The Muslims were quickly forced back from the *Real*; the Spanish troops made it as far as the *Sultana*'s mainmast before they were stopped; its intricate walnut decking was soon slippery with oil and blood as both sides hacked and slipped in the muck. Each ship was supported from behind by other galleys that fed a transfusion of fresh men up rear ladders as those at the bows collapsed and died. At close range, missiles were deadly. A man armored in a breastplate and back plate could be skewered right through by a single arrow or felled by a bullet. Don Bernardino de Cardenas on the *Real* was hit on the breastplate by a shot from a swivel gun; it failed to rupture his armor but he died later from the force of the blow. Islam's green banner was peppered with shot, but the Christians were forced back.

Both sides understood that the flagships were key to the battle. Makeshift barricades were erected at the mast stations to thwart boarders, so that the fight for the boats resembled street fighting in a narrow alley. So close were the men that they were massacred in droves; more were fed in from behind. Flights of arrows from the *Sultana* whipped across the sky, hitting the deck of the *Real* so fast they seemed to be growing out of it; according to one eyewitness, the Christian ships bristled like porcupines. The fortunes on the flagships reversed and the Ottomans stormed back up the *Real*. In the midst of this mayhem, Don Juan's pet marmoset was seen pulling out arrows from the mast, breaking them with its teeth, and throwing them into the sea.

On either side of the *Real* and all down the line, the fighting was furious. Venier, trying to come up to the aid of the flagship, hit the *Sultana* amidships but was surrounded on both sides. Only the appearance of two Venetian galleys from the reserve saved his life. Both their captains were killed. Bazán's reserve galleys, kept back to buttress the line at critical moments, were now being pumped in to stem the tide of battle. Colonna repulsed the galley of Mehmet Bey with Ali's sons aboard. Farther up the line the galleys of the corsairs Kara Hodja and Kara Deli attempted to storm the *Griffin*, Kara Hodja running at the front of his men, but the arquebus fire was starting to tell. "Giambattista Contusio felled Kara Hodja with an arquebus and one after another until there weren't six Turks left alive." And the Spanish pikemen, who had learned to fight in organized drills in the Alpujarras, were deadly at close range. Once aboard an enemy ship, they swept down the deck, impaling resisters and butting them into the sea. Aurelio Scetti recorded the desperate courage of his fellow Christian galley slaves liberated from their chains to fight: "There was a high number of deaths among the Turks when the Christian prisoners jumped aboard the enemy ships, telling themselves, 'Today we either die or we earn our freedom.' "

The fighting on the *Sultana* and the *Real* continued for over an hour. A second rush up the deck was again repulsed, but there was a gradual weakening of Ottoman firepower. Don Juan himself fought from the prow with his two-handed sword and received a dagger thrust in the leg. On the poop of his adjacent galley, the eighty-year-old Venier stood bareheaded and fired off crossbow bolts at turbaned figures as fast as his man could reload.

Bazán's reinforcements were beginning to swing the battle, and the heavyweight galleasses came blasting back into the fray. Pertev Pasha's ship had its rudder shot away; Pertev jumped ship into a rowing boat manned by a renegade and slipped off, the oarsman calling out in Italian, "Don't shoot. We're also Christians!" Pertev cursed Ali's recklessness as he went. Ships were now closing in on the *Sultana*, snuffing out the supply of men able to reinforce Ali Pasha's vessel. The pasha's sons made a desperate attempt to help their father, but were repulsed. Colonna and Romegas captured one galley, then turned to consider the next target.

"What shall we go for next?" asked Colonna. "Take another galley or help the *Real*?" Romegas seized the tiller himself and turned the ship toward the *Sultana*'s right flank. Venier was closing in from the other side, sweeping the deck with fire. "My galley, with cannon, arquebuses, and arrows, didn't let any Turk make it from the poop to the prow of the pasha's ship," he wrote. A third wave of men swept up the *Sultana*'s deck; a last-ditch stand was taking place at the poop deck behind makeshift barricades. Ali Pasha was still furiously dispatching arrows from his bow as the last defenses were blown away. Men were throwing themselves into the sea to avoid the hail of fire.

There are a dozen different accounts of Ali's last moments, according different degrees of heroism to the pasha. Most probably the admiral, an easy target in his bright robes, was felled by an arquebus shot; a Spanish soldier hacked off his head and raised it aloft on a spear. There were shouts of "Victory!" as the league's flag was run up to the masthead. Don Juan jumped onto the deck of the *Sultana*, but realizing the fight was over, retired to his own ship. Resistance on the *Sultana* collapsed. Ali's head was taken to Don Juan, who according to some accounts was gravely offended that his adversary had been so ungallantly decapitated, and ordered the object to be thrown into the sea. The Spanish soldiers mopped up.

Ottoman resistance in the center began to collapse. Ali's sons were captured on the flagship of Mehmet Bey; others surrendered or tried to flee. According to Caetani, the decks of both the *Real* and the *Sultana* had been reduced to a shambles: "On the *Real* there were an infinite number of dead." On the *Sultana*, pitching on the slow sea with its crew decimated to the last man, "an enormous quantity of large turbans, which seemed to be as numerous as the enemy had been, rolling on the deck with the heads inside them."

BUT FOR THE OTTOMANS the battle was not yet lost. While both fleets were fully engaged at the center, there was still a possibility of snatching victory. Gian'Andrea Doria and Uluch Ali had been playing a game of cat and mouse on the seaward wing, still maneuvering for position an hour after the centers collided.

Doria was a figure of controversy and suspicion in the Christian fleet. His reluctance for this battle, his concern for his own galleys, and his innate caution became grounds for growing concern as Don Juan gazed up at the struggle unfolding to the south. It appeared from the central battle group that Doria was moving too far out to sea, as if trying not to engage. Don Juan dispatched a frigate to summon him back.

More likely Doria had understood from the start the gravity of his position and was working furiously to avoid being caught out. Uluch Ali had more ships; the possibility of outflanking the Christians was considerable. If the Ottomans could outdistance him on the outer wing, they could decimate their enemy from behind. Uluch Ali slid his squadron farther and farther south, pulling Doria with him and enlarging the space between the Christian center and its right wing. A gap opened up, a thousand yards wide. Some of the Venetian ships, fearing treachery by Doria, turned back, fragmenting his line. Uluch Ali, who "could make his galley do what a rider could do with a well-trained horse," was working with conscious intent. A shrill blast on the whistle and a section of his squadron spun about and headed for the gap, now outflanking Doria on the inside. The Genoese admiral had been outplayed. Before he could react, the Ottomans were bearing down on the flank of the Christian center.

IT WAS A BRILLIANT MANEUVER and a sudden reversal of fortune. Uluch had engineered the kind of broken mêlée the Ottomans wanted to fight. With the wind now behind him, Uluch and his corsairs caught a batch of scattered ships at a serious disadvantage. Ahead of him were the Venetian galleys from Doria's wing, isolated and in disarray, then the small group of Sicilian galleys, and three vessels flying the familiar white cross on a red ground—Uluch's most hated enemy, the Maltese galleys of the Knights of Saint John. These detachments were hopelessly outnumbered and already exhausted from the fight. It was now three, four, five to one. Uluch "delivered an immense carnage on these ships." Seven Algerian ships fell on the Maltese galleys, raking them with a hail of bullets and arrows. The heavily armored but hopelessly

outnumbered knights went down fighting. The Spanish knight, Geronimo Ramirez, riddled with arrows like some Saint Sebastian, kept
boarders at bay until he fell dead on the deck; the flotilla commander,
Prior Pietro Giustiniani, wounded by five arrows and taken alive, was
the last man standing on a vessel otherwise devoid of life. The Sicilian
galleys pulled up to help but were immediately engulfed in a storm of
fire; the *Florence* was overrun by a galley and six corsair galliots; every
soldier and Christian slave was killed. On the *San Giovanni* a row of
chained corpses slumped at the oars; the soldiers were all dead and the
captain felled by two musket balls. There were no survivors on the Genoese flagship of David Imperiale or on five of the Venetian galleys. The
flagship of Savoy would be found later drifting on the water, totally
silent, not a man left to tell the tale.

There were extraordinary moments of thoughtless bravery on
these stricken Christian ships. The young prince of Palma boarded a
galley single-handed, fought the crew back to the mainmast, and lived
to tell the tale. On the stricken *San Giovanni*, the Spanish sergeant
Martin Muñoz, lying below with fever, heard the enemy clattering up
the deck overhead, and leaped from his bed determined to die. Sword in
hand, he hurled himself at the assailants, killed four, and drove them
back before collapsing on a rowing bench, studded with arrows and
with one leg gone, calling out to his fellows "Each of you do as much."
On the *Doncella*, Federico Venusta had his hand mutilated by the explosion of his own grenade. He demanded a galley slave cut it off. When
the man refused, he performed the operation himself and then went
to the cook's quarters, ordered them to tie the carcass of a chicken over
the bleeding stump, and returned to battle, shouting at his right hand
to avenge his left. A man hit in the eye by an arrow plucked it out, eye-
ball and all, tied a cloth around his head, and fought on. Men grappling
their assailants on deck dragged them overboard to drown together in
the bloody sea. The *Christ over the World*, surrounded and overrun, blew
itself up, taking the encircling galleys with it.

Despite this resistance, Uluch Ali was tearing a hole in the Christian line, collecting prizes as he went. He took in tow the Maltese flagship, strewn with dead bodies, as a trophy for the sultan. A little sooner
and he might well have tipped the battle, but with the Ottoman center
now collapsing, his chance was ebbing away. Doria regrouped to attack
Uluch's ships from one side; Colonna, Venier, and Don Juan brought

their galleys around to confront him from the other. The wily corsair certainly had no intention of dying in a lost cause; he cut the towrope on the Maltese flagship, leaving the wounded Giustiniani to tell the tale but prudently taking its standard as a trophy. Steering to the north with fourteen galleys, he slipped off.

The Christian ships turned to mopping up and looting. The battlefield was a devastated scene of total catastrophe. For eight miles guttering vessels burned on the water; others floated like ghost ships, their crews all dead. The surviving Muslims fought courageously to the last. There were moments of grotesque comedy. Some ships refused to surrender; running out of missiles, they picked up lemons and oranges and hurled them at their attackers. The Christians, wrote Diedo, "out of disdain and ridicule, retaliated by throwing them back again. This form of conflict seems to have occurred in many places towards the end of the fight, and was a matter for considerable laughter." Elsewhere men still thrashed and fought in the water, clung to spars, or casually drowned. Chroniclers struggled to convey the scale of the carnage. "The greater fury of the battle lasted for four hours and was so bloody and horrendous that the sea and the fire seemed as one, many Turkish galleys burning down to the water, and the surface of the sea, red with blood, was covered with Moorish coats, turbans, quivers, arrows, bows, shields, oars, boxes, cases, and other spoils of war, and above all many human bodies, Christian as well as Turkish, some dead, some wounded, some torn apart, and some not yet resigned to their fate struggling in their death agony, their strength ebbing away with the blood flowing from their wounds in such quantity that the sea was entirely coloured by it, but despite all this misery our men were not moved to pity for the enemy. . . . Although they begged for mercy they received instead arquebus shots and pike thrusts." There was looting on a grand scale. Men put out rowing boats to fish the dead out of the water and rob them; "the soldiers, sailors and convicts pillaged joyously until nightfall. There was great booty because of the abundance of gold and silver and rich ornaments that were in the Turkish galleys, especially those of the pashas." Aurelio Scetti took two Moorish prisoners in the hope of securing his subsequent release from the galleys; he would live to be disappointed.

It was a scene of staggering devastation, like a biblical painting of the world's end. The scale of the carnage left even the exhausted victors shaken and appalled by the work of their hands. They had witnessed killing on an industrial scale. In four hours 40,000 men were dead, nearly 100 ships destroyed, 137 Muslim ships captured by the Holy League. Of the dead, 25,000 were Ottoman; only 3,500 were taken alive. Another 12,000 Christian slaves were liberated. The defining collision in the White Sea gave the people of the early modern world a glimpse of Armageddon to come. Not until Loos in 1916 would this rate of slaughter be surpassed. "What has happened was so strange and took on so many different aspects," wrote Girolamo Diedo, "it's as if men were extracted from their own bodies and transported to another world."

The day drew to its mournful close; the bloody water, heaving thickly with the matted debris of the battle, reddened in the sunset. Burning hulks flared in the dark, smoking and ruined. The wind got up. The Christian ships could barely sail away, according to Aurelio Scetti, "because of the countless corpses floating on the sea." The survivors left with pitiful shouts from the water still ringing in their ears. "Even though many Christians were not dead, nobody would help them." As the winners sought secure anchorages on the Greek shore, a

*Galley from the stern*

storm churned the surface of the sea, scattering the debris, as if the ocean were wiping the battlefield away with a great hand.

THE OTTOMAN CHRONICLER PECHEVI wrote his own obituary for the battle. "I saw the wretched place where the battle took place myself. ... There has never been such a disastrous war in an Islamic land, nor in all the seas of the world since Noah created ships. One hundred eighty vessels fell into enemy hands, along with cannon, rifles, other war resources and materials, galley slaves, and Islamic warriors. All other losses were proportional. There had been one hundred twenty men in even the smallest ships. With this, the total reckoning of men lost was twenty thousand." And Pechevi was undercounting.

It was Cervantes, hit in the chest by two arquebus shots and permanently maimed in the left hand, who summed up the Christian mood. "The greatest event witnessed by ages past, present and to come," he wrote.

# CHAPTER 22

# Other Oceans

1572–1580

AT ELEVEN A.M. on October 19 a single galley came rowing into the Venetian lagoon. A ripple of alarm spread among those standing on the water's edge of the piazzetta of Saint Mark. The vessel appeared to be manned by Turks, yet it came confidently forward. Nearer, the swelling crowd could discern Ottoman banners trailing from its stern; then the bow guns fired a bursting victory salute. News of Lepanto swept through the city. No one had risked more, played for higher stakes, or experienced such extremes of emotion as the Venetians. They had seen Ottoman warships in their lagoon, watched the ransacking of their colonies, lost Cyprus, and endured the terrible fate of Bragadin. Venice exploded with pent-up emotion. There were bells and bonfires and church services. Strangers hugged in the street. The shopkeepers hung notices on their doors—CLOSED FOR THE DEATH OF THE TURK—and shut for a week. The authorities flung open the gates of the debtors' jail and permitted the unseasonal wearing of carnival masks. People danced in the squares by torchlight to the squeal of fifes. Elaborate floats depicting Venice triumphant, accompanied by lines of prisoners in clanking chains, wound through Saint Mark's square. Even the pick-pockets were said to take a holiday. All the shops on the Rialto were decorated with Turkish rugs, flags, and scimitars, and from the seat of a gondola you could gaze up at the bridge where two lifelike turbaned heads stared at each other, looking as if they had been freshly severed from the living bodies. The Ottoman merchants barricaded themselves in their warehouse and waited for the city to calm down. Two months later, in an unaccustomed fit of religious zeal, the Venetians remembered the butcher who had taken his knife to Bragadin, and expelled all the Jews from their territories.

Each of the main protagonists reacted to the news in his own way. According to legend, the pope had already been apprised of the out-

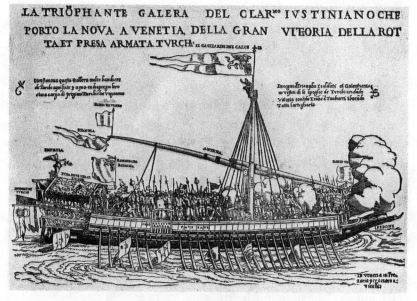

*Carrying the news to Venice*

come by divine means. At the moment Ali Pasha fell to the deck, the pope was said to have opened his window, straining to catch a sound. Then turned to his companion and said, "God be with you; this is no time for business, but for giving thanks to God, for at this moment our fleet is victorious." None had worked harder for this outcome. When word reached him by more conventional means, the old man threw himself to his knees, thanked God, and wept—then deplored the exorbitant waste of gunpowder in firing off celebratory shots. For Pius, it was the justification of his life. "Now, Lord," he murmured, "you can take your servant, for my eyes have seen your salvation." Philip was at church when the news reached him in Madrid. His reaction was as phlegmatic as Suleiman's after Djerba: "He didn't show any excitement, change his expression or show any trace of feeling; his expression was the same as it had been before, and it remained like that until they finished singing vespers." Then he soberly ordered a Te Deum.

LEPANTO WAS EUROPE'S TRAFALGAR, a signal event that gripped the whole Christian continent. They celebrated it as far away as Protestant London and Lutheran Sweden. Don Juan was instantly the hero of the age, the subject of countless poems, plays, and news sheets.

The papacy declared October 7 henceforward to be dedicated to Our Lady of the Rosary. James VI of Scotland was moved to compose eleven hundred lines of Latin doggerel. The Turkish wars became the fit subject for English dramatists—Othello returns from fighting "the general enemy Ottoman" on Cyprus. In Italy, the great painters of the age set to on monumental canvases. Titian has Philip holding his newborn son up to winged victory while a bound captive kneels at his feet, his turban rolling on the floor, and Turkish galleys explode in the distance. Tintoretto portrays Sebastiano Venier, gruff and whiskery in black armor, gripping his staff of office before a similar scene. Vasari, Vicentino, and Veronese produce huge battle scenes of tangled fury, full of smoke, flame, and drowning men, all lit by shafts of light from the Christian heaven. And everywhere, from Spain to the Adriatic, church services, processions of victors and captive Turks, weeping crowds, and the dedication of Ottoman battle trophies. Ali Pasha's great green banner hung in the palace in Madrid, another in the church at Pisa; in the red-tiled churches of the Dalmatian coast they displayed figureheads and Ottoman stern lanterns and lit candles in memory of the part their galleys played on the left wing.

In the wake of all this euphoria there were small acts of chivalry. Don Juan was said to have been personally upset by Ali Pasha's death; he recognized in the kapudan pasha a worthy opponent. It is an ironic note that these two most humane commanders, bound by a shared code of honor, had contrived such great slaughter. In May 1573, Don Juan received a letter from Selim's niece—the sister of Ali's two sons—to beg for their release. One had died in captivity; the other Don Juan returned, along with the gifts she had sent and a touching reply. "You may be assured," he wrote, "that, if in any other battle he or any other of those belonging to you should become my prisoner, I will with equal cheerfulness as now give them their liberty, and do whatever may be agreeable to you." This prompted a response from the sultan in person, still, as ever, "Conqueror of Provinces, Extinguisher of Armies, terrible over lands and seas," to Don Juan, "captain of unique virtue [courage]. . . . Your virtue, most generous Juan, has been destined to be the sole cause, after a very long time, of greater harm than the sovereign and ever-felicitous House of Osman has previously received from Christians. Rather than offence, this gives me the opportunity to send you gifts."

Others were harder-hearted. The Venetians understood that naval supremacy rested less in ships than in men. To the pope's horror, they sent Venier urgent orders to kill all the skilled Ottoman mariners in his power "secretly, in the manner that seems to you most discreet," and requested that Spain do the same. With such measures they hoped and believed that the maritime power of the Turk had been decisively broken: "It can now be said with reason that their power in naval matters is significantly diminished."

In time the Venetians discovered that the tough-minded Ottomans were not shattered by this shattering defeat. The tone was set by Mehmet, Ali's seventeen-year-old son, two days after the battle. In captivity, he met a Christian boy who was crying. It was the son of Bernardino de Cardenas, mortally wounded at the prow of the *Real*. "Why is he crying?" asked Mehmet. When he was told the reason, he replied, "Is that all? I have lost my father, and also my fortune, country, and liberty, yet I shed no tears."

Selim was in Edirne when news of the disaster reached him. According to the chronicler Selaniki, he was initially so deeply affected that he did not sleep or eat for three days. Prayers were recited in the mosques and there was fear verging on panic in the streets of Istanbul that, with its fleet destroyed, the city could be attacked by sea. It was a moment of crisis for the sultanate, but its response, under the assured guidance of Sokollu, was prompt. Selim hurried back to Istanbul; his presence, as he rode through the streets with the vizier at his side, seems to have stabilized the situation.

The Ottomans came to use a euphemism for this heavy defeat: the battle of the dispersed fleet. Uluch Ali's initial report had tried to soften the blow by suggesting that the navy had been scattered rather than annihilated. "The enemy's loss has been no less than yours," he wrote to the sultan. As the full scale of the catastrophe sank in, it was received with acceptance, as Charles had taken the shipwreck at Algiers. "A battle may be won or lost," Selim declared. "It was destined to happen this way according to God's will." Sokollu wrote to Pertev Pasha, one of the few leaders to escape with his life (though not with his position), in a similar vein. "The will of God makes itself manifest in this way, as it has appeared in the mirror of destiny. . . . We trust that all-powerful God will visit all kinds of humiliation on the enemies of the religion." It was a setback, not a catastrophe. The Turks even tried to find positives in God's scourge, quoting a sura of the Koran, "But it may happen that you hate a thing which is good for you." Yet within the sultan's domain there could be no clear analysis of the underlying causes. All blame was heaped on the dead Ali Pasha, the admiral who "had not commanded a single rowing boat in his life." The true reasons for the defeat—the attempt to overmanage the campaign from Istanbul, the struggle for power between the court factions under a weak sultan, the motives for appointing Ali Pasha—these remained hidden. Sokollu himself was suspiciously implicated in these dealings but the subsequent crisis only served to demonstrate his ability and strengthen his grip on power. He moved swiftly and efficiently to manage the situation; orders and requests for information were fired off to the governors of Greek provinces; Uluch Ali was appointed de facto kapudan pasha—all other potential candidates were dead.

By the time Uluch Ali sailed back into Istanbul, he had managed to scrape together eighty-two galleys along the way to make some sort of show, and he flew the standard of the Maltese knights as a battle trophy. This display was pleasing enough to Selim for him not only to spare Uluch's life but also to confirm the corsair as kapudan pasha—admiral of the imperial navy. And as if to signal a great triumph, the sultan also conferred an honorific name on his commander. Henceforth Uluch was to be known as Kilich (sword) Ali. The knight's banner was hung in the Aya Sofya mosque as a token of victory. And the Ottoman administration, now under the undisputed control of Sokollu, swung into furious action. Over the winter of 1571–1572, the enlarged imperial dockyards completely rebuilt the fleet in an effort worthy of Hayrettin. When Kilich expressed concern that it might be impossible to fit the ships out properly, Sokollu gave a sweeping reply. "Pasha, the wealth and power of this empire will supply you, if needful, with anchors of silver, cordage of silk, and sails of satin; whatever you want for your ships you have only to come and ask for it." In the spring of 1572, Kilich sailed out at the head of 134 ships; they had even produced eight galleasses of their own, though they never got the hang of managing them. So rapid was this reconstruction that Sokollu could taunt the Venetian ambassador about their relative losses at Cyprus and Lepanto: "In wrestling Cyprus from you we have cut off an arm. In defeating our fleet you have shaved our beard. An arm once cut off will not grow again, but a shorn beard grows back all the better for the razor."

And almost immediately the Holy League started to falter. It had recognized the importance of consolidating its victory but proved unable to do so. There was bickering over booty. Then Pius died the following spring. He was spared the gradual collapse of his Christian enterprise. During the campaigning season of 1572, Philip kept his fleet at Messina and Don Juan cooling his heels, preferring a strike in North Africa to further war in the east. Colonna and the Venetians dispatched a substantial fleet anyway to confront the Ottomans off the west coast of Greece, but Kilich was too wily to be caught and did what Ali Pasha should have done: kept his ships in a secure anchorage and let his opponents waste their strength. The following year Don Juan did at least sail to the Maghreb and take back Tunis, but by this time Venice could no longer sustain the fight; in March 1573 they had signed a separate peace with Selim, ceding territory and cash to the sultan on highly unfavorable terms. Philip received the news with "a slight ironical twist of his lips." Then he smiled to himself. He was blamelessly rid of the expense of the league and the troublesome Venetians; it was their ambassador who was forcibly ejected from the room by the furious Pope Gregory XIII. In 1574 even Don Juan's triumph at Tunis turned to dust. Kilich Ali sailed to the Maghreb with a larger fleet than either side had mustered at Lepanto and took the city back. He returned to Istanbul with guns firing and captives on the deck; it was like the old days again. The Ottomans were as strong in North Africa as ever; Selim's mastery of the White Sea seemed to have been fully restored.

NOW THAT THE EXPLOSIVE FEELINGS that Lepanto released in Europe have been largely forgotten—the pope returned the Ottoman flags to Istanbul in 1965—some modern historians have tended to play down the significance of the battle. What seemed at the time to be Europe's iconic sea battle that would determine the contest for the center of the world is no longer viewed as a pivotal event like the Battle of Actium fought in the same waters fifteen hundred years earlier to decide control of the Roman Empire, nor that of Salamis, which shattered the Persian advance into Greece. In modern times Lepanto has been labeled "the victory that led nowhere," on the Christian side a fluke, on the Ottoman side an aberration soon mended. Like the battlefield itself, the Battle of Lepanto appears to have been swallowed by time and the devouring sea.

Yet this verdict underestimates the sheer terror in which Christendom lived in the middle years of the sixteenth century, and the material and psychological consequences of momentary success. No one standing on the banks of the Golden Horn in August 1573 watching Kilich Ali's triumphant return from Tunis—the banners, the displayed captives, the cannon shot salutes to the sultan, the nighttime illuminations surrounding the shores of the great city with a ring of fire—could know that Lepanto had sounded the death knell for such Ottoman maritime victories, or that Kilich himself was the last of the great corsair descendants of Hayrettin. In 1580, Philip signed a peace with the sultan that ended the imperial contest for the Mediterranean at a stroke. It was couched in the familiar ringing terms of Ottoman imperial documents and conceded no majesty to anyone:

> Your ambassador who is currently at our imperial court submitted a petition to our throne and royal home of justice. Our exalted threshold of the centre of greatness, our imperial court of omnipotent power is indeed the sanctuary of commanding sultans and the stronghold of the rulers of the age.
>
> A petition of friendship and devotion came from your side. For the safety and security of state and the affluence and tranquility of subjects, you wished friendship with our home of majestic greatness. In order to arrange a structure for peace and to set up conditions for a treaty, our justice-laden imperial agreement was issued on these matters. . . .
>
> It is necessary . . . when it arrives, that is to say after petitioning to our abode of happiness on the basis of sincerity and frankness, that your irregulars and corsairs who are producing ugliness and wickedness on land and sea do not harm the subjects of our protected territories and that they be stopped and controlled. . . .
>
> On the point of faithfulness and integrity let you be staunch and constant and let you respect the conditions of the truce. From this side also no situation will come into existence at all contrary to the truce. Whether it be our naval commanders on the sea, our volunteer captains [corsairs] or our commanders who are on the frontiers of the protected territories, our world-obeyed orders will be sent and damage and difficulties will not reach your country or states and the businessmen who come from that area....

In our imperial time and at our royal abode of happiness it is indeed decided that the prosperity of times come into being. In the same manner, if the building of peace and prosperity and the construction of a treaty and of security are your aims, without delay send your man to our fortunate throne and make known your position. According to it our imperial treaty will be commanded.

It reads like a statement of Ottoman victory; it was certainly no defeat. By this time Philip had defaulted on the crown's payments to its creditors and his attention was being drawn west and north—to the conquest of Catholic Portugal and a proposed invasion of Protestant England. What the treaty recognized was the hardening of a fixed frontier in the Mediterranean between the Muslim and the Christian worlds. With the capture of Cyprus, the Ottomans had virtually cleared the eastern sea, though Venetian Crete still awaited; the failure of Malta and the disaster at Lepanto had scotched grandiose Ottoman schemes of proceeding to Rome. Conversely, with the strategic recapture of Tunis it was clear to Spain that North Africa was cemented into the Ottoman Empire. Charles's hopes of Constantinople had also long gone. The year 1580 was the end of the Crusading dream; the end of great galley wars too. The empires of the sea had fought themselves to a standstill.

YET IF CHRISTENDOM could not win the battle for the Mediterranean, it might certainly have lost it. The year after the battle, old Don Garcia de Toledo was still blanching at the sheer risk of Lepanto. Don Juan had hazarded everything on a single throw of the dice. Don Garcia knew that the consequences of failure would have been catastrophic for the shores of the Christian Mediterranean—and that the margin of victory had been far narrower than its spectacular outcome. With defeat, and the absence of any defending fleet, would have come the rapid loss of all the major islands of the sea—Malta, Crete, the Balearics—a last-ditch defense of Venice, and then, from these launchpads, a push into the heart of Italy, to Rome itself, Suleiman's ultimate goal. Southern Europe could have looked very different indeed if Shuluch Mehmet had turned the Venetian wing, if the heavily gunned galleasses had not disrupted Ali Pasha's center, or Uluch Ali had punctured Doria's line an hour earlier. As it was, the check at Malta

victory at Lepanto stopped dead Ottoman expansion in the
the sea. The events of 1565–1571 fixed the frontiers of the
Mediterranean world.

And though the Ottomans shrugged off defeat, damage had been
done. At Lepanto, the empire suffered its first military catastrophe
since the Mongol warlord Tamerlane shattered the army at Ankara in
1402. These were huge psychological gains for Christian Europe.
Christendom's sense of military inferiority had become so deeply in-
grained that resigned acceptance had become the normal reaction to
each successive defeat. The explosion of fervor in the autumn of 1571
signaled a belief that the balance of power might be starting to tilt.
Cervantes put into the mouth of Don Quixote an expression of just
what difference the few hours at Lepanto had made: "That day . . . was
so happy for Christendom, because all the world learned how mistaken
it had been in believing that the Turks were invincible at sea."

THE BATTLE BETWEEN ISLAM AND CHRISTIANITY for the center
of the world did not begin with the siege of Rhodes, nor did it entirely
end with Lepanto, but between 1520 and 1580 the contest achieved a
special definition when religious impulse and imperial power combined
to produce a conflict of terrible intensity that was fought on the cusp of
two distinct eras of human history. The styles of warfare were at once
primitive and modern; they looked back to the visceral brutality of the
Homeric bronze age, and forward to the clinical devastation of artillery
weapons. At that moment, Charles and Suleiman believed that they
were fighting for control of the earth. What Lepanto and its aftermath
revealed was that even with shattering victories, the Mediterranean
was no longer worth the fight. The middle sea, hemmed in by cluster-
ing landmasses, could now not be easily won by oared galleys, whatever the resources available. Both sides had participated in a hugely
expensive arms race for an elusive prize. The conflict stressed the
human and material reserves of both the protagonists more than they
were prepared to admit. Cyprus and Lepanto cost the Ottomans up-
ward of eighty thousand fighting men. Despite their huge population,
the supply of skilled soldiers was not inexhaustible, and when the
bishop of Dax saw the proudly rebuilt fleet, he was not impressed:
"Having seen . . . an armada leave this port made up of new vessels,
built of green timber, rowed by crews which never held an oar, pro-

vided with artillery which had been cast in haste, several pieces being compounded of acidic and rotten material, with apprentice guides and mariners, and armed with men still stunned by the last battle ..." As the Spanish found after Djerba, the special conditions of naval warfare made specialist skills hard to replace. After 1580, there was a growing distaste for maritime ventures; the Ottoman fleet lay rotting in the still waters of the Horn. The glory days of Barbarossa would never return.

Both sides were soon afflicted by economic malaise. Philip defaulted on his debts in 1575; the years after 1585 saw fiscal crisis start to rack the Muslim world too. The slogging maritime war, and the particular cost of rebuilding the fleet after Lepanto, increased the steepening gradient of taxation in the sultan's realms. At the same time, the influx of bullion from the Americas was beginning to hole the Ottoman economy below the waterline, in ways that were barely understood. The Ottomans had the resources to outstay any competitor in the business of war, but they were powerless to protect their stable, traditional, self-sufficient world against the more pernicious effects of modernity. There were no defensive bastions proof against rising European prices and the inflationary effects of gold. In 1566, the year after Malta, the gold mint at Cairo—the only one in the Ottoman world, producing coins from limited supplies of African gold—devalued its coinage by 30 percent. The Spanish real became the most appreciated currency in the Ottoman empire; it was impossible to strike money of matching value. The silver coins paid to the soldiers grew increasingly thin; they were "as light as the leaves of the almond tree and as worthless as drops of dew," according to a contemporary Ottoman historian. With these forces came price rises, shortages, and the gradual erosion of the indigenous manufacturing base. Raw materials and bullion were being sucked out of the empire by Christian Europe's higher prices and lower production costs. From the end of the sixteenth century globalizing forces started stealthily to undermine the old social fabric and bases of Ottoman power. It was a paradigm of Islam's whole relationship with the West.

THE TREATY OF 1580 RECOGNIZED a stalemate between two empires and two worlds. From this moment, the diagonal frontier that ran the length of the Mediterranean between Istanbul and the Gates of Gibraltar hardened. The competitors turned their backs on each other, the Ottomans to fight the Persians and confront the challenge of Hungary and the Danube once more, Philip to take up the contest in the Atlantic. After the annexation of Portugal he looked west and symbolically moved his court to Lisbon to face a greater sea. He had his own Lepanto still to come—the shipwreck of the Spanish armada off the coast of Britain, yet another consequence of the Spanish habit of sailing too late in the year. In the years after 1580, Islam and Christendom disengaged in the Mediterranean, one gradually to introvert, the other to explore.

Power started to swing away from the Mediterranean basin in ways that the Ottomans and the Hapsburgs with their overcentralized bureaucracies and their hidebound belief in God-given rights could hardly foresee. It was Protestant seamen from London and Amsterdam with their stout sailing ships financed by an entrepreneurial middle class who started to conjure wealth from new worlds. The Mediterranean of the oared galleys would become a backwater, bypassed by new forms of empire. The life—and death—of the cartographer Piri Reis symbolized the Ottomans' lost opportunity to turn outward and explore the empirical world. An anonymous Ottoman mapmaker, writing in the 1580s, crystallized an awareness of the threat that new voyages to the Indies would bring. "It is indeed a strange fact and a sad affair that a group of unclean unbelievers have become strong to the point of voyaging from the west to the east, braving the violence of the winds and calamities of the sea, whereas the Ottoman empire, which is situated at half the distance in comparison with them, has not made any attempt to conquer [India]: this despite the fact that voyages there yield countless benefits, [bringing back] desirable objects, and articles of luxury whose description exceeds the bounds of the describable and explicable." Ultimately Spain would be outflanked too.

After 1580 the corsairs also deserted the sultan's cause and returned to man-taking on their own account along the barren shores of the Maghreb. The sea at the center of the world would face another two hundred miserable years of endemic piracy that would funnel millions of white captives into the slave markets of Algiers and Tripoli. As late as 1815, the year of Waterloo, 158 people were snatched from Sardinia; it took the New World Americans finally to scotch the menace of the Barbary pirates. Venice and the Ottomans, permanently locked into the tideless sea, would contest the shores of Greece until 1719, but the power had long gone elsewhere.

# *Traces*

IN JULY 1568, IN THE HEAT of a Maltese summer day, Jean Parisot de La Valette suffered a severe stroke as he was riding home from a day's hawking in the woods. The gruff old warrior lingered for a few weeks, long enough to free his household slaves, forgive his enemies, and commit his soul to God. The people watched in silence as his coffin was carried through the streets of Birgu—renamed Vittoriosa after the siege—lifted onto a black galley, and rowed across the harbor. He was buried in the chapel of Our Lady of Victory, in the new capital that bore his name, Valletta, constructed on the hills of Mount Sciberras— where the Turks had placed their guns—and the ruins of Saint Elmo. His tomb is decorated with a Latin epitaph, composed by his English secretary, Sir Oliver Starkey: "Here lies La Valette, worthy of eternal honour. The scourge of Africa and Asia, and the shield of Europe, whence he expelled the barbarians by his holy arms, he is the first to be buried in this beloved city which he founded."

After him, the other participants of the great maritime conflict fell away one by one. Selim slipped in his bathhouse in 1574, apparently dizzy from an attempt to give up drinking; Sokollu, his power waning, was stabbed to death in 1578; Uluch Ali died in the arms of a Greek slave girl in 1587; Gian'Andrea Doria lived until 1606, tainted to the end with suspicions of cowardice. Philip wrote his last memorandum in 1598. And in a quiet corner of Italy, the town records of Correggio noted an entry for December 12, 1589, on the man whose eyewitness account—dedicated to "the most serene señor Don Juan of Austria"— has preserved so much detail on the siege of Malta: "It is believed that the death of Francisco Balbi di Correggio, a wandering poet who wrote in Italian and Spanish and who was ever persecuted by men and by fortune, occurred on this date away from his native land."

None endured a sadder fate than Don Juan himself, so eager for glory and a crown of his own. Lepanto won him few plaudits from the cautious Philip, who shackled his ambitions and snuffed out his dreams.

In the end, the king dispatched him to Flanders to crush the Dutch revolt, where the dashing prince who had danced galliards on his own deck died of typhoid and disappointment in 1578. No career had a more startling trajectory, like the path of the comet bursting briefly across the night sky before Lepanto, then gone into the dark sea. Only two months after the battle he wrote a sad description of his own fate: "I spend my time building castles in the air, but in the end all of them, and I, blow away in the wind." It is an epitaph that might serve all the empire builders of the violent century.

Memorials to these people and events dot the Mediterranean shore. They make a picturesque backdrop for tourism: the dark, forbidding gateways of Venetian fortresses entered under the watchful eye of Saint Mark's lion; ruined watchtowers on the headlands of Southern Italy; the massive bastions of Malta; lonely coves where abandoned villages, cleared by pirate raids, crumble into dust beneath the shade of pines; rusting cannon and neat pyramids of stone balls on seaside promontories; the immense, vaulted chambers of galley pens. Barbarossa sleeps in a fine mausoleum on the banks of the Bosphorus, from where his spirit can watch tankers sliding up to the Black Sea, and the wealth of Cyprus went to pay for the astonishing minarets of Selim's mosque in Edirne. Turgut Reis had his home port on the Turkish coast renamed in his honor, while the people of Le Castella in Calabria have forgiven the renegade Uluch Ali to the extent of erecting a statue. Suleiman himself lies in a mausoleum near his great mosque, the Suleymaniye, that looks down over the Golden Horn and the site of the arsenal. As for Bragadin, the martyr of Famagusta is forever being flayed alive in a lurid fresco in the church of Saint John and Saint Paul in Venice. The skin itself followed him home. Someone stole it back from Istanbul in 1580 so that it now nestles in the wall behind his monument.

Period prints and paintings allow us to get some idea of the sheer intensity of the contest these men fought. Ottoman janissaries, their ostrich-feathered shakos flickering like snakes' tongues, mass in trenches before the Maltese redoubts; doubleted defenders in steel casques shoulder arquebuses; cannons roar; plumes of smoke embellish the air; fleets clash on seas jammed solid with masts under apocalyptic skies; drowning figures gasp and wave. But of the galleys that made all this happen—unloading troops and raiding coasts and advancing in great crescents to the thumping of drums and blaring of war trumpets—almost nothing remains beyond random battle trophies in museums: faded banners bearing the names of God in Arabic or Latin, stern lanterns, weapons, and clothes. The ships have all been taken by the sea.

# I L   F I N E.

# Author's Note and Acknowledgments

OUR KNOWLEDGE OF THE HISTORY of the Mediterranean in the sixteenth century is a testament to the invention of printing and the spread of literacy. Where the great event of the Mediterranean world in the fifteenth century—the fall of Constantinople in 1453—is recorded in a mere handful of short accounts, the siege of Malta, the battle of Lepanto, and all the major events and protagonists in this book are the subjects of numerous vivid chronicles, personal testaments, pamphlets, ballads, prints, and news sheets, produced in all the languages of Western Europe for a receptive audience. In addition to this explosion of printed material, there are literally millions of memoranda, letters, secret briefings, and diplomatic exchanges about the events of the time, dictated by the major players and scribed and dispatched across the sea by professional secretariats in Madrid, Rome, Venice, and Istanbul. For example, it has been suggested that no one person has ever read all the correspondence of Philip II of Spain, who ruled half the world from his study desk for forty-two years, and who could produce twelve hundred items of correspondence in a good month. In the face of such engulfing torrents of material, it is inevitable that a short, general work of this nature owes a huge debt to generations of scholars who have given their lives to heroically mining the archives of the world. Among those whose work I have particularly valued are Fernand Braudel, the father of Mediterranean studies in the sixteenth century; Kenneth Setton, whose wonderful four-volume work *The Papacy and the Levant* is a treasure trove of source material; and Ismail Danişmend. From more recent times I am extremely grateful to Stephen Spiteri, whose compendious book *The Great Siege* is an ultimate source on everything to do with events on Malta in 1565.

One vexing issue that has arisen in the writing of this book is the question of the form of names of places and people. The names by which the protagonists are known vary considerably from language to language; many confusingly change their names during the course of the story, have multiple nicknames, and, in the case of the Ottomans,

294 | AUTHOR'S NOTE AND ACKNOWLEDGMENTS

common names that reoccur frequently: two different Mustaphas commanded the sultan's army within a six-year period. I have tried to be as clear about this as possible, without being too long-winded. The Ottoman admiral at Lepanto—or again Inebahtı, to give it the Turkish name—is properly called Müezzinzade Ali. For simplicity's sake, I have called him Ali Pasha throughout. In general I have chosen the form of name by which a person is known in his own language. For example, the corsair who died at Malta is usually referred to in Christian sources as Dragut. I have preferred his Turkish name, Turgut. In addition, I have chosen to transliterate Turkish words for English-speaking readers—Şuluç has become Shuluch, Oruç, Oruch, Çavus, Chaush—but I cannot claim that my phonetically approximate renderings are an exact science.

IN THE ACTUAL CREATION of this book, I am extremely grateful to a large number of individuals and organizations. First, to Jonathan Jao and the team at Random House for their enthusiasm and professionalism, and to my agent, Andrew Lownie. In all matters to do with the Knights of Saint John and the siege of Malta, research was helped enormously by the use of the wonderful library of the Order of Saint John at Clerkenwell, London (www.sja.org.uk). My thanks to Pamela Willis, the librarian. I am grateful a second time to Dr. Stephen Spiteri. Not only did *The Great Siege* clearly explain what a ravelin looks like, its author also generously allowed me to reproduce his reconstructions of St. Elmo. I commend his website (www.fortress-explorer.org) for all kinds of information about the fortifications on Malta.

Many friends and casual bystanders have been unwittingly drawn into this project. Stan Ginn saved the initial proposal from even more serious structural flaws than it now contains; Elizabeth Manners and Stephen Scoffham read and commented on the manuscript; John Dyson provided books from Istanbul; Jan Crowley, Christopher Trillo, Annamaria Ferro, and Andrew Kirby helped with translation; Henrietta Naish had me to stay; Deborah Marshall-Warren sat down for a cup of coffee in the square in Birgu and found herself corralled into finding source material. To all these people I am very grateful. And again, my thanks and love to Jan for supporting the strange enterprise of book writing in good health and bad. Some aspects of it were probably tolerable—the trips to the Venetian lagoon, the landscapes of Malta, and the ramparts of Famagusta—but the business of observing at close quarters books being written is a dull chore at best. Last, a posthumous salute to my father, George Crowley, who knew the sea well in peace and war, and who introduced me to Malta when I was ten. Without that marvelous first glimpse of the Mediterranean, this book would not have come about.

# Source Notes

All the quotations in the book are from primary and other sixteenth-century sources. References refer to the books from which the quotations have been taken, as listed in the bibliography.

**EPIGRAPH**

 ix "The inhabitants of the Maghreb" Brummett, p. 89

**PROLOGUE: PTOLEMY'S MAP**

 xiii "as the spirit of God" Crowley, p. 233
 xiii "despoiled and blackened as if by fire" ibid., p. 232
 xiv "one empire, one faith" ibid., p. 240
 xiv "sovereign of two seas" ibid.
 xv "In mid-sea sits a waste land" Grove, p. 9
 xvi "cruellest enemy of Christ's name" Setton, vol. 2, p. 292
 xvii "He has daily in his hand" ibid., vol. 3, p. 175
 xvii "He pays attention" ibid., p. 174

*Part One* CAESARS: THE CONTEST FOR THE SEA

**CHAPTER 1: THE SULTAN PAYS A VISIT**

 3 "Suleiman the sultan" Brockman, p. 114
 3–4 "Conqueror of the Lands of the Orient and the Occident" Finkel, p. 115
 4 "in the interest of the world order" Crowley, p. 51
 4 "The sultan is tall" Alan Fisher, p. 2
 7 "if all the other Christian princes" Setton, vol. 2, p. 372
 8 "These corsairs are noted" Rossi, p. 26
 8 "evil sect of Franks" ibid., p. 26
 8 "How many sons of the Prophet" ibid., p. 27
 8 "The said Rhodians" Setton, vol. 3, p. 122
 8 "They don't let the ships" Rossi, p. 27
 8 "head of Muhammad's community" Alan Fisher, p. 5
 8 "the vipers' nest of Franks" Rossi, p. 26
 9 "Brother Philip Villiers de L'Isle Adam" Brockman, pp. 114–5
 9 "Sire, since he became Grand Turk" ibid., p. 115
 9 "Now that the Terrible Turk" Setton, vol. 3, p. 172
 10 "numerous as the stars" Crowley, p. 102
 10 "galleasses, galleys, pallandaries" Bourbon, p. 5
 10 "and he feared" ibid., p. 11

10  "decked their men . . . trumpets and drums" Bourbon, p. 12

11  "the damnable workers of wickedness" Rossi, p. 26

11  "The Sultan Suleiman to Villiers de L'Isle Adam" Brockman, pp. 115–6

13  "a most brilliant engineer" Bosio, vol. 2, p. 545

13  "beseeching St John to take keeping" Bourbon, p. 17

13  "to make murder of the people" ibid., p. 19

14  "falling to the ground they broke" ibid., p. 20

14  "the handgun shot was innumerable and incredible" ibid., p. 19

14  "a mountain of earth" Porter, vol. 1, p. 516

15  "with great strokes of the sword" Bourbon, p. 28

15  "fell from the walls as he went to see his trenches" ibid., p. 28

15  "26 and 27, combat" Hammer-Purgstall, vol. 5, p. 420

16  "On this occasion" ibid., p. 421

16  "even before the hour of morning prayer" Brockman, p. 134

16  "The attack is repulsed" Hammer-Purgstall, vol. 5, p. 421

16  "and finally to ruin and destroy all Christendom" Setton, vol. 3, p. 209

17  "It was an ill-starred day for us" ibid.

18  "pleasure-house" Porter, vol. 1, p. 516

18  "We had no powder" ibid., p. 517

18  "insistent and interminable downpours" Rossi, p. 41

19  "could not think the city any longer tenable" Caoursin, p. 516

19  "all Turkey should die" Setton, vol. 3, p. 212

20  "The Great Turk is very wise, discreet . . . chair was of fine gold" Porter, vol. 1, p. 516

20  "it was a common thing to lose cities" Bosio, vol. 2, p. 590

20  "It saddens me to be compelled" Caoursin, p. 507

21  "In this way" Rossi, p. 41

22  "agile as serpents" Brummett, p. 90

## CHAPTER 2: A SUPPLICATION

23  "On its mainsail was painted" Merriman (1962), vol. 3, p. 27

24  "It is for Austria to rule the entire earth" ibid., p. 446

24  "Spain, it's the king" ibid., p. 28

25  "approaching covertly" ibid., p. 28

26  "There is more at the back of his head" Beeching, p. 11

28  "It was the start of all the evils" López de Gómara, p. 357

29  "God had made him" Seyyd Murad, p. 96

29  "I am the thunderbolt of heaven" Achard, p. 47

31  "go and tell your Christian kings" Sir Godfrey Fisher, p. 53

33  "kissing the imperial decree" Seyyd Murad, p. 125

## CHAPTER 3: THE KING OF EVIL

36  "if the parents of any of the dead" Seyyd Murad, p. 121

36  "which destroyed twenty-six great ships" López de Gómara, p. 135

36  "It's not Peru" Heers, p. 171

37  "Because of the story of the great riches" Haëdo, p. 26
37  "like the sun among the stars" Seyyd Murad, p. 96
37  "I will conquer . . . God's protection" Belachemi, p. 222
37  "drawn from life" Heers, p. 226
38  "Barbarossa, Barbarossa, you are the king of evil" Belachemi, p. 400
41  "that they could not move" Seyyd Murad, p. 164
41  "It was the greatest loss" López de Gómara, p. 399
41  "Barbarossa impaled with many other Spaniards" ibid.
41  "Hayrettin spread his name and reputation" Seyyd Murad, p. 164
41  "Caesar, Charles, Emperor!" Necipoğlu, p. 174
42  "Unless this disaster is reversed" Tracy, p. 137
42  "sailing with a great armada" ibid.
42  "Explosion of mines . . . The snow continues to fall." Hammer-Purgstall, vol. 5, p. 452
43  "bestowing on the Knights" Attard, p. 12

## CHAPTER 4: THE VOYAGE TO TUNIS

45  "the rumour here" Tracy, p. 27
45  "Just as there is only one God" Clot, p. 79
45  "Spain is like a lizard" Finlay, p. 12
46  "He detests the emperor" Necipoğlu, p. 173
46  "The king of Spain has for a long time" Merriman (1962), vol. 3, p. 114
46  "In the light of duty" Tracy, p. 138
46  "with great ceremony and pomp" Necipoğlu, p. 173
46  "continuous rain" Hammer-Purgstall, vol. 5, pp. 480–1
47  "the miserable fugitive had fled" Clot, p. 86
48  "amid the firing of numerous salutes" Kâtip Çelebi, p. 47
49  "Barbarossa was continually in the arsenal" Bradford (1969), p. 129
49  "In all he had 1,233 Christian slaves . . . the expectation of plunder" López de Gómara, p. 522
50  "The supremacy of Turkey" Bradford (1969), p. 123
51  "massacring many men" Sandoval, vol. 2, p. 474
51  "From the Strait of Messina" ibid., p. 487
52  "to attack the enemy" Tracy, p. 147
52  "Show me your ways, O God" Merriman (1962), vol. 3, p. 114
54  "with lance in hand" Tracy, p. 147
54  "the holy enterprise of war" ibid., p. 156
55  "Your glorious and incomparable victory" Clot, p. 106

## CHAPTER 5: DORIA AND BARBAROSSA

58  "to multiply the difficulties of the Emperor" Heers, p. 73
58  "I cannot deny" Clot, p. 137
58  "The Turk will make some naval expedition" Necipoğlu, p. 175
58  "to build two hundred vessels" Kâtip Çelebi, p. 66
59  "Venetian infidels" ibid., p. 56

59 "as we observe that all" Setton, vol. 3, p. 410

60 "laid waste the coasts of Apulia" Bradford (1969), p. 152

60 "the common enemy" Setton, vol. 3, p. 433

61 "this year the Venetians possessed twenty-five islands" Kâtip Çelebi, p. 61

62 "tore his beard and took to flight" ibid., p. 64

62 "Such wonderful battles" ibid., p. 64

62 "the proclamation of the victory was read" ibid., p. 64

64 "I can guarantee that" Heers, p. 163

65 "We must thank God for all" Brandi, p. 459

65 "nobody could have guessed" ibid.

## CHAPTER 6: THE TURKISH SEA

66 "To see Toulon" Bradford (1969), p. 197

67 "ceaselessly spewing . . . black as ink" Maurand, p. 109

67 "the famous, imperial, and very great city of Constantinople" ibid., p. 183

68 "It's an extraordinary thing" ibid., pp. 67–9

68 "God in his mercy . . . except for some Turks who escaped by swimming" ibid., p. 97

70 "out of spite . . . only answer we ever got" ibid., p. 129

70 "much given to sodomy" ibid., p. 127

70 "the tears, groans, and sobs" ibid., p. 133

71 "the king of the sea" Kâtip Çelebi, p. 69

71 "numerous salvoes from cannon" Haëdo, p. 74

72 "They grabbed young women and children" Davis, p. 43

73 "As to me" ibid., p. 209

73 "the outrage done to God . . . dozens of years after death" ibid., pp. 41–2

74 "Christian stealing" ibid., p. 27

74 "as friends and Christians . . . boys and girls as slaves" Maurand, p. 165

75 "the lady named Huma" Setton, vol. 4, p. 840

77 "That least tolerable and most to be dreaded employment" Davis, p. 77

79 "Turgut has held the kingdom of Naples" Braudel, vol. 2, p. 993

79 "He is seen for days on end" ibid., p. 914

81 "as pleasing to Turkish eyes . . . with the Turkish galleys" Setton, vol. 4, p. 765

## Part Two EPICENTER: THE BATTLE FOR MALTA

## CHAPTER 7: NEST OF VIPERS

85 "We must draw strength from our weaknesses" Braudel, vol. 2, p. 986

85 "for two months now, the said King of Spain" ibid., p. 1010

86 "corsairs parading crosses" Mallia-Milanes, p. 64

89 "The Turk is still alive" Alan Fisher, p. 7

89 "You will do no good" Bradford (1999), p. 17

90 "would redound to the harm of Christendom" Guilmartin (1974), p. 106

90 "to enlarge the empire" Bosio, vol. 3, p. 493

91 "I intend to conquer the island of Malta" Cassola (1995), p. 19

92 "a Sicilian character with a mixture of African" The Great Siege 1565, p. 4

93  "The question of grain is very important" Cassola (1995), p. 325 et seq.
95  "furiously" Braudel, vol. 2, p. 1015
95  "wanted more than once to go" Setton, vol. 4, p. 845
95  "that he should treat Piyale" Bosio, vol. 3, p. 501
95  "I am relying on you . . . to help Malta" Cassola (1995), p. 7
96  "lead, rope, spades . . . sails for making defences" Balbi (2003), p. 33
96  "and different pictures in the Turkish style" Cirni, fol. 47
96  "in an atmosphere of triumph" Balbi (2003), p. 34
97  "Here are two good-humored men" Peçevi, p. 288

## CHAPTER 8: INVASION FLEET

98  "On the morning of March 29" Setton, vol. 4, p. 949
98  "He is tall and well made" Balbi (1961), p. 29
101  "A people of little courage" Spiteri, p. 117
101  "hoes, picks, shovels" Bosio, vol. 3, p. 499
102  "the Turkish fleet will be coming" Braudel, vol. 2, p. 1015
102  "At one in the morning" ibid., p. 1016
102  "has withdrawn into the woods" Setton, vol. 4, p. 847
102  "must be coming to . . . the division of Christendom" ibid., p. 852
102  "serious, of good judgement and experience" Bosio, vol. 3, p. 497
103  "on which the salvation . . . as long as possible" ibid., p. 499
103  "The enemy could get in" ibid.
104  "because experience has shown" ibid.
104  "each man was required" Bradford (1999), p. 48
105  "bringing with them" Balbi (1961), p. 50
105  "At fifteen or twenty miles" Bosio, vol. 3, p. 512
106  "five to a bench" ibid., p. 512

## CHAPTER 9: THE POST OF DEATH

110  "A well-ordered camp" Balbi (2003), p. 49
111  "devoutly imploring" Bosio, vol. 3, p. 521
112  "I do not come to Malta" ibid., p. 522
113  "that part of the island" Cirni, fol. 52
113  "The Turkish army covered the whole countryside . . . rattle of our muskets" Bosio, vol. 3, p. 523
113  "not one man" Balbi (1961), p. 53
114  "was so low" Balbi (2003), p. 48
115  "the key to all the other fortresses of Malta" Bosio, vol. 3, p. 526
115  "on a very narrow site and easy to attack" ibid., p. 525
115  "Their plan is to take the castle" Setton, vol. 4, p. 842
115  "four or five days . . . all hope of rescue" Bosio, vol. 3, p. 525
116  "secure the fleet" ibid.
116  "We could see ten or twelve bullocks" Balbi (1961), p. 58
118  "no equal in the world at earthworks" Bosio, vol. 3, p. 539
118  "with marvelous diligence and speed" ibid., p. 528

119 "a consumptive body" Cirni, fol. 53

120 "In truth it was a remarkable thing" Bosio, vol. 3, pp. 531–2

121 "in superb order" ibid., p. 532

121 "a wise and experienced warrior" ibid., p. 531

122 "that it was extraordinary" ibid., p. 539

122 "even at the cost of many good soldiers" ibid., p. 533

## CHAPTER 10: THE RAVELIN OF EUROPE

123 "a fortress without a ravelin" Cirni, fol. 63

124 "as if he were still alive" Bosio, vol. 3, p. 540

124 "with the roar of the artillery" ibid., p. 541

125 "The fort could not be held for long" Balbi (2003), p. 68

125 "It was impossible to get the ravelin back" Bosio, vol. 3, p. 542

126 "for nothing pleases soldiers more than money" Balbi (1961), p. 68

126 "by Vespers they had repaired it again" Bosio, vol. 3, p. 548

126 "there was not a safe place in St Elmo" Balbi (1961), p. 69

126 "because their defences had been levelled" ibid., p. 71

126 "so that it seemed as though" Bosio, vol. 3, p. 547

127 "For every one who came back" ibid., p. 553

130 "in the language that . . . as dearly as possible" ibid., p. 553

130 "all said with one voice" Balbi (1961), p. 74

130 "These consisted of barrel hoops" ibid., p. 75

131 "and hurled them into the ditch again" Bosio, vol. 3, p. 556

131 "baskets, mattresses and unravelled rope" Balbi (1961), p. 76

132 "The pashas were reproaching the janissaries" Balbi (2003), p. 79

132 "on the promise of his head" Bosio, vol. 3, p. 558

133 "so that the earth and the air shook" ibid., p. 561

133 "painted with extraordinary designs . . . according to the devotion of each man" ibid., p. 562

134 "with our minds split" Cirni, fol. 65

134 "fighting like one inspired" Balbi (2003), p. 82

134 "to enter the fort or die together" Bosio, vol. 3, p. 563

134 "Those who remained . . . crowned and encircled with fire" Balbi (1961), p. 79

134 "crowned and encircled with fire" Bosio, vol. 3, p. 563

134 "so that the enemy" ibid.

134 "Victory and the Christian faith!" Bosio, vol. 3, p. 564

134 "Keep quiet" ibid., p. 564

## CHAPTER 11: THE LAST SWIMMERS

136 "We, for our part, did not" Balbi (2003), p. 86

137 "the sun was like a living fire" Bosio, vol. 3, p. 571

137 "covered in flames and fire" ibid., p. 570

137 "Victory! Victory!" ibid.

137 "everyone resolved with one accord" ibid., p. 572

138 "God knows what the grand master felt" Balbi (2003), p. 88

138   "made themselves ready . . . to have mercy on their souls" Balbi (1961), p. 86

138   "At sunrise" Balbi (1961), p. 86

139   "Kill! Kill!" Bosio, vol. 3, p. 571

139   "but as soon as they saw" Balbi (2003), p. 90

139   "which made our hair stand on end on Birgu" Bosio, vol. 3, p. 573

139   "by your god" Cirni, fol. 71

140   "some mutilated, some without heads" Balbi (2003), p. 93

141   "drank the sherbet" Peçevi, p. 289

## CHAPTER 12: PAYBACK

142   "It grieved us all" Balbi (1961) pp. 88–9

143   "I had put all our forces" Spiteri, p. 606

143   "without which we're dead" Bosio, vol. 3, p. 596

143   "at the hour of vespers" ibid., p. 581

143   "with all your people, your property and your artillery" Balbi (2003), p. 97

143   "in a terrible and severe voice" Bosio, vol. 3, p. 581

143   "saying that he was only" Balbi (2003), pp. 98–9

145   "his heart touched . . . to the Catholic Faith" Bosio, vol. 3, p. 587

145   "Turks, Turks!" ibid., p. 586

148   "heavily armed and very fat" ibid., p. 589

148   "These poor creatures" Balbi (1961), p. 104

149   "With an enormous flash" Bosio, vol. 3, p. 597

151   "in cloth of gold . . . and magnificent bows" Balbi (2003), p. 111

151   "strangely dressed . . . and chanting imprecations" Bosio, vol. 3, p. 603

151   "if it had not been so dangerous" Balbi (2003), p. 111

151   "yet in spite of this" ibid., p. 112

152   "I don't know . . . throwing one another back, falling and firing" Bosio, vol. 3, p. 606

152   "with pikes, swords, shields, and stones" ibid., p. 605

153   "wearing a large black headdress" Balbi (2003), p. 114

153   "but before giving up" Balbi (1961), p. 113

154   "Relief! Victory!" Bosio, vol. 3, p. 604

154   "the Greek traitor" ibid.

154   "Kill! Kill! . . . dispatched them" ibid., p. 605

155   "like the Red Sea . . . battle had been fought" ibid.

155   "a great deal of hashish" Balbi (2003), p. 116

155   "Saint Elmo's pay" Bosio, vol. 3, p. 605

## CHAPTER 13: TRENCH WARS

156   "I sent you over to Malta" Cassola (1995), pp. 26–7

156   "make sure that" ibid., pp. 26–7

157   "We realise in how great peril" Setton, vol. 4, p. 858

157   "mostly a rabble and" ibid., p. 855

157   "If Malta is not helped" Merriman (1962), vol. 4, p.117

158   "Its loss would be greater" Setton, vol. 4, p. 869

158 "if he had not aided your Majesty" ibid., p. 866

159 "a bombardment so continuous" Cirni, fol. 85

162 "by the will of God" Balbi (2003), p. 133

163 "trying to amuse him" ibid., p. 130

163 "Omer has performed outstanding service" Cassola (1995), p. 147 et seq.

164 "When the admiral" Peçevi, p. 290

165 "He doubted that the water would hold out" Cirni, fol. 87

165 "like a moving earthquake" ibid.

165 "These we found in the same condition" Bonello, p. 142

166 "I can't see any of these dogs" Balbi (1961), p.137

167 "This is the day to die" Balbi (2003), p. 144

167 "pike in hand, as if he were a common soldier" ibid.

167 "Seeing it" Balbi (2003), pp. 144–5

167 "The assaults on this day" Balbi (1961), p. 138

167 "without heads, without arms and legs" Cirni, fol. 97

168 "Victory and relief!" Balbi (2003), p. 145

169 "to the affront to the sultan's name" Bosio, vol. 3, p. 636

170 "The *chaush* Abdi" Cassola (1995), p. 32

170 "I have often left guards" Bonello, p. 142

171 "an enjoyable game hunt" Bosio, vol. 3, p. 645

171 "out of sheer joie de vivre" ibid.

## CHAPTER 14: "MALTA YOK"

173 "Our men are in large part dead" Bonello, p. 147

174 "We were sometimes so close" Balbi (2003), p. 165

174 "some of the Turks . . . three loaves and a cheese" Cirni, fol. 114

174 "that God did not want Malta to be taken" ibid.

175 "Due to the urgent need" Spiteri, p. 635

175 "that their bolts could pierce" Balbi (1961), p. 160

175 "stick in hand" Bosio, vol. 3, p. 678

176 "They did not move" Balbi (1961), p. 158

176 "Four hundred men still alive . . . don't lose an hour" Merriman (1962), vol. 4,
p. 118

176 "providing it could be done" Fernandez Duro, p. 83

177 "from the water both from the sky and the sea" Bosio, vol. 3, p. 678

177 "They continued to bombard" Balbi (1961), p. 165

178 "miserable and horrible" Bosio, vol. 3, p. 687

179 "who by his clothing and bearing" ibid., p. 693

179 "And having done that" ibid.

182 "Relief, relief! Victory! Victory! . . . of the most holy reputation" ibid., p. 694

183 "Not even at the point" Balbi (1961), p. 184

184 "so great that I maintain . . . many died" ibid.

184 "Kill them!" Bosio, vol. 3, p. 701

185 "We could not estimate" Balbi (2003), pp. 185–6

185 "arid, ransacked, and ruined" Bosio, vol. 3, p. 705

185 "could not walk in the streets" Braudel, vol. 2, p. 1020

186 "who fought during the Siege of Malta" Cassola (1995), p. 36
186 "He has given orders" Braudel, vol. 2, p. 1021
186 "Sultan of Sultans" Alan Fisher, p. 4
187 "This chimney is still burning" Hammer-Purgstall, vol. 6, p. 233

## Part Three ENDGAME: HURTLING TO LEPANTO

### CHAPTER 15: THE POPE'S DREAM

191 "by nature irascible" Lesure, p. 56
192 "Turkish expansion is like the sea" Crowley, p. 35
192 "too high an estimation of himself" Lesure, p. 56
193 "He is extremely skillful" ibid., pp. 57–8
194 "a slave of wickedness" Beeching, p. 135
194 "a good man" Braudel, vol. 2, p. 1029
194 "We should like it even better" ibid.
195 "No one alone can resist it" Setton, vol. 4, p. 912
197 "The Turk is only interested" Braudel, vol. 2, p. 1045
198 "To carry out war" Bicheno, p. 103
199 "It is better to treat all enemy rulers" Mallett, p. 216
201 "to give heart and help to the Moors of Granada" Braudel, vol. 2, p. 1066
202 "It was the saddest sight in the world" ibid., p. 1072
202 "with a fine present" Setton, vol. 4, p. 934

### CHAPTER 16: A HEAD IN A DISH

204 "an island thrust into the mouth of the wolf" Setton, vol. 4, p. 1032
205 "All the inhabitants of Cyprus are slaves" Hill, p. 798
207 "Selim, Ottoman Sultan" ibid., p. 888
208 "the forces of his Catholic Majesty" Setton, vol. 4, p. 955
209 "His Holiness has demonstrated the truth" Parker (1979), p. 110
209 "It is clear that one of the principal reasons" Braudel, vol. 2, p. 1083
209 "He is one of the greatest dissimulators" Parker (1998), p. 33
210 "If we have to wait for death" ibid., p. 65
210 "please the Pope and provide always for Christendom's need" Capponi, p. 130
211 "You shall obey Marc'Antonio Colonna . . . would bring upon Christendom" Bicheno, p. 175
211 "that there would be no combat" Setton, vol. 4, p. 973
212 "the king commands and wishes" Capponi, p. 133
213 "obligation of preserving intact the fleet of Your Majesty" Setton, vol. 4, p. 978
213 "and all this was done" ibid.
213 "the eye of the island" Hill, p. 861
214 "the finest and most scientific construction" ibid., p. 849
214 "had neither muskets nor swords" Excerpta Cypria, p. 129
214 "Would to God we had lost him too!" ibid., p. 128
215 "No liberty did they get" ibid., p. 132
216 "We were anxious to harass" ibid., pp. 133–4

216 "I saw but little charity" ibid., p. 136
217 "Everyone shall know at this crisis" ibid., p. 133
217 "acquire honour by my goods" Capponi, p. 153
217 "Though he pretends he is willing" Hill, p. 922
218 "who had on a breastplate" *Excerpta Cypria*, p. 138
218 "our men were cut in pieces" ibid.
218 "The Coadjutor fell killed by a musket ball" ibid.
218 "You dogs, enemies of God" ibid.
219 "but with no kind of order" ibid., p. 139
219 "we took a great cross and exhorted them . . . and a few escaped" ibid., p. 140
219 "here I say, we have the traitor" ibid.
219 "Then a drunken Greek hoisted" ibid.
219 "but the change was a sad and mournful one" ibid.
219 "The victors kept cutting off the heads" ibid.
220 "I have seen your letter" Bicheno, pp. 167–70

## CHAPTER 17: FAMAGUSTA

221 "the loss of Nicosia" Setton, vol. 4, p. 990
221 "God knows whether Famagusta" ibid., p. 999
221 "to render the Venetians more satisfactory service" ibid., p. 993
223 "I have no doubt" ibid., p. 1009
223 "A very fair stronghold" Hill, p. 857
223 "as long as there was a drachm of food" Setton, vol. 4, p. 999
225 "to find and immediately attack" Inalcik, pp. 187–9
226 "as a sign of joy and gladness" Setton, vol. 4, p. 1015
226 "with lively and loving words" ibid.
227 "as the League is now" Parker (1979), p. 110
227 "It will look very fine on paper" Braudel, vol. 2, p. 1092
229 "Long live St Mark" Setton, vol. 4, p. 1013
229 "I shall make you walk" Morris, p. 110
229 "The wine is finished" Setton, vol. 4, p. 1032
230 "I, Mustapha Pasha" ibid.

## CHAPTER 18: CHRIST'S GENERAL

231 "I see that, where naval warfare is concerned" Parker (1998), p. 72
231 "The domination of the Turk must extend as far as Rome" Lesure, p. 61
232 "You must keep yourself" Bicheno, p. 156
233 "With due humility and respect" Petrie, p. 135
234 "He is a prince so desirous" Bicheno, p. 208
234 "brave and generous" Peçevi, pp. 310–1
234 "coming from and growing up" ibid., p. 311
235 "The original sin of our court" Setton, vol. 4, p. 1021
235 "Everybody was surprised and delighted" Stirling-Maxwell, p. 356
235 "Today at 23 hours" Setton, vol. 4, p. 1024
236 "Take, fortunate prince" Stirling-Maxwell, p. 359

237 "You must know that by the commission" Setton, vol. 4, p. 1034

237 "having discharged our debt" ibid.

238 "Up to that hour" ibid., p. 1038

239 "Since the Divine Majesty has determined" ibid., p. 1039

239 "You shan't have a noble" Peçevi, p. 346

239 "Those Muslim captives . . . broken the treaty" Gazioğlu, p. 65

240 "Do I not know . . . in my army" Hill, p. 1029

240 "Tie them all up!" Setton, vol. 4, p. 1040

240 "Behold the head" ibid., p. 1030

240 "I am a Christian" ibid., p. 1042

240 "Look if you can see your fleet" ibid., p. 1032


CHAPTER 19: SNAKES TO A CHARM

242 "Thank God that we are all here" Stirling-Maxwell, p. 377

243 "Your Excellency should always try" *Colección de Documentos Inéditos*, p. 275

244 "If I were in charge" ibid., p. 8

244 "For the love of God . . . to destroy it" Bicheno, p. 211

245 "You should be warned" *Colección de Documentos Inéditos*, pp. 13–14

245 "In reality it's not possible" ibid., p. 25

246 "but rather have the enemy" Bicheno, p. 215

246 "Not everyone willingly agrees to fight" Capponi, p. 239

246 "like snakes drawn by the power of a charm" ibid., p. 224

246 "Although their fleet is superior" Stirling-Maxwell, p. 385

249 "he fasts three times a week" Bicheno, p. 224

249 "If the [enemy] fleet appears" Lesure, p. 80

249 "Now I order that" Inalcik, pp. 188–9

250 "In the embarkation of these men" Stirling-Maxwell, p. 235

251 "By the Blood of Christ" Thubron, p. 137

252 "a man pessimistic by nature" Peçevi, p. 350

253 "The shortage of men is a reality" ibid.

253 "What does it matter if . . . my life" ibid.

254 "God showed us a sky and a sea" Capponi, p. 247


CHAPTER 20: "LET'S FIGHT"

255 "like a forest" Capponi, p. 254

255 "We felt great joy" Lesure, p. 120

256 "Sir, I say that" Brantome, p. 125

256 "Gentlemen, this is not the time" Capponi, p. 255

257 "if this happens" *Colección de Documentos Inéditos*, p. 9

257 "One could never get" Lesure, p. 123

260 "lived in virtuous and Christian fashion . . . what we can" Beeching, p. 197

261 "Victory and long live Jesus Christ!" Lesure, p. 127

261 "My children, we are here to conquer" Stirling-Maxwell, p. 407

262 "with pork flesh still stuck" Capponi, p. 258

263 "Friends, I expect you today" Stirling-Maxwell, p. 410

263    "Blessed be the bread" Capponi, p. 258

264    "like drowned hens" Thubron, p. 145

264    "inspired with youthful ardor" Lesure, p. 129

264    "Hurtling towards each other" Caetani, p. 202

265    "It was so terrible that" ibid., p. 134

265    "God allow us" Capponi, p. 266

265    "and already the sea" Setton, vol. 4, p. 1056

CHAPTER 21: SEA OF FIRE

266    "Shuluch and Kara Ali" Thubron, p. 46

267    "In this vast confusion" ibid., p. 150

267    "It was an appalling massacre" ibid.

268    "In war the death" Bosio, vol. 3, p. 499

268    "and all our shots" Caetani, p. 134

269    "So great was the roaring of the cannon" ibid.

270    "a mortal storm of arquebus shots" Capponi, p. 273

270    "a great number of them" Caetani, p. 207

271    "Giambattista Contusio felled Kara Hodja" ibid., p. 135

271    "There was a high number" Scetti, p. 121

272    "Don't shoot. We're also Christians!" Capponi, p. 279

272    "What shall we go for next" Brântome, p. 126

272    "My galley, with cannon" Lesure, p. 136

272    "On the *Real*" ibid., p. 135

272    "an enormous quantity of large turbans" ibid.

273    "could make his galley do" ibid., p. 138

273    "delivered an immense carnage" ibid.

274    "Each of you do as much" Stirling-Maxwell, p. 422

275    "out of disdain and ridicule" Thubron, pp. 156–7

275    "The greater fury of the battle" Bicheno, pp. 255–6

275    "the soldiers, sailors and convicts" Thubron, p. 157

276    "What has happened was so strange" Caetani, p. 212

276    "because of the countless corpses . . . nobody would help them" Scetti, p. 122

277    "I saw the wretched place" Peçevi, pp. 351–2

277    "The greatest event witnessed" Cervantes, p. 76

CHAPTER 22: OTHER OCEANS

279    "God be with you" Stirling-Maxwell, p. 443

279    "Now, Lord" Pastor, vol. 18, p. 298

279    "He didn't show any excitement" *Colección de Documentos Inéditos*, p. 258

280    "the general enemy Ottoman" *Othello*, Act I, Scene 3, line 50

280    "You may be assured" Petrie, p. 192

280    "Conqueror of Provinces" Bicheno, p. 270

281    "secretly, in the manner" Lesure, p. 151

281    "It can now be said" Setton, vol. 4, p. 1068

281    "Why is he crying . . . yet I shed no tears" Stirling-Maxwell, p. 428

281  "The enemy's loss has been" Setton, vol. 4, p. 1069

281  "A battle may be won or lost" Inalcik, p. 190

281  "The will of God" Lesure, p. 182

281  "But it may happen" Hess (1972), p. 62

282  "had not commanded" Yildirim, p. 534

282  "Pasha, the wealth and power" Setton, vol. 4, p. 1075

282  "In wrestling Cyprus" Stirling-Maxwell, p. 469

283  "a slight ironical twist of his lips" Setton, vol. 4, p. 1093

284  "Your ambassador" Hess (1972), p. 64

286  "That day . . . was so happy" Cervantes, p. 138

286  "Having seen . . . an armada" Setton, vol. 4, p. 1091

287  "as light as the leaves" Braudel, vol. 2, p. 1195

288  "It is indeed a strange fact" Soucek (1996), p. 102

## EPILOGUE: TRACES

289  "Here lies La Valette" Bradford (1972), p. 173

289  "the most serene señor" Balbi (1961), p. 7

289  "It is believed that the death of" ibid., p. 5

290  "I spend my time" Bicheno, p. 260

# Bibliography

Achard, Paul, *La Vie Extraordinaire des Frères Barberousse*, Paris, 1939

Anderson, R. C., *Naval Wars in the Levant, 1559–1853*, Liverpool, 1952

Attard, Joseph, *The Knights of Malta*, Malta, 1992

Babinger, Franz, *Mehmet the Conqueror and His Time*, Princeton, 1978

Balbi di Correggio, Francisco, *The Siege of Malta, 1565*, trans. Ernle Bradford, London, 2003

Balbi di Correggio, Francisco, *The Siege of Malta, 1565*, trans. Henry Alexander Balbi, Copenhagen, 1961

Barkan, Omer Lutfi, "L'Empire Ottoman face au monde chrétien au lendemain de Lépante" in Benzoni

Beeching, Jack, *The Galleys at Lepanto*, London, 1982

Belachemi, Jean-Louis, *Nous les Frères Barberousse, corsaires et rois d'Alger*, Paris, 1984

Benzoni, Gino, *Il Mediterraneo nella seconda metà del '500 alla luce di Lepanto*, Florence, 1974

Bicheno, Hugh, *Crescent and Cross: The Battle of Lepanto 1571*, London, 2004

Bonello, G., "An Overlooked Eyewitness's Account of the Great Siege" in *Melitensium Amor, Festschrift in Honour of Dun Gwann Azzopardi*, ed. T. Cortis, T. Freller, and L. Bugeja, pp. 133–48, Malta, 2002

Bosio, G., *Dell'istoria della sacra religione et illustrissimia militia di San Giovanni Gierosolimitano*, vols. 2 and 3, Rome, 1594–1602

Bostan, Idris, *Kürekli ve Yelkenli Osmanlı Gemileri*, Istanbul, 2005

Bourbon, J. de, "A brief relation of the siege and taking of the city of Rhodes" in *The Principal Navigations, Voyages, Traffiques and Discoveries of the English Nation* by Richard Hakluyt, vol. 5, Glasgow, 1904

Bradford, Ernle, *The Great Siege: Malta 1565*, London, 1999

Bradford, Ernle, *Mediterranean: Portrait of a Sea*, London, 1970

Bradford, Ernle, *The Shield and the Sword: The Knights of St. John*, London, 1972

Bradford, Ernle, *The Sultan's Admiral: The Life of Barbarossa*, London, 1969

Brandi, Karl, *The Emperor Charles V*, London, 1949

Brântome, P. de Bourdeille, Seigneur de, *Oeuvres complètes*, ed. L. Lalanne, vol. 3, Paris, 1864

Braudel, Fernand, "Bilan d'une bataille," in Benzoni

Braudel, Fernand, *The Mediterranean and the Mediterranean World in the Age of Philip II*, trans. Siân Reynolds, 2 vols., Berkeley, 1995

Bridge, Antony, *Suleiman the Magnificent, Scourge of Heaven*, London, 1983

Brockman, Eric, *The Two Sieges of Rhodes, 1480–1522*, London, 1969

Brummett, Palmira, *Ottoman Seapower and Levantine Diplomacy in the Age of Discovery*, Albany, 1994

Büyüktuğrul, Afif, "Preveze Deniz Muharebesine ilişkin gerçekler" *Beleten*, vol. 37, 1973

Caccin, P., and Angelo M., *Basilica of Saints John and Paul*, Venice, 2004

Caetani, O., and Diedo, G., *La Battaglia di Lepanto, 1571*, Palermo, 1995

Caoursin, Will, and Afendy, Rhodgia, *The History of the Turkish War with the Rhodians, Venetians, Egyptians, Persians and Other Nations*, London, 1683

Capponi, Niccolò, *Victory of the West: The Story of the Battle of Lepanto*, London, 2006

Cassar, George, ed. *The Great Siege 1565*, Malta, 2005

Cassola, A., *The 1565 Ottoman Malta Campaign Register*, Malta, 1988

Cassola, A., *The Great Siege of Malta (1565) and the Istanbul State Archives*, Malta, 1995

Cervantes, Miguel de, *El Ingenioso Hidalgo Don Quijote de la Mancha*, Glasgow, 1871

Cirni, A. F., *Commentari d'Anton Francesco Cirni, Corso, ne quale se descrive la Guerra ultima di Francia, la celebratione del Concilio Tridentino, il Soccorso d'Orano, l'Impresa del Pignone, e l'Historia dell'Assedio di Malta*, Rome, 1567

Clot, André, *Suleiman the Magnificent*, trans. Matthew J. Reisz, London, 2005

*Colección de Documentos Inéditos para la Historia de España*, vol. 3, Madrid, 1843

Crowley, Roger, *1453: The Holy War for Constantinople and the Clash of Islam and the West*, New York, 2005

Danişmend, I. H., *Izahlı Osmanlı tarihi kronolojisi*, vol. 2, Istanbul, 1948

Davis, R. C., *Christian Slaves, Muslim Masters: White Slavery in the Mediterranean, the Barbary Coast, and Italy, 1500–1800*, London, 2003

Deny, Jean, and Laroche, Jane, "L'expédition en Provence de l'armée de Mer du Sultan Suleyman sous le Commandement de l'admiral Hayreddin Pacha, dit Barberousse (1543–1544)" *Turcica*, vol. 1, Paris, 1969

Elliot, J. H., *Imperial Spain 1469–1716*, London, 1990

*Encyclopaedia of Islam*, 11 vols., Leiden, 1960

*Excerpta Cypria: Materials for a History of Cyprus*, trans. Claude Delaval Cobham, Cambridge, 1908

Fernandez Duro, Cesareo, *Armada Española desde la Union de los Reinos de Castilla y de Aragon*, vol. 2, Madrid, 1896

Finkel, Caroline, *Osman's Dream: The Story of the Ottoman Empire, 1300–1923*, London, 2005

Finlay, Robert, "Prophecy and Politics in Istanbul: Charles V, Sultan Süleyman, and the Habsburg Embassy of 1533–1534" *The Journal of Early Modern History*, 1998, vol. 2

Fisher, Alan, "The Life and Family of Süleyman I" in *Süleyman the Second and His Time*, ed. Halil Inalcik and Cemal Kafadar, Istanbul, 1993

Fisher, Sir Godfrey, *Barbary Legend: War, Trade, and Piracy in North Africa, 1415–1830*, Oxford, 1957

Fontanus, J., *De Bello Rhodio*, Rome, 1524

Friedman, Ellen G., *Spanish Captives in North Africa in the Early Modern Age*, London, 1983

Galea, J., "The Great Siege of Malta from a Turkish Point of View" *Melita Historica* IV, Malta, 1965

Gazioğlu, Ahmet C., *The Turks in Cyprus: A Province of the Ottoman Empire (1571–1878)*, London, 1990

Gentil de Vendosme, P., *Le Siège de Malte par les Turcs en 1565*, Paris, 1910

Ghiselin de Busbecq, Ogier, *The Turkish Letters of Ogier Ghiselin de Busbecq: Imperial Ambassador at Constantinople*, trans. Edward Seymour Forster, Oxford, 1927

Glete, Jan, *Warfare at Sea 1500–1650*, London, 2000

Goffman, Daniel, *The Ottoman Empire and Early Modern Europe*, Cambridge, 2002

Grove, A. T., and Rackham, Oliver, *The Nature of Mediterranean Europe: An Ecological History*, London, 2001

Guglielmotti, P. Alberto, *Storia della Marina Pontificia*, vol. 5, Rome, 1887

Guilmartin, John Francis, *Galleons and Galleys*, London, 2002

Guilmartin, John Francis, *Gunpowder and Galleys: Changing Technology and Mediterranean Warfare at Sea in the Sixteenth Century*, Cambridge, 1974

Guilmartin, John, "The Tactics of the Battle of Lepanto Clarified" at www.angelfire.com/ga4/guilmartin.com

Güleryüz, Ahmet, *Kadırgadan Kalyona Osmanlıda Yelken*, Istanbul, 2004

Haëdo, Diego de, *Histoire des Rois d'Alger*, trans. H. de Grammont, Saint-Denis, 1998

Haji Khalifeh, *The History of the Maritime Wars of the Turks*, trans. James Mitchell, London, 1831

Hammer-Purgstall, J., *Histoire de L'Empire Ottoman*, vols. 4–6, Paris, 1836

Heers, Jacques, *The Barbary Corsairs: Warfare in the Mediterranean, 1480–1580*, London, 2003

Hess, Andrew, "The Battle of Lepanto and Its Place in Mediterranean History" *Past and Present* 57, Oxford, 1972

Hess, Andrew, "The Evolution of the Ottoman Seaborne Empire in the Age of Oceanic Discoveries, 1453–1525" *American Historical Review* 75, no. 7 (December 1970)

Hess, Andrew, *The Forgotten Frontier: A History of the Sixteenth Century Ibero-African Frontier*, Chicago, 1978

Hess, Andrew, "The Ottoman Conquest of Egypt (1517) and the Beginning of the Sixteenth-Century World War" *International Journal of Middle East Studies* 4 (1973)

Hill, Sir George, *A History of Cyprus, volume III: The Frankish period, 1432–1571*, Cambridge, 1972

Housley, Norman, *The Later Crusades 1274–1571*, Oxford, 1992

Imber, Colin, "The Navy of Süleyman the Magnificent" in *Archivum Ottomanicum, VI* (1980)

Imber, Colin, *The Ottoman Empire: The Structure of Power*, Basingstoke, 2002

Inalcık, Halil, "Lepanto in the Ottoman Documents" in Benzoni

Inalcık, Halil, *The Ottoman Empire: The Classical Age, 1300–1600*, London, 1973

Inalcık, Halil, and Camal Kafadar, *Süleymân the Second and His Time*, Istanbul, 1993

*Islam Ansiklopedisi*, 28 vols., Istanbul, 1988

Jurien de La Gravière, Jean Pierre, *Doria et Barberousse*, Paris, 1886

Jurien de La Gravière, Jean Pierre, *La Guerre de Chypre et la Bataille de Lépante*, 2 vols., Paris, 1888

Jurien de La Gravière, Jean Pierre, *Les Chevaliers de Malte et la Marine de Philippe II*, 2 vols., Paris, 1887

Kamen, Henry, *Philip of Spain*, London, 1997

Kâtip Çelebi, *The History of the Maritime Wars of the Turks*, trans. J. Mitchell, London, 1831

Kunt, Metin, and Christine Woodhead, eds., *Süleyman the Magnificent and His Age*, Harlow, 1995

Lane, Frederic C., *Venice: A Maritime Republic*, Baltimore, 1973

Lesure, M., *Lépante, la Crise de L'Empire Ottoman*, Paris, 1972

Longworth, Philip, *The Rise and Fall of Venice*, London, 1974

López de Gómara, Francisco, *Cronica de los Barbarrojas*, in *Memorial Historico Español: Colección de Documentos, Opusculos y Antiguedades*, vol. 6, Madrid, 1853

Luttrell, Anthony, *The Hospitallers of Rhodes and Their Mediterranean World*, Aldershot, 1992

Lynch, John, *Spain Under the Hapsburgs, vol 1: Empire and Absolutism 1516–1598*, Oxford, 1964

Mallett, M. E., and Hale, J. R., *The Military Organization of a Renaissance State: Venice, c. 1400 to 1617*, Cambridge, 1984

Mallia-Milanes, Victor, *Venice and Hospitaller Malta, 1530–1798: Aspects of a Relationship*, Malta 1992

Mantran, Robert, "L'écho de la bataille de Lépante a Constantinople" in Benzoni

Maurand, Jérome, *Itinéraire de J. Maurand d'Antibes à Constantinople (1544)*, Paris, 1901

Merriman, Roger Bigelow, *The Rise of the Spanish Empire in the Old World and in the New*, vols. 3 and 4, New York, 1962

Merriman, Roger Bigelow, *Suleiman the Magnificent, 1520–1566*, Cambridge, Massachusetts, 1944

Morris, Jan, *The Venetian Empire: A Sea Voyage*, London, 1980

Mulgan, Catherine, *The Renaissance Monarchies, 1469–1558*, Cambridge, 1998

Necipoğlu, Gülru, "Ottoman-Hapsburg-Papal Rivalry" in *Süleyman I and His Time*, ed. Halil Inalcik and Cemal Kafadar, Istanbul, 1993

Norwich, John Julius, *A History of Venice*, London, 1982

Parker, Geoffrey, *The Grand Strategy of Philip II*, London, 1998

Parker, Geoffrey, *Philip II*, London, 1979

Pastor, Louis, *Histoire des Papes*, vols. 17–18, Paris, 1935

Peçevi, Ibrahim, *Peçevi Tarihi*, vol. 1, Ankara, 1981

Petit, Édouard, *André Doria: un amiral condottiere au XVIe siècle (1466–1560)*, Paris, 1887

Petrie, Sir Charles, *Don Juan of Austria*, London, 1967

Phillips, Carla Rahn, "Navies and the Mediterranean in the Early Modern Period" in *Naval Policy and Strategy in the Mediterranean: Past, Present, and Future*, ed. John B. Hattendorf, London, 2000

Piri Reis, *Kitab-ı bahriye*, vols. 1 and 2, ed. Ertuğrul Zekai Ökte, Ankara, 1988

Porter, Whitworth, *The Knights of Malta*, 2 vols., London, 1883

Prescott, W. H., *History of the Reign of Philip the Second, King of Spain*, 3 vols., Boston, 1855–58

Pryor, John H., *Geography, Technology, and War: Studies in the Maritime History of the Mediterranean, 649–1571*, Cambridge, 1988

Rosell, Cayetano, *Historia del Combate Naval de Lepanto*, Madrid, 1853

Rossi, E., *Assedio e Conquista di Rodi nel 1522 secondo le relazioni edite e inedite de Turchi*, Rome, 1927

Sandoval, Fray Prudencio de, *Historia de la Vida y Hechos del Emperador Carlos V*, vols. 2–4, Madrid, 1956

Scetti, Aurelio, *The Journal of Aurelio Scetti: A Florentine Galley Slave at Lepanto (1565–1577)*, trans. Luigi Monga, Tempe, Arizona, 2004

Setton, Kenneth M., *The Papacy and the Levant, 1204–1571*, vols. 2–4, Philadelphia, 1984

Seyyd Murad, *La Vita e la Storia di Ariadeno Barbarossa*, ed. G. Bonaffini, Palermo, 1993

Shaw, Stanford, *History of the Ottoman Empire and Modern Turkey*, vol. 1, Cambridge, 1976

Sire, H.J.A., *The Knights of Malta*, London, 1994

Soucek, Svat, *Piri Reis and Turkish Mapmaking After Columbus: The Khalili Portolan Atlas*, London, 1996

Soucek, Svat, "The Rise of the Barbarossas in North Africa" in *Archivum Ottomanicum 3*, 1971

Spiteri, Stephen C., *The Great Siege: Knights vs. Turks MDLXV—Anatomy of a Hospitaller Victory*, Malta, 2005

Stirling-Maxwell, Sir William, *Don John of Austria*, vol. 1, London, 1883

Testa, Carmel, *Romegas*, Malta, 2002

Thubron, Colin, *The Seafarers: Venetians*, London, 2004

Tracy, James D., *Emperor Charles V, Impresario of War*, Cambridge, 2002

Turan, Şerafettin, "Lala Mustafa Paşa hakkında notlar" *Beletin 22*, 1958

Uzunçarşılı, Ismail Hakkı, *Osmanlı Tarihi, Vols. 2 and 3*, Ankara, 1988

Vargas-Hidalgo, Rafael, *Guerra y diplomacia en el Mediterraneo: Correspondencia inédita de Felipe II con Andrea Doria y Juan Andrea Doria*, Madrid, 2002

Yildirim, Onur, "The Battle of Lepanto and Its Impact on Ottoman History and Historiography" in *Mediterraneo in Armi*, ed. R. Cancila, Palermo, 2007

Zanon, Luigi Gigio, *La Galea Veneziana*, Venice, 2004

# Index

Pages numbers on which illustrations occur are *italicized*

## About the Author

ROGER CROWLEY was born in 1951 and spent part of his childhood in Malta. He read English at Cambridge University. After university he taught English in Istanbul, where he developed a strong interest in the history of Turkey. He has traveled throughout the Mediterranean basin over many years and has a wide-ranging knowledge of its geography and its past. He is the author of *1453: The Holy War for Constantinople and the Clash of Islam and the West*. His website is www.rogercrowley.co.uk.

## About the Type

The text of this book was set on the Monotype in a typeface called Bell. The Englishman John Bell (1745–1831) was responsible for the original cutting of this design. The vocations of Bell were many—among others, bookseller, printer, publisher, type founder, and journalist. His types were considerably influenced by the delicacy and beauty of the French copper-plate engravers. Monotype Bell might also be classified as a delicate and refined rendering of Scotch Roman.